Happy Birthday...
Charlie!

Many, many more!

Draughtons

Frank Davis Cooks
Cajun, Creole, and Crescent City

Also by Frank Davis

The Frank Davis Seafood Notebook
Frank Davis Cooks Naturally N'Awlins
The Frank Davis Fishing Guide
to Lake Pontchartrain and Lake Borgne

ABOUT THE COVER

The Hermann-Grima Historic House at 820 St. Louis Street is generally considered to be the earliest and best example of American architecture in New Orleans' French Quarter. Built in 1831, it has been meticulously restored to depict the gracious life-style of a prosperous Creole family in the years from 1830 to 1860. The museum complex also includes two flower-filled courtyards, a stable, a cast-iron cistern, and a working 1831 French kitchen where Frank shot this cover. The kitchen is used for cooking demonstrations utilizing the open hearth, baking oven, and potager.

Accredited by the American Association of Museums and a designated National Historic Landmark, the Hermann-Grima Historic House is open to the public Monday through Saturday. Housed in the stable, the museum shop features specialty items highlighting New Orleans' unique traditions and cuisine.

Jacket photograph by Sonny Randon

FRANK DAVIS
Cooks Cajun, Creole, and Crescent City

Frank Davis

**Foreword by
Albert Barrocas, M.D., F.A.C.S.**

**Illustrations by
Shelby Wilson**

PELICAN PUBLISHING COMPANY
Gretna 1994

Library of Congress Cataloging-in-Publication Data

Davis, Frank, 1942-
    Frank Davis cooks Cajun, Creole, and Crescent City / Frank Davis ; foreword by Albert Barrocas ; illustrations by Shelby Wilson.
        p.   cm.
    Includes index.
    ISBN 1-56554-055-7
    1. Cookery, American—Louisiana style.   2. Cookery, Cajun.
3. Cookery, Creole.   I. Title.
TX715.2.L68D377 1994
641.59763—dc20   93-44631
                                                                            CIP

Text illustrations by Shelby Wilson

Manufactured in the United States of America

Published by Pelican Publishing Company, Inc.
1101 Monroe Street, Gretna, Louisiana 70053

To Elisabeth Clare, little Elise,
the greatest little granddaughter
in the whole wide world!
Paw-Paw loves you!

Contents

Foreword

Hundreds of "recipe" books are written each year in the United States. At the same time, the increasing interest in wellness, disease prevention, and health promotion has resulted in a captive audience of millions of people looking for "diet" and "healthy living" books.

With each passing day, new warnings are issued about our diet, water supply, and the environment. Yet all too often these proclamations appear to be contradictory and confuse the public. It is little wonder that recent surveys indicate Americans are easing up on health-conscious diets. Actually, we may not be far from the day that the Surgeon General will decree: *"WARNING! LIVING MAY BE HAZARDOUS TO YOUR HEALTH!"*

In this addition to his outstanding and best-selling cookbook series, Frank Davis has taken the public's concern into account. He has once again infused his human genius and his culinary experience into each of the almost two hundred recipes, providing us with a variety of foods and ingredients to accommodate diverse tastes and health needs. This is by no stretch of the imagination a "diet cookbook," but the message of moderation and adaptation is interwoven into the fabric of the entire volume.

I have had the opportunity to fish, cook, and exercise with Frank. We have a strange but wonderful relationship. He considers some of my advice strange, while I consider his cooking to be wonderful! Seriously though, in all our years of collaborating and blending health and nutrition with New Orleans cuisine we've learned from each other and have come to the conclusion that healthy dining can be fun.

Frank understands the public and how to reach them with simple to understand, guilt-free, and tasteful messages. He has incorporated the KISS philosophy—*Keep It Simple and Sensible*—into this book, as he does on an everyday basis, whether on his Tuesday morning television cooking show or at the myriad of cooking classes and demonstrations he does each year around the country.

The typical reader of this new book will be able to enjoy these authentic New Orleans recipes, yet still have an insight as to how to healthfully modify and adapt them as needed or desired. The "Chef's Notes" he includes at the end of many of the recipes not only give the reader additional preparation information but dietetic substitution information as well for individuals on restricted or limited diets. Furthermore, the book provides some fat, sodium, and cholesterol alterations an individual cook can make to modify the recipes to specific needs.

Individually developed and tested New Orleans recipes are presented here as in previous volumes, but unique to this edition is the inclusion of helpful health tips. Frank has succeeded in presenting a balance of good taste along with good nutrition and health. He clearly demonstrates that disease prevention and health promotion through nutrition does not have to be painful or tasteless ... even in a city like New Orleans!

All too often the best intention to follow a specific diet is abandoned at the first deviation from it. We have all felt guilty at times about having butter or cream sauces. But enjoying a "sometimes"-type recipe allows many of us to stay on a course of healthy dining longer than the more restrictive regimens that offer us an "all or none" alternative, which is usually expensive and doomed for failure from the outset.

Make no mistake about it—many of Frank's New Orleans recipes include the so-called "forbidden" foods. But it's the very nature of these dishes! They are sacred and they shouldn't be tampered with! From a health-conscious point of view, the reader need not do without them. Simply modify the quantity to allow for healthy compliance. In other words, have a *serving* instead of a New Orleans *"helping"* or two.

Maintaining the New Orleans flavor while still preparing a healthy meal requires the genius of an expert chef and the perseverance exhibited by a few unique individuals. Frank Davis is such an individual.

So ... eat hearty and healthy; enjoy; come con gana; mangez; con salute; buen provecho; essen—any way you say it, enjoy your dining. Enjoy your health!

ALBERT BARROCAS, M.D., F.A.C.S.

Introduction

First there was *The Frank Davis Seafood Notebook,* the Matthew, Mark, Luke, and Frank of cooking seafood the way we cook it in New Orleans.

Then came *Frank Davis Cooks Naturally N'Awlins,* a full-spectrum cookbook that ran the gamut from soups to salads to entrées to desserts, all done in the true traditions of old New Orleans.

And now you have in front of you the newest compilation, *Frank Davis Cooks Cajun, Creole, and Crescent City,* all the old and new ethnic, downhome, make-you-slap-your-momma-twice recipes I couldn't squeeze into the last two cookbooks.

So what can I tell you about it?

I can tell you that all the recipes have been tested over and over again so that they're guaranteed to work not only in my kitchen but in yours as well.

I can tell you that all the recipes are authentic Cajun, Creole, and New Orleans in flavor and origin because this is how folks here have cooked these dishes in their homes for generations.

I can tell you that like my other cookbooks I've written this one in the narrative, just as if I were standing right beside you in front of the stove, guiding you through each step and sparing no explanation so that you understand the principles of cooking.

I can tell you that for the most part if you eat the standard New Orleans "helping" rather than the traditional "serving" you're going to gain weight, because each recipe is chock-full of rich, succulent flavors that make second helpings a must rather than an option!

I can tell you that none of the recipes is hard to do. Even a novice cook, if he sits down and reads the directions, can cook from this book and have every single dish turn out perfectly.

I can tell you that in spite of the fattening appeal of each dish, you will find tips throughout the book that will teach you how to make health-conscious substitutions to cut some of the fats, sodium, and cholesterol if you're interested in doing that.

I can tell you that like my other books neither should this one be stashed away on a shelf in the library. I really recommend you keep it in the kitchen (*or better yet, in the bathroom*) and read it from cover to cover. It's not a list of recipes—it's a full-blown *cooking school* complete with all the courses befitting the culinary sciences.

I can tell you it's a fun book. It's fun to use, it's fun to read, and it's fun to watch the mouth-watering taste satisfaction you'll see on the faces of the folks for whom you prepare the recipes.

And finally I can also tell you that once you get to the last page, if you've followed all the directions and employed all the hints and tricks I've shared with you, you genuinely will have mastered a small part of the art of cooking Cajun, Creole, and Crescent City!

The Basics of Nutrition

This cookbook is so chocked full of tasty recipes you're going to be motivated to prepare every single one of them, which means it's going to be extremely difficult to lose any weight once you start cooking. In fact, some experts rumor that you may even gain a few pounds!

But let's say that instead of giving up all these good New Orleans dishes you're just going to cut back on your portions and keep an eye on what you eat.

That's a good idea. But if you do that, if that's your plan, you're going to have to have some idea of how much fat and cholesterol you can have every day and still stay healthy (while cooking these recipes!).

Well, I'm not a doctor nor a registered dietitian. But I know a bunch of doctors and registered dietitians who know all about this stuff. So to help y'all out, they've helped me simplify some nutritional basics for you.

EVERYTHING YOU NEED TO KNOW ABOUT FAT FACTS

All fat in foods is not identical. Fat is a combination of different types of fatty acids—saturated, monounsaturated, and polyunsaturated.

Saturated fat is the really bad stuff. It's the fat you get from animal foods, such as meat, butter, coconut and palm oil, and some dairy products. This kind of fat raises your blood cholesterol and increases your risk of heart disease. Experts say that of the total 30 percent of all fat calories you're allowed every day, keep the amount of saturated fat at 10 percent of the calories or even less.

Monounsaturated fat is found in olive oil, canola oil, and peanut oil. Recent evidence indicates that substituting this fat (in moderation) for saturated fat helps lower blood cholesterol and reduces the risk of heart disease.

Polyunsaturated fat mainly comes from vegetable oils such as soybean, corn, cottonseed, sunflower, and safflower. This fat (in moderation) is not only helpful in lowering blood cholesterol, but removes cholesterol from the body!

Shortenings and margarine contain both monounsaturated and polyun-saturated fats. Lard and butter contain saturated fat!

Foods high in saturated fat include:
Beef round steak, beef roast, beef porterhouse, ground beef, whole milk, most cheeses, hot dogs, luncheon meats, doughnuts, cake, pork chops, ham, sausage, bacon, butter, ice cream, French fries, 2 percent milk, potato chips, nondairy coffee creamer.

Foods low in saturated fat include:
Fruit, vegetables, roasted skinless turkey breast, baked or broiled skin-less chicken, broiled or grilled fish, skim milk, low-fat yogurt, 1 percent cottage cheese, pork tenderloin, Canadian bacon, dried beans, dried prunes, cereal, pasta without cheese or meat, rice, popcorn without butter, whole-grain breads.

One of the most significant ways to lower your blood cholesterol is to reduce your intake of foods that are high in saturated fat. In fact, blood cholesterol reductions of 15 to 25 percent, which is achievable by diet alone, in just two weeks can reduce the risk of heart disease by up to 30 to 50 percent!

Don't believe that all foods labeled *"cholesterol free"* are good for you. Many products on the grocery shelf with no dietary cholesterol are filled with saturated fat. See what kind of oils are used in the product. Coconut oil, palm oil, and hydrogenated oil are all very high in saturated fat. Read the labels!

GETTING SPECIFIC ...

Remember that meat loses about 25 percent of its weight during cook-ing. So if you subscribe to the recommended dietary guidelines of 3 ounces of cooked meat per serving, you should begin with 4 ounces of raw meat to get to that point.

You should eat no more than 6 ounces of cooked meat, fish, or poultry every day.

Egg yolks are high in cholesterol. Egg whites have no cholesterol. So to maintain a healthy life-style, try to eat no more than 3 egg yolks a week. Incidentally, to keep within these parameters, when you prepare scram-bled eggs and omelets a good trick is to use several egg whites but only one egg yolk per portion. Nobody will ever know you did it if you don't tell! And when other recipes call for whole eggs, go ahead and substitute just the whites instead. All you have to do is *double* the number of eggs called for in the recipe.

The average daily intake of dietary cholesterol is 304 milligrams for women and 435 milligrams for men. The experts recommend that to be "heart healthy" you should have no more than 300 milligrams of cholesterol per day.

The National Academy of Sciences says that a normal healthy adult needs no more than 500 milligrams of sodium for an entire day. Be sure to read sodium labels on the foods you buy also and try to keep the amount as low as possible.

When you shop for a margarine, choose a brand that has "liquid oil" listed as the first ingredient. Remember, any oil that turns solid at room temperature contains "saturated" fat. So if you have a solid margarine, you can bet the fat is of the saturated variety.

Most store-bought biscuits, muffins, pancakes, pastries, and croissants are not made with healthful oils. Read the labels or make your own at home. Or buy a plain angel food cake for dessert! Angel food cake has no fat at all! Fig bars and gingersnaps are also good cookie selections.

One cup of premium ice cream contains 14.7 grams of saturated fat. One cup of frozen yogurt has only 1.9 grams of saturated fat!

So here's the bottom line. By no stretch of the imagination is this a "diet cookbook." It was never intended to be. Each of the recipes is prepared authentically, with all the traditional ingredients, most of them high in fat, sodium, and cholesterol.

But as you go through the cookbook, as you prepare the dishes for you and your family, you'll find the potential and the opportunities on almost every page to make changes and substitutions. This is why I've included this section in the book—to teach you basically how to handle the alterations.

Of course, some recipes are not conducive to change. To achieve their classic tastes you just have to accept the fattening consequences. In these cases, I recommend reduced portions instead of abstinence! But there are enough recipes included that can withstand a reduction in salt, for example, or an olive oil substitution for butter, or the use of a rich fat-free stock instead of heavy cream.

Feel free to experiment to suit your health and your tastes. You'll be surprised just what you can do with a little basic understanding and a lot of creativity!

*Sources: U.S. Department of Health & Human Services,
American Dietetic Association

FIBERIZE YOUR DIET!

All of the latest medical studies say that one of the healthiest things you can do for digestion and your overall intestinal tract is to eat a lot of *fiber!*

But unless you're a magna cum laude nutritionist, you just don't know what's high in fiber and what isn't. Well ... that's what this page in the book is for! Here's the current list of all your high-fiber foods!

Fresh apples (with the skin on), raw bananas, red beans (in fact, most beans!), rice, strawberries, blackberries. blueberries, raspberries, beets, oat- and wheat-bran cereals, corn on the cob, steamed broccoli, brussels sprouts, coleslaw, stir-fried cabbage, carrots, oatmeal, fresh figs, kiwi fruit, mushrooms, toasted almonds, dry-roasted cashews, green peas, raisins, baked potatoes, sweet potatoes, dried prunes, and pumpkins.

AND CUT THE FATS!

The new thing with dietitians now is: "If you want to drop a few pounds, forget about counting calories—cut the fat!" So again, which foods are fat and which ones aren't? Here's your list!

Low-fat foods include:
Fresh apples, fresh apricots, fresh bananas, all dried beans, fresh green beans, fresh limas, a small filet mignon, beets, all fresh berries, wheat, corn and oat bran (*but not rice bran!*), steamed broccoli, steamed brussels sprouts, boiled cabbage, fresh carrots, cauliflower, cooked oatmeal, low-fat cottage cheese, raw cherries, fresh corn on the cob, cranberries, cucumbers, eggplant (unless fried or smothered in olive oil), fresh figs, bass, sac-a-lait, cobia, cod, flounder, snapper, triggerfish, speckled trout, croaker, lakerunner, striped bass, white bass, grouper, steamed clams, boiled lobster (but don't dip it in drawn butter!), boiled shrimp, pink grapefruit, lettuce, fresh spinach, kiwi fruit, lemons, limes, cantaloupes, watermelons, skim milk, peaches, nectarines, oranges, mushrooms, onions, papayas, all pastas, pears, green peas, bell peppers, chili peppers, pineapples, grilled pork tenderloin, baked potatoes, plums, dried prunes, pumpkins, raisins, brown rice, winter squash, sweet potatoes, tomatoes, asparagus, turkey white meat (skinless), chicken breast (skinless), and plain nonfat yogurt.

High-fat foods include:
Avocados, London broil steak, extra-lean ground beef, regular ground beef (very high!), rice cereal, Edam cheese, cheddar cheese, feta cheese, mozzarella cheese (moderate to high), Monterey Jack cheese, Parmesan cheese, Romano cheese, eggs, blue crabs and oysters (moderately high), pompano, gar, salmon, spadefish, catfish, drum, tuna, bluefish, bluegill,

dolphin, king mackerel, Spanish mackerel, lamb, whole milk, almonds, cashews, peanuts, pecans, solid shortenings, veal roast, and plain whole-milk yogurt.

UNDERSTANDING THIS "FAT FREE" THING!

The whole world population has gone "fat free"!

At least they think they have. But that may not be the case at all. Understanding what fat free really means can be unbelievably confusing—and sometimes downright deceiving, because in many cases it's not what it appears to be!

For example, if a package label says a product is *99 percent fat free,* the maker wants you to believe that 99 percent of the calories are *not* coming from fat! Only 1 percent is. But how accurate is that?

Well, unless you do a little mathematics on your own, it may or may not be so. Technically and, yes, legally, it could mean that the product is 99 percent fat free *by weight,* which is something altogether different from content! Let me try to explain.

Take a pound of butter. It's 100 percent fat, right? But now add 1 pound of marbles to the butter and mix it together. By *weight,* the butter is now 50 percent fat free. By content, though, it's still 100 percent fat! You get the picture?

Manufacturers often add water to their products, as in the case of sliced ham, sliced turkey, sliced salami, and other cold cuts. Water contains 0 percent fat. But it also increases the weight of the product. If you add enough water to increase the weight by 97 percent, couldn't you then say that it was 97 percent fat free (by weight)? Absolutely! And food manufacturers do that all the time!

So how do you know what the real fat content is? Well, you have to learn some simple nutrition.

1—There are 9 calories in 1 gram of fat.

2—The USDA recommends that your daily diet contain no more than 30 percent fat (27 percent is better).

3—If the food package label says the product contains 6 grams of fat, you multiply 9 times 6 to get the number of calories from fat.

9 x 6 = 54 calories coming from fat

---

*Keep in mind that the moderate and high fat content found in seafoods are unsaturated or monounsaturated fats and can still be heart-healthy, provided the dietary intake does not exceed 30 percent of the total calories as fats.

4—You then take the number of calories per serving (let's say it's listed as 130 on the package label). Divide that into the calories coming from fat (54).

54 divided by 130 = .40

That means in every serving you have 40 percent fat content! If your mathematics give you a total of 40 percent and the guidelines say no more than 27 percent ... you're way over!

But you can't do all this multiplication and division while standing in the middle of the grocery store. So there is an easy way to read food labels at a glance to figure out the true percentage of fat.

1—Find out the number of calories per serving. (Let's say it's 130.)
2—Now move the decimal two places to the left. (That gives you 1.3.)
3—Then multiply 1.3 times 3 (since there are 9 calories in 1 gram of fat and 3 x 9 = 27, which is the percent of calories you should get from fat every day).
4—So you get 1.3 x 3 = 3.9. (That's good! That's 27 percent fat and within the guidelines.)

Now read the product label again. If it says that each serving contains 6 grams of fat and you shouldn't have any more than 3.9, you know it's high, it's not fat free, it's not low fat, and it should stay right there on the shelf if you're trying to cut your fat intake and you haven't figured this particular food into your daily fat allowance! It's just that easy!

Of course, the main thing to remember is to not become fanatical about this fat thing. So okay—one particular food you like is high in fat. Don't give it up! Don't do without it! Go ahead and have it ... but make it fit into the total daily fats you're allowed.

For example, let's say you get an intense craving for a piece of fried chicken for lunch. You know that's going to be way over your guideline numbers. So do you skip the fried chicken? No! Just make up for the difference by reducing the amount of fat you eat at supper. Remember—we're talking about "daily totals," not each meal!

YOUR PERSONAL FAT NUMBER

So how much fat should you take in every day for your weight and still be within the 27 percent guideline? Easy!

First you multiply your weight by 10 (since it takes 10 calories per pound to maintain body weight).

Then move the decimal point two places to the left and multiply by 3.

Let's say you weigh 150 pounds. Multiply that by 10.

$$150 \times 10 = 1,500$$

Now move the decimal point to get 15.00.

$$15 \times 3 = 45$$

That means you can have a total of 45 grams of fat every day and still be within the guideline of 27 percent of your calories from fat.

Oh, just for the record, if you reduce your caloric intake by 500 calories every day, you will lose one pound a week. Just be careful not to ever go under 1,000 calories per day without a doctor's or registered dietitian's supervision.

YOUR PERSONAL CALORIE NUMBER ... AND YOUR LIFE-STYLE

People ask their doctors all the time, "How do I know how many calories I should eat every day?" Well, there's an easy way to figure it out.

If you consider yourself to be a normal individual (which means you don't have some kind of glandular problem), who does some type of moderate exercise on a regular basis, you can figure that *10 calories per pound per day* will maintain your present weight. As in the example above, if you weigh 150 pounds, **150 x 10 = 1,500 calories,** which means that if you take in 1,500 calories a day, you won't gain any weight—but you won't lose any either.

But there's good news and bad news here.

The good news is that if you reduce your caloric intake by 500 calories every day, you'll *lose* a pound a week. The bad news is that if you increase that number by 500 calories per day, you'll *gain* a pound a week.

Remember, though, that your one-pound weight loss or weight gain is figured on a weekly basis. Let's say Alfonse invites you to his fishing camp Wednesday and you pig out on fried trout and French fried potatoes. Don't feel as if you are doomed forever! As the line from *Gone with the Wind* says, "Tomorrow's another day!" So make up for your over-indulgences tomorrow.

Instead of taking in your usual 1,500 calories on Thursday, reduce the number to 1,000. It'll put you right back on track if you're good the rest of the week.

The bottom line is ... for a dietary program to work, you must base it on sound nutrition. Don't expect to take off 20 pounds in two weeks by starving yourself, then turning around and going back to your old way of eating. You're just going to gain it all back plus some! Understand what foods do, how they affect your well-being, and how you can accomplish your goals without guilt and stress. It's not called "diet"! It's called "life-style."

Make watching what you eat something you do every day of your life and you won't ever have to go on a diet again!

SO HOW MUCH IS LOW SALT AND LOW CHOLESTEROL?

As a rule of thumb, if the food you eat contains 300 milligrams or less of cholesterol for the entire day it is generally considered to be **"low cholesterol."** The number drops down to 200 mg or less for high-risk individuals or persons with known high cholesterol levels.

By the same token, **"low sodium"** is generally considered to be food that contains less than 2,000 milligrams (or 2 grams) per day. The truth of the matter is, however, your body can do quite well with 500 mg of sodium every day. So to stay within these numbers it's a good idea to avoid shaking on the salt whenever possible.

Food Guide Pyramid
A Guide to Daily Food Choices

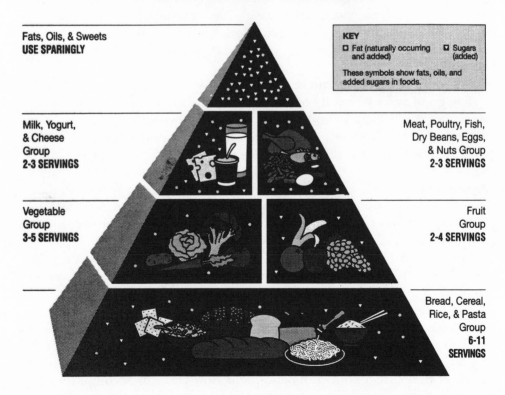

KEY
◻ Fat (naturally occurring and added)   ▨ Sugars (added)

These symbols show fats, oils, and added sugars in foods.

Fats, Oils, & Sweets
USE SPARINGLY

Milk, Yogurt, & Cheese Group
2-3 SERVINGS

Meat, Poultry, Fish, Dry Beans, Eggs, & Nuts Group
2-3 SERVINGS

Vegetable Group
3-5 SERVINGS

Fruit Group
2-4 SERVINGS

Bread, Cereal, Rice, & Pasta Group
6-11 SERVINGS

UNDERSTANDING THE FOOD GUIDE PYRAMID

Remember the old food "pie chart" we all learned back in health class in grammar school? Well, over the years it has become stale and has been thrown out.

Today there's the "food guide pyramid," first published in 1992 by the United States Department of Agriculture. Its basic thrust is to (1) build your diet on a base of grains, vegetables, and fruits; (2) add only moderate amounts of lean meats, eggs, nuts, and dairy products; and (3) limit your intake of fats and sweets.

Of course, that's not the way New Orleanians grew up eating. Nathan Pritikin once said that in New Orleans, we even fry the chairs! So if folks here (and all along the bayou for that matter) are going to learn a healthful way of eating for the future, based on the pyramid, a little explanation and education is in order.

As simply as I can make it, you should continue to eat a variety of foods because your body needs more than 40 different nutrients for good health. And since no single food can supply all these nutrients, variety is crucial. However, you need to learn to eat the right things in the right quantities. According to the pyramid:

1—Eat more bread, cereal, rice, and pasta than anything else. And the recommendation is that you eat 6 to 11 servings of these each day. All these foods are rich in nutrients, they're low in fat, they supply body energy, and they furnish all the fiber you need every day.

2—Vegetables come next. They are extremely good for you, they're easy on the waistline because they're low in calories, and you should have 3 to 5 servings every day. Of course, don't cover them up with all the butter and melted cheese! I know how y'all think—I'm a native New Orleanian too!

3—Fruits are next on the pyramid. And the fresh kind is best of all. Of course, if you have to opt for the canned variety be sure you choose a variety that's packed in light syrup or their own natural juices. You should plan to include 2 to 4 servings in your meals every day.

4—Now we start getting into the no-no stuff ... the things New Orleanians like best. Milk, yogurt, and cheese should be a part of your daily diet but you should enjoy them in limited quantities. According to the pyramid, you want to eat only 2 to 3 servings of these foods every day.

5—The restriction gets a little tighter when you get to meat, poultry, fish, dry beans, eggs, and nuts. The daily servings are still in the 2 to 3 range, but selection becomes more important. For example, instead of fried chicken, which you can have in moderation every now and then, select skinless broiled chicken for your daily meals; instead of a rib-eye steak, which you can eat on special occasions, select a lean cut of veal or beef (and not more than 3 ounces in weight after cooking); and instead of scoffing down a whole can of cashew nuts while sitting in front of the TV set, sprinkle a little of them over a scoop of yogurt once in a while for a dessert treat. Are you getting the drift?

We're talking nothing more than moderation and a little bit of common sense here. Oh by the way, just in case you're interested, a half-cup of cooked dry beans (yep! red beans and rice), 1 egg, or 2 tablespoons of peanut butter each equals precisely 1 ounce of lean meat. So if you want to make a swap-out, you know what to swap.

6—And finally on the pyramid there's fats, oils, and sweets. You see how it's the smallest block right at the top? That's because you're supposed to eat those in small quantities. Actually, the dietary guidelines recommend using fats, oils, and sugar very sparingly. And to take this a step farther, you can clump salt and alcohol in this category as well.

So go ahead and enjoy your favorite foods. But enjoy them sparingly. See, I know that the majority of you are not going to give up Saturday-night fish fries at your neighbor's house. I also know that you're not going to stop bringing home the fried-chicken specials from Popeyes and the Blue Bell Ice Cream from A&P. But you really don't have to. All you have to do is keep the *pyramid* in mind on a daily basis and think common sense. It's really not all that difficult to do!

SERVINGS VS. HELPINGS … NEW ORLEANS STYLE

There's been a lot of talk lately about reading product labels to determine the nutritional value of foods. Sodium, fat, protein, carbohydrates, cholesterol—they're all spelled out in grams on the side panels of cans, cartons, boxes, bags, and wrappers. But also included on the lists is something called *"serving size."*

Believe it or not, folks in Louisiana have a hard time understanding what a serving size really is. Oh, we know what a *"helping"* is! Helpings always come in numerical units of twos and threes and are served in platefuls. For example:

"This gumbo is so good I'm on my third helping!"

"Son, you want another helping of barbecued shrimp?"

"What's the matter, dear? You only had three helpings of roasted duck and andouille dressing."

Well, the truth of the matter is that if in each of those examples the "helpings" were true "servings," we'd all be a lot lighter with a narrower midriff bulge.

Just so you have a bench mark to gauge from, here are the true definitions of some common "single servings":

1 slice of bread	1 oz. ready-to-eat cereal
½ cup cooked rice	3 to 4 saltine crackers
1 cup raw leafy vegetables	½ cup other vegetables
¾ cup vegetable juice	1 medium apple or banana
¾ cup fruit juice	1 cup milk or yogurt
1½ oz. natural cheese	2 oz. processed cheese
3 oz. cooked lean meat	3 oz. cooked poultry
3 oz. cooked fish	½ cup cooked beans
1 egg	2 tbsp. peanut butter

No wonder we have a problem controlling our weight! None of these quantities comes anywhere near what is considered to be a "New Orleans helping."

So if you want to follow the recommendations of the food guide pyramid and start eating servings instead of helpings, check the food labels again. Almost every one of them lists the serving size.

**Frank Davis Cooks
Cajun, Creole, and Crescent City**

CHAPTER 1

Breads

Black Skillet Corn Bread

I know that most cookbooks and side-panel packaging tell you that you can make a pan of corn bread in a square baking dish, in a muffin tin, or in a corn-stick pan. But I'm here to tell you that if you want the absolute best corn bread you ever had in your born days, you gotta make it in a buttered black cast-iron skillet! And that's all there is to it! No exceptions!

2 cups self-rising yellow cornmeal	1½ cups cultured buttermilk
1 tbsp. granulated sugar	1 heaping tbsp. finely chopped chili
½ tsp. baking soda (not powder!)	peppers
1 large egg, slightly beaten	1 stick sweetcream butter

The first thing you do is preheat your oven to 425 degrees.

Then take your cast-iron skillet and put it on the stove over medium-low heat.

Meanwhile, in a large mixing bowl, mix together the cornmeal, granulated sugar, and baking soda. Then, thoroughly whip in the egg and the buttermilk until the mixture is smooth and lump-free. At this point, stir in the chili peppers and let the mix rest for a few minutes on the countertop.

While the cornmeal is resting, drop the butter into the skillet and melt it down … *but don't let it burn.* When it's hot, swirl the butter around in the skillet to completely coat the bottom and the sides. Then pour the corn-bread mix into the skillet, slide the skillet into the oven, and bake the bread for about 25 minutes until it turns a golden-brown color with a crispy top and sides.

I suggest you serve it piping hot right from the oven, drizzled with a little extra butter or cane syrup on top!

Oooooo-weeee!

Chef's Note: *You can jazz up your corn bread by adding to the mix whole kernel or white shoepeg corn (but be sure it's thoroughly drained), finely crumbled bacon bits, Louisiana hot sauce, finely chopped green onions, shredded cheddar cheese, or just anything else you fancy. The creativity is up to you, but there's nothing wrong with this corn bread just the way it is!*

The best way to be sure your corn bread is done is to insert a wooden toothpick in the center. When it comes out dry and clean, slice the corn bread up and serve it!

Baked Cheese-n-Garlic Bread

This stuff is great with Italian gravy and pasta, with Sicilian-baked chicken, with N'Awlins fried shrimp … in fact, this stuff is even great for dessert!

1 loaf fresh-baked French bread	⅔ cup imported Romano cheese,
¾ cup extra-virgin olive oil	shredded
3 tsp. garlic powder	1 cup shredded provolone cheese

All you do is take a bread knife, split the loaf in half from end to end, and place both insides up.

Then, with a large pastry brush, generously paint on the olive oil, making sure that every square inch of the bread is thoroughly coated.

Now, lightly sprinkle the garlic powder evenly over the olive oil.

And finally, liberally sprinkle the Romano cheese evenly over the garlic powder and sprinkle the provolone over the Romano.

All that's left is to cut the loaf into serving-size portions, place all the pieces on a sheet pan—*dressed side up*—and bake at 375 degrees in the center of the oven for about 10-12 minutes or until the cheeses melt and turn gooey and toasty.

Enjoy, paisano!

Real Sicilian Garlic Bread Mix

There's nothing more Italian than a good garlic bread. In fact, I know Sicilians who, when the meal is over, will have one more piece of garlic bread for dessert! It's that good! And with a little trick, you can have garlic bread anytime you want it. Here's how!

1 loaf French bread	2 tbsp. finely chopped parsley
2 whole heads garlic	Extra chopped parsley for topping
1 lb. Parkay Squeeze Margarine	1 cup grated Romano cheese
½ cup extra-virgin olive oil	

First, take the loaf of French bread, cut it lengthwise, and set it aside for the moment.

Then take the garlic and cut off the tops of the pods—kinda like cutting the tops off an artichoke (you want to leave the head intact, but remove the tops of the cloves). When the garlic heads are trimmed, place them in a shallow pie pan, cover them with some olive oil, slide them into a preheated 400-degree oven, and bake them for about 40 minutes or until the garlic begins popping out of the pods. Now, set them aside to cool.

Next, take a 4-cup mixing bowl and empty out the contents of the Parkay Squeeze Margarine. When no more margarine can be shaken from the bottle, pour the ½ cup of olive oil into the margarine bottle, replace the cap, close the spout, and shake the oil well. Then pour out the oil into the bowl too.

Now transfer the olive oil-margarine mixture to the food processor, squeeze all the baked garlic cloves out of the pods and drop them into the margarine, add the parsley to the mix, and turn the processor on—*for about 10 to 15 seconds.*

At this point, take a spoon and spread the garlic-margarine mixture evenly over the French bread, sparsely sprinkle on a little fresh parsley, liberally sprinkle on the Romano cheese, and bake the bread in a 400-degree oven until it starts to brown.

Then quickly toast the top under the broiler and serve it piping hot!

Chef's Note: *If you'd like to make up a batch of the garlic-margarine mix and store it in the refrigerator (it will keep for about a month), I suggest you also put the parsley and the Romano cheese into the mixture before putting it back into the margarine bottle. That way, it's handy whenever you get a hankering for garlic bread.*

And you need not use it just on French bread, either. It goes great on sliced bread, "peewee" rolls, Italian bread, San Francisco sourdough, whatever … to say nothing of using it as a "baste" for pork chops, chicken, fish, shrimp, and other meats.

Roman Bruschetta

If you like the taste of garlic bread, you're going to love this extra-rich Roman-style bread. It's made with olive oil, fresh garlic, anchovy paste, Parmesan cheese, fresh tomatoes, and a dash of basil. And honestly, it's great with anything!

6 slices coarse-textured bread	1 lb. shredded Parmesan cheese
3 cloves fresh-minced garlic	3 very thinly sliced tomatoes
½ cup extra-virgin olive oil	Dash of basil
3 anchovy fillets	Salt and black pepper

First, place the bread on a shallow cookie sheet and toast it lightly in a 400-degree oven.

While the bread is toasting, take your food processor and whip the garlic, olive oil, and anchovies into a puree. Then, while the bread is still hot—*right out of the oven*—take a pastry brush and liberally brush the puree over each slice, sprinkle on a teaspoon or two of the Parmesan, top with a slice of tomato, and season with a dash of basil, salt, and lots of black pepper.

Finally place the dressed bread slices under the broiler and toast them until the tomatoes wilt and sizzle.

Serve 'em immediately, paisano.

Chef's Note:

1—For best results, the bread should be cut into slices about ⅜ to ½ inch thick.

2—While dried basil can be used to make bruschetta, a pinch of finely minced fresh basil is better. No, it's best!

CHAPTER 2

Salads

Sour-Cream Potato Salad

There's Cajun potato salad, German potato salad, hot potato salad, and cold potato salad ... but try *this* potato salad, especially the next time you serve rump roast, grilled filet mignon, barbecued chicken, or London broil! It's great!

10 large red potatoes	**2 tbsp. horseradish**
1 cup sour cream	**1 cup thinly sliced green onions**
2 cups real mayonnaise	**¾ cup minced fresh parsley**
1 tsp. celery seed	**Salt and black pepper to taste**

First, boil the potatoes in their own skins until tender. Then, *while they are still warm* (and this is important since it brings the starch to the surface and enriches the flavor), peel them and cut them into small dice-sized pieces and place them into a 12-by-14 Pyrex baking pan.

Next, in a separate mixing bowl, thoroughly whip together the remaining ingredients (except the salt and pepper), cover, and allow the mixture to "marry" on the countertop for about an hour (of course, this is ten times as good if you allow it to "rest" in the fridge overnight!).

Then when you're ready to eat, place the potatoes in the oven (covered) at 350 degrees and warm them (this should take only about 15 minutes). Then, using a rubber spatula, gently—*but thoroughly*—fold in the dressing mixture, making sure that every single piece of potato is coated.

Finally, season to taste with salt and pepper and serve immediately.

Chef's Note: *For a cold potato salad, prepare the dish fully and chill thoroughly in the refrigerator. You can also let this potato salad set overnight in the fridge, but keep in mind that the flavors will intensify considerably and the spices will get richer!*

Potato Salad Like Yo' Momma Usta Make

Here's a potato salad I guarantee you're gonna love. Rich and creamy to the bottom of the bowl, it reminds you of those times when you snuck into the refrigerator long after supper for just one mo' bite. Try this one for Momma!

10 red (Irish) potatoes, boiled and peeled
½ medium-size white onion, finely chopped
¼ cup finely sliced green onions
½ cup finely chopped celery
2 sweet pickles, finely diced
6 hard-boiled eggs, whites and yolks separated

2 cups Blue Plate mayonnaise
2 tbsp. yellow prepared mustard
2 tbsp. Creole mustard
2 tsp. Louisiana hot sauce
2 tsp. paprika
Salt and white pepper to taste

Start off by chopping your potatoes until they are in chunks about an inch or so square—*they shouldn't look like mashed potatoes, y'all!*

Next, mix into the potatoes—*one ingredient at a time*—the onions, the green onions, the celery, and the pickles. Then when everything is thoroughly blended, coarsely chop the egg whites and stir them in. Now gently fold—*evenly!*

Next, in a separate bowl, cream together the mayonnaise, the egg yolks, the yellow mustard, the Creole mustard, and the Louisiana hot sauce. And I do mean *cream it* until you end up with nothing but a yellowish paste that is smooth and silky. This is the secret step to making a good-tasting potato salad. It's what gives you the harmony of flavors in every single bite.

At this point, you want to gently fold the egg yolk and mayonnaise paste into the potatoes—being careful not to mash too many of the potato chunks. Then stir in half of the paprika and season the salad to taste with the salt and white pepper. But be careful not to oversalt or you'll lose the delicate enhancement of the individual ingredients.

Finally, sprinkle on the remaining paprika to garnish and color the top. Then cover the potato salad with plastic wrap and chill it in the refrigerator for at least an hour before you serve it.

This is good stuff! And it goes good with almost anything, from baked redfish to barbecued chicken to pot-roasted pork to boiled crawfish!

Chef's Note: *Use small Irish potatoes in this dish, not "B"-size creamer potatoes.*

Variation: *To make Cajun-Style Potato Salad, try adding ½ cup finely chopped smoked sausage to the recipe.*

Sicilian Green Bean and Olive Salad

The next time you're looking for that perfect salad, and you're tired of the plain old lettuce and tomato routine, make this one for your family. They'll love it ... whether they're Sicilian or not!

½ head lettuce, shredded
4 cans Italian green beans, drained
1 medium tomato, cut in small dice
1 medium yellow onion, coarsely
   chopped
½ cup extra-virgin olive oil
3 tbsp. white wine vinegar

1 tsp. sweet basil
½ tsp. oregano
1 tsp. garlic powder
1 cup pitted green olives
½ cup crumbled bacon bits
Salt and black pepper to taste
Grated Romano cheese for topping

In a large shallow salad bowl, toss together the lettuce, green beans, tomato, and chopped onion until they are uniformly mixed.

Then in a separate bowl, make a salad base by mixing together well the olive oil, vinegar, sweet basil, oregano, and garlic powder. When the base is thoroughly blended fold in the olives and the bacon bits and season the dressing to taste with salt and pepper. Now allow the mixture to *rest* at room temperature for about an hour.

At this point, pour the dressing over the salad and toss it gently—you don't want to break up the beans, but you want to make sure that every bit of the salad is coated.

Finally, cover the dish with plastic wrap and place it in the refrigerator to chill (preferably overnight, but no less than 2 hours).

When you're ready to eat, spoon out a heaping helping of the salad in a cold bowl, top with Romano cheese, and serve with crackers, croutons, melba toast, or breadsticks.

Chef's Note: *For easier preparation and a more authentic Sicilian flavor, simply sprinkle on a couple of teaspoonfuls of Frank Davis "Strictly N'Awlins" Sicilian Seasoning instead of the basil, oregano, and garlic powder. To order these spices by direct mail, call 1-800-742-4231.*

Original New Orleans Wop Salad

I remember as a child how much I relished the delicious fried chicken from Jim's on Carrollton Avenue. There was something special about the batter, or maybe it was the marinade, or the seasoning mix. I don't know! And there was something else special about Jim's Fried Chicken—that great-tasting "wop salad" they served with it! Well, this is as close as you're gonna get to the good old days.

3 cups torn lettuce

1 large Creole tomato, cut in wedges

⅔ cup peeled celery, cut in bite-size chunks

¼ cup green olives with pimientos

¼ cup pitted black olives

½ cup fresh diced bell pepper

¼ cup red wine vinegar

½ cup finely chopped onion

2 cups extra-virgin olive oil

12 flat anchovies, oil reserved

1 tsp. garlic powder

Salt and coarse-ground black pepper to taste

¼ cup grated Pecorino Romano cheese

1 clove fresh garlic

3 hard-boiled eggs, quartered

In a large wooden or plastic salad bowl, vigorously toss all the salad vegetables—the lettuce, tomato, celery, green olives, black olives, and bell pepper. Then place the bowl in the refrigerator to get everything cold.

While the salad fixings are chilling, take a large cold mixing bowl—preferably stainless steel—pour in the red wine vinegar, and add the finely chopped onions. Then, with a wire whisk or an electric hand mixer, begin whipping in the olive oil in a thin stream until it blends with the vinegar.

Next, pour in the oil from the anchovies and whip that in as well. Then sprinkle in the garlic powder, along with the salt and coarsely ground black pepper, and whip them in too.

At this point, remove the salad vegetables from the refrigerator, pour the dressing evenly over the top, drop in the anchovies and the Romano cheese, and toss everything vigorously again. Now, put the salad back into the fridge for about 30 minutes so that the vegetables pick up the flavors.

Then, when you're ready to eat, take the salad bowls you're going to serve in—*and for authenticity you should serve wop salad in wooden bowls*—rub the insides thoroughly with the clove of fresh garlic to season them, and spoon up the salad ... decorated and garnished with the boiled eggs.

Hey, y'all! Is that like you had at Jim's, or what?

Summertime Gumbo Salad

If you take the word literally, "gumbo" means everything good mixed all together. But you don't have to mix it together in a traditional roux! I've taken bacon, shrimp, and chicken, combined them with a rich boiled-egg base—kinda like an egg salad—spiced it up N'Awlins style, and chilled it all into a perfect light meal for those steamy Crescent City summers! Go ahead—whip up a batch of your own. You'll love it!

1 qt. water
1 cup white wine (Chablis or
  Chenin Blanc)
2 whole carrots, coarsely chopped
1 medium onion, coarsely chopped
3 ribs celery, coarsely chopped
3 deboned skinless chicken breasts
1 lb. thick-sliced bacon
8 boiled eggs, coarsely chopped
1 cup finely chopped onions
⅔ cup finely chopped celery
½ cup finely sliced green onions

2 whole shallots, finely minced
2 cups real mayonnaise
1 tsp. yellow prepared mustard
1 tsp. chicken base (or 1 bouillon
  cube)
2 tsp. liquid crabboil
2 lb. tiny salad shrimp, precooked
1 tsp. salt
½ tsp. black pepper
½ tsp. paprika
¼ cup finely minced parsley for
  garnish

First, pour the quart of water and the cup of white wine into a 3-quart saucepan, along with the 2 carrots, the medium onion, and the 3 ribs of celery. Then bring the mixture to a *slow boil* and let it simmer for at least 15 minutes so that a rich-flavored "poaching stock" can develop.

When it's ready, drop in the 3 chicken breasts and let them poach in the liquid for about 12-15 minutes, depending upon the size of the breasts. Remember, you want them fully cooked but just tender—if you overcook them, they'll come out dry. Keep in mind, too, that "poaching" means the water just barely bubbles—you don't want to *boil* the chicken.

While the chicken is poaching, put the bacon into a frypan and cook it nice and crisp, rendering out all the excess fat. Then drain the bacon on paper towels and chop it into small bite-size chunks.

At this point, take a large mixing bowl and drop in the hard-boiled eggs, the cup of finely chopped onions, the ⅔ cup of chopped celery, the ½ cup of green onions, the chopped bacon, and the minced shallots. Now mix all the ingredients together until they are uniformly blended.

Meanwhile, in a separate bowl, thoroughly whip together the mayonnaise, the mustard, and the chicken base until the mixture becomes smooth and creamy. Set it aside momentarily.

Now take the chicken breasts out of the poaching liquid and set them on a cutting board to cool. But don't discard the poaching stock! Bring it back to a boil and pour in the liquid crabboil. Then drop in the salad shrimp; and when the water comes back to a boil, turn the fire off, remove the pot from the burner, and let the shrimp soak for 3 minutes.

While the shrimp are soaking, cut up the chicken into small bite-size pieces and add them to the main mixing bowl. Then take a colander, drain the shrimp thoroughly, and place them in the main mixing bowl, too, along with all the vegetables you used in the poaching stock.

Once again, with a large spoon, mix all the ingredients together until uniformly blended. Then, using a large rubber spatula, fold in the seasoned mayonnaise base—*do this gently so that you don't break up the shrimp, but make sure that every single morsel is coated with the mayo.*

All that's left is to taste the final mix for salt and black pepper and add what you need. To finish the recipe, place the salad in a large glass casserole dish, sprinkle it lightly with paprika, garnish it with parsley, and chill it in the refrigerator for at least 3 hours so that the full flavor can develop.

I suggest you serve the gumbo salad with fresh-baked French pistolettes, on a cold lettuce leaf with wheat thins or corn chips, stuffed into a chilled Creole tomato or half of an avocado, or plain and simple on a saucer surrounded by saltine crackers and washed down with a glass of iced tea.

Any way you serve it, it makes summertime special!

Chef's Note:
1—When I refer to shallots, *I'm not talking about green onions. I mean real shallots—those little purple bulbs that taste like a cross between an onion and a garlic.*

2—You should be able to find a jar of chicken base on your grocery shelf near the seasonings and spices. But if you can't find it where you shop, take a chicken bouillon cube and drop it into just enough hot water to dissolve it into a light paste. Remember, though, that if you have to use a bouillon cube, you'll also have to reduce the amount of salt you put in the finished dish because bouillon cubes are always salty.

3—Be careful not to overseason the gumbo salad with salt and pepper. It may not taste as if you've seasoned it properly at the outset; but as it "rests" in the refrigerator the seasonings will become stronger as the flavors marry.

Italian Salad with Caesar Dressing

With a chilled bottle of Frascati or Lambrusco or Chianti and a fresh-baked loaf of Italian bread … this can be a whole meal!

Salad Fixings:

In a large wooden or stainless-steel bowl, prepare the following ingredients and place them in the refrigerator to chill:

½ head iceberg lettuce, broken in bits

1 head romaine lettuce, broken in bits

6 radishes, thinly sliced

8 Italian plum tomatoes (or cherry tomatoes), chopped

1 small zucchini, sliced

2 ribs celery, in bite-size chunks

10 fresh mushrooms, quartered

1 small cucumber, sliced

1 large carrot, peeled and julienned

½ green bell pepper, sliced

½ red bell pepper, sliced

½ yellow bell pepper, sliced

4 hard-boiled eggs, sliced

12 anchovies, rolled with capers

½ cup green olives, chopped

½ cup black olives, whole

⅔ cup shredded mozzarella cheese

1 large clove garlic, peeled

The Caesar Dressing:

2 whole eggs

2 tbsp. red wine vinegar

2 tbsp. fresh lemon juice

1 tbsp. garlic puree (or 3 baked garlic cloves)

2 tsp. Worcestershire sauce

8 minced flat anchovies plus the anchovy oil

2 heaping tbsp. Grey Poupon mustard

1½ cups extra-virgin olive oil

½ cup grated Romano

Salt and black pepper to taste

In a large bowl, beat the eggs until superfrothy. Then, with a whisk, beating continuously, begin adding the other ingredients one at a time until they are all blended smoothly together and the olive oil is in "suspension."

When you're ready to eat, spoon out the salad fixings into ice-cold bowls, top them with the dressing, and toss everything together well.

And that's all there is to it!

Chef's Note: *It is okay to use a blender or food processor (or even electric beaters) to make this dressing if you can't work the whisk.*

Oh—and I suggest you serve the salad with garlic sticks or fresh-baked Italian bread brushed with olive oil.

Frank's Famous Italian Salad Mix

Next to the mix the Tusa Brothers make at Central Grocery on Decatur Street in New Orleans, you won't find an Italian salad mix better than this one anyplace this side of Palermo!

1 cup finely chopped onions
½ cup finely diced carrots
½ cup finely chopped cauliflower
¾ cup finely diced celery
¼ cup chopped pimientos
½ cup chopped marinated artichoke hearts
1 cup commercial olive salad mix

2 cups chopped green olives
2 cups chopped black olives
¼ cup capers
¼ cup chopped anchovies
4 cups extra-virgin olive oil
½ cup red wine vinegar
3 tsp. salt
2 tsp. black pepper

In a large stainless-steel, glass, or plastic bowl, mix together all the ingredients thoroughly. Then cover the mixture tightly with plastic wrap and allow it to *cure* in your refrigerator at least overnight.

The next day, you can package it in either plastic or glass containers and store it in your refrigerator for up to 30 days.

Chef's Note: *I suggest you remove the mix from the refrigerator and allow it to set at room temperature for at least 3 hours before using it on salads, muffalettas, and pasta so that the olive oil will become liquid (it will harden slightly in the refrigerator).*

Also note that the liquids that the bottled olives and marinated artichoke hearts come packed in should be added to the mixture and not discarded.

CHAPTER 3

Chowders, Soups, and Gumbos

Cajun Chowder Cordon Bleu

Slowly simmer rich Cajun tasso, tender chunks of chicken, and creamy melted Swiss cheese in a butter-roux milk stock that you've transformed into a thickened chowder … and you've got yourself one of the best bowls of gourmet Louisiana you've ever savored! You won't believe how tasty this stuff is!

½ stick butter
2 cups sliced fresh mushrooms
4 tbsp. all-purpose flour
2 gal. water
2 cups coarsely chopped onions
2 cups coarsely chopped celery
1 cup coarsely chopped bell pepper
3 whole bay leaves
4 cloves garlic, chopped
3 whole carrots, coarsely chopped
2 tsp. poultry seasoning

2 whole fryer-broiler chickens
2 qt. whole milk
2 cups julienned tasso
2 cups finely diced peeled carrots
Salt and black pepper to taste
4 cups finely diced Irish potatoes
1 cup shredded Swiss cheese
Thinly sliced green onions for
    topping
Butter for topping

First, in a heavy 12-inch skillet, melt the ½ stick of butter over medium-high heat and sauté the sliced mushrooms until they are tender and most of the liquid from the mushrooms has evaporated. Then sprinkle the flour into the skillet evenly, reduce the heat to low, and cook for 5 minutes—stirring constantly—to make a butter roux (but do not let the flour brown!). Set the mixture aside to cool when it's done.

Meanwhile, in a large stockpot, bring 2 gallons of water to a rapid boil and drop in the onions, celery, bell pepper, bay leaves, garlic, carrots, and poultry seasoning. After the seasoning vegetables soften in the stock (which should take about 15 minutes), put the whole chickens in the pot and poach them—covered—at a slow boil for about an hour or so.

When the chickens are done, remove them from the pot to let them cool (they'll probably fall apart, but that's what you want them to do!). Then strain the poaching stock, throw away all the seasoning vegetables, put the stock back into the pot, and reduce it over medium heat to about one-half of its original volume (don't skip this part because this is what concentrates the flavor of the chicken). If you plan to serve the chowder as soon as it's done, I also suggest you take a ladle and meticulously skim all the excess floating fat off the stock.

At this point, you can begin to build the chowder!

First, pick all the meat from the chicken, being careful to discard the skin, gristle, and bones. Then after the stock has been reduced to 2 quarts and defatted, stir in the milk and bring the mixture to a slow boil. Now drop in the chicken meat, along with the sliced tasso and the mushroom-butter roux, and let the chowder cook for 10 minutes, stirring constantly so that it begins to thicken slightly. If it becomes too thick (remember, you want it the consistency of melted ice cream), simply add more whole milk as necessary.

Now stir in the diced carrots, cover the pot, reduce the heat to low, and simmer the chowder for 30 minutes. Then 15 minutes before you're ready to eat, season the chowder with salt and pepper to taste and drop in the diced potatoes (as the chowder cooks, you may have to add a little more milk to the mixture to compensate for the thickening effect of the potatoes).

Just before you're ready to serve, either drop the Swiss cheese into the chowder and stir it in rapidly to cause it to melt, or sprinkle a handful of the cheese over each bowl as you serve it.

All that's left is to garnish each bowl with a teaspoon or two of thinly sliced green onions, top it with a pat of butter, and serve it up piping hot with a side-stack of crispy table wafers. Ummmmmmmmm!

Chef's Note: *Tasso is spicy, fully cooked pork used to flavor beans, soups, stews, and other Cajun dishes. In South Louisiana, it is marketed principally by Savoie in half-pound packages and is available in most supermarkets.*

If the chicken stock you end up with is not flavorful enough to suit your taste, dissolve a couple of tablespoons of prepared chicken base into the stock to enrich the taste.

I don't suggest you skin the chicken before poaching it, because there is a tremendous amount of flavor in the skin. Besides, it's too easy to completely defat the stock after it's made. Simply chill it in the refrigerator until the fat floats to the top and hardens ... then scoop it off in chunks.

If Frank Davis "Strictly N'Awlins" Poultry Seasoning is not available where you shop, it can be ordered by calling 1-800-742-4231.

Making a Great Leftover Turkey Chowder

Every year after Thanksgiving and Christmas, you're probably confused about what to do with leftover turkey. Oh, sure ... you can make turkey po' boys or turkey casserole or turkey potpie. But lemme suggest that this year you fix a great turkey chowder. Here's how you do it!

Cut up some green onions, celery, and parsley—about 2 cups of green onions, 1 cup of celery, and 1 cup of parsley. Then take a skillet, melt down a half-stick of butter (or better yet, take some of the turkey fat from the drippings), and sauté the vegetables until they wilt. Now, with the fat removed (either by skimming it off or by lifting it off once it's refrigerated) pour all the drippings from the turkey you baked into the sautéed vegetables and cook them for about 15 minutes at a slow simmer. I also suggest you drop in your leftover turkey, including all the turkey debris—the little pieces of turkey meat that fell off the bones while you were doing the carving.

Okay—here comes the coup de grace! Turn up your fire to high, bring the concoction to a boil, and immediately begin stirring in some heavy cream. But do it a little at a time. You want just enough cream to accent the turkey flavor—you don't want the mixture to taste like a "turkey cream sauce." You'll be able to tell—I suspect you should be able to get by with about a half-pint.

Then let it cook on high—reducing—until the liquid thickens slightly. When it's just the way you want it, ladle it out over some angelhair pasta or a bowl full of fettucini—whichever you prefer. I'd also sprinkle it with some fresh basil (finely chopped) and top it off with a dash or two or imported Romano. Lemme tell y'all—Julius Caesar should have had it this good!

N'Awlins Homemade Vegetable-Beef Soup

Contrary to what you've always heard, making a *good pot* of soup is not just throwing everything together in a Dutch oven and letting it boil for 3 hours. There's a method to making really good vegetable soup ... and here's the method.

2 lb. lean chuck roast
6 qt. water
1 small head fresh broccoli, florets only
1 medium head cabbage, shredded
2 cups whole-kernel corn
¼ lb. fresh green beans
1 large potato, diced
1 large turnip, diced
6 ribs celery, chopped semicoarse
1 large onion, diced
2 green onions, chopped coarse
3 large carrots, julienned and chopped
1 large fresh tomato, peeled and diced
1 tsp. summer savory
Salt and black pepper to taste
½ stick butter
1 cup cooked Ronzoni soup pasta—No. 44
Grated Romano cheese for garnish

First off, when you buy your beef make sure you get all the bones it was cut from—then get another pound or so of extra bones ('cuz you can't make "good beef soup" without a rich beef stock; and we're not cooking this soup in water ... *we're cooking it in stock!*).

So the first thing you do is dice your beef into 1-inch squares, put the diced beef and all the bones into a baking pan, and roast them at 400 degrees until they turn a nice rich brown (approximately 20 minutes). Now, while the meat is browning, bring your water to a boil (and for the best soup ever, I recommend you use bottled water instead of tap water).

When your beef and bones have browned, drop them into the boiling water in the stockpot and let them cook at a "slow bubble" for at least *4 hours* (8 hours is even better), skimming the surface for scum occasionally. Then when your stock is ready, strain it, pick the meat from the bones, and finely chop half of the diced beef.

Now you're ready to make soup!

Put all the beef back in the stock and start adding vegetables. And the best tip I can give you is to *cut up all the vegetables in equal-size pieces and add them a little at a time so that you don't reduce the cooking temperature of the stock.* In other words, you want the stock to keep on boiling the entire time you add the vegetables.

Continue to add vegetables until they are all in the soup. Then toss in the summer savory, reduce the fire to medium-low, and let the soup *"just bubble"* until all the vegetables tenderize (about 2 hours generally). By the way, you should cook the soup covered for all but the last *half-hour* (it needs a half-hour to "reduce").

Then, about 10 minutes before you're ready to eat, add your salt and pepper to taste, stir in the butter, and drop in the soup pasta. I suggest you serve the soup piping hot in deep bowls, accompanied by croutons and topped with grated Romano. We're talking magnifico, here!

Chef's Note:

1—Chop only half of the beef, leaving the other half in squares. It will make a nicer presentation.

2—To make the soup "fat free," ideally you should make the stock the day before cooking the soup, refrigerate it, and remove the congealed fat from the top of the stock. To make the soup the same day you make the stock, just skim off the greasy layer. Of course, you will have to leave out the butter at the end of the cooking time, too.

3—To peel the fresh tomato easily, put it in the freezer until it becomes almost frozen. Then let it sit out at room temperature until just the outer skin starts to loosen. It will come right off with one or two swipes. You can also drop the tomato into boiling water for a minute or two and remove the peel that way as well.

4—If you don't have soup pasta on hand, break some uncooked fettucini noodles or spaghetti in pieces about 1/2 inch long and drop in the soup. By the time they cook and swell, they'll be perfect for the soup.

5—And to add a little bit of elegance to the vegetable-beef soup, stir in about a tablespoon of a really good brandy about 10 minutes before you serve it. You'll be surprised at how tremendously it enhances the flavor!

Old N'Awlins Split Pea Soup

New Orleanians love their split pea soup at two important times during the year … at Mardi Gras, and whenever it gets cold! And since we need a robust soup to ready the taste buds for a Christmas brisket, here's my split pea recipe. I guarantee, you're gonna love it!

6 strips lean bacon	4 carrots, cubed
4 tbsp. bacon drippings	2 qt. homemade chicken stock
1 lb. smoked ham, cut in small cubes	2 tsp. Worcestershire sauce
1 lb. split green peas, dried	1/2 tsp. black pepper
2 cups diced onions	3 smoked ham hocks
2 ribs celery, finely chopped	Salt to taste
	Parsley to garnish

First, take a skillet and render down the bacon strips until they turn crisp. Then drain them on paper towels and crumble them into small pieces.

Meanwhile, reheat the bacon drippings in the skillet to high, drop in the cubed ham, and stir-fry the cubes until they brown slightly. Now toss into the pan the peas, onions, celery, and carrots and sauté—*agitating constantly*—until the vegetables begin to wilt. (Remember that by quick-frying the peas, you'll soften them more easily and make a much smoother soup.)

While the mix is sautéing, add the chicken stock to a 5-quart Dutch oven and bring it to a boil.

Then when the vegetables are tender-crisp (cooked but still a little crunchy) add them to the chicken stock.

Now bring the mixture to a full boil and—*constantly stirring*—add the Worcestershire sauce, black pepper, ham hocks, and crumbled bacon. This is also when you salt the soup to taste, but I suggest you go lightly since you have a variable amount of salt already in the ham and bacon.

At this point, reduce the heat to low, cover the pot tightly, and simmer the soup for about 2 hours, stirring occasionally so that the peas don't stick and burn on the bottom.

After 1 hour of cooking time, though, take a slotted spoon, remove the ham hocks, cut the meat off the bones, and return the meat to the soup. Then cover the pot again and continue cooking.

When you're ready to eat, ladle the piping hot soup into deep bowls, sprinkle on a pinch of parsley for garnish, and serve with saltines, breadsticks, or hot buttered French bread.

Chef's Note: *For thick, creamy split pea soup, cook 15 minutes longer with the pot cover removed. To thin the soup should it become too thick, add a little extra chicken stock or whole milk.*

Shrimp and Okra Gumbo

If you like a good rich-tasting shrimp and okra gumbo … this is the one you've been looking for! Chock-full of okra, shrimp, fresh New Orleans seasoning vegetables, and spiced with just the right amount of peppery smoked sausage, it's the one I want you to try the next time you get a craving for a taste of real New Orleans food!

½ cup vegetable oil
½ cup all-purpose flour
2 cups diced onions
1 cup diced bell peppers
1 cup finely chopped celery
6 cloves garlic, chopped
¼ cup minced parsley
¼ cup sliced green onions
½ lb. hot country smoked sausage, sliced
4 cans Trappey's cut okra, drained
1 can Rotel tomatoes with chilies

2 tbsp. apple cider vinegar
6 cups chicken stock
2 cups shrimp stock
¾ oz. dried shrimp
3 bay leaves
½ tsp. thyme
2 tsp. basil
1 tbsp. Kitchen Bouquet
Salt, black, and red pepper to taste
3 lb. peeled and deveined shrimp (25-30 count)
6 cups cooked long-grain rice

This is one of those recipes that starts off with a traditional New Orleans roux—that's equal parts of all-purpose flour and vegetable oil, cooked slowly over medium heat until you get a rich, nutty-flavored brown paste. Keep in mind that you may have to cook the mixture for a half-hour or more to get the right consistency and color.

Then when the roux is ready, drop in the seasoning vegetables and stir them in thoroughly. This does two things: it lowers the temperature of the roux and keeps it from browning any further, and the residual heat from the roux cooks the vegetables to the proper doneness.

At this point, set the roux aside for awhile and begin preparing the rest of the gumbo. Here's how you do it.

In a deep-sided skillet, fry the sausage slices over medium-high heat until they begin to brown and render out any excess fat (this should take about 10 minutes). Then drop in the drained okra and the tomatoes, pour in the vinegar (it cuts the okra slime!), and fry over high heat until the okra is softened and tender (another 10 minutes or so).

Now in a 6- to 8-quart gumbo pot, start combining your ingredients. First, pour in the chicken and shrimp stock and bring it to a boil over high heat. Then spoon in the okra-sausage mixture, along with the roux, and stir everything together until it is uniformly blended. Then, when the mixture starts to bubble, reduce the heat to medium-low, cover the pot, and cook the gumbo for about 15 minutes so that the roux can thicken ever so slightly.

Here's where all the rest of your ingredients—*except the fresh shrimp and the rice!*—go in. Stir in the dried shrimp, bay leaves, thyme, basil, Kitchen Bouquet, salt, and peppers. Then cover the pot once more, reduce the heat to low, and simmer the gumbo again for another 30 minutes, stirring occasionally to make sure the okra isn't sticking to the bottom of the pot.

After the allotted cooking time, *taste* the gumbo, adjust the seasoning—add more salt or pepper if you want—and adjust the thickness by adding either more stock or more roux as you desire. Ideally, New Orleans gumbo should have the consistency of a semithick soup, but if you like yours a little watery, feel free to add more stock to thin it out. By the way, this gumbo is best if cooked *very very slowly* for about 3 or 4 hours or longer. All you do is add stock as you need it and stir it occasionally.

Now, *about 15 minutes before you're ready to eat,* drop the fresh shrimp into the gumbo, stir them in well, put the lid back on the pot, and let them cook over low heat. To add them before the last 15 minutes will overcook them and cause them to be rubbery and grainy.

Then when you're ready to chow down, spoon up a big bowl of steamed rice, ladle the gumbo over it, and serve it piping hot alongside a tall stack of buttered saltine crackers and your favorite frosty drink.

Babe, there ain't nothing better, anytime!

Chef's Note: Don't leave out the dried shrimp! *They contribute immensely to the "shrimpy flavor" of the gumbo.*

If you prefer not to use canned okra (personally, I like it for gumbo), you can substitute 4 packages of frozen okra in its place. Just remember that you're going to have to extend the cooking time to get the okra tender.

I also suggest you make extra roux and extra stock. If for some reason your gumbo comes out too thin, just spoon in a little extra roux and cook it until it thickens to your liking. If for some reason your gumbo turns out too thick, just pour in a little extra shrimp (or chicken) stock and cook it until it thins out the way you want it. Don't add water instead of stock or you'll dilute the flavor.

One more thing—I don't recommend you use any more sausage than the amount I've indicated. Because shrimp are so delicate, it's easy to overpower the gumbo with sausage flavor. Just a hint of sausage piques the shrimp.

Oh—and by frying the okra with a couple tablespoons of vinegar you eliminate most of the "rope" (slime) that comes from okra when it's cooking.

Pure-Cajun Chicken-Sausage Gumbo

This is one of the richest, tastiest gumbos you're ever gonna eat ... and it's made with three different kinds of sausage. I want you to try it the next time you get a craving for some real down-home Cajun food!

1 stewing hen (about 3 to 4 lb.)
½ lb. Cajun andouille sausage, sliced
½ lb. hot sausage, sliced
1 lb. country smoked sausage, sliced
Salt and pepper to taste
Drippings from sausage
3 carrots, coarsely diced
2 large bay leaves

2 large onions, quartered
2 ribs celery, coarsely diced
½ lb. mushrooms, sliced
⅔ cup peanut oil
1 cup all-purpose flour
1½ cups diced onions
1 cup finely chopped celery
½ cup diced bell peppers
4 cloves garlic, chopped
6 cups cooked long-grain rice

Start off by skinning the hen, cutting it in pieces, and deboning the meat. Then in a large pot filled with just enough water to cover, cook the bones and chicken skin at a "slow boil" for about an hour or so.

When they're done, remove the bones and skin from the boiling pot and allow them to cool ... *but save the boiling liquid and set it back on a low fire for awhile.*

Next take a skillet and slowly sauté the sausages until you render out most of their fat. While they're cooking, salt and pepper the deboned chicken pieces and dust them lightly in flour. Then pan-sauté the chicken in the sausage drippings until they slightly brown. At the same time, place the cooked sausage in a stockpot containing enough water to cover them and boil the pieces until they are tender (which should take about 30 minutes).

Now pick the meat from the cooled chicken bones. Then combine both the boiled chicken and the sautéed chicken and set the mixture aside.

At this point, put the bones and chicken skin back into the pot you have on the low fire and simmer the stock again—this time along with the carrots, the bay leaves, the onions, and the celery—until a rich broth is brewed. Incidentally, to develop that richness it is best to cook the stock slowly for about 3 to 4 hours or longer. All you do is keep adding water as needed.

Meanwhile, in the skillet with the leftover sausage drippings, sauté the mushrooms until they brown. Then remove the mushrooms and set them aside. Now add the peanut oil to the drippings, bring the combined fats to the point of them "almost smoking," whisk in the flour, and make your roux *(and by the way, you want it to reach a dark brown color)*. When it's ready, stir in the fresh aromatics (onions, celery, bell peppers, and garlic) and blend them thoroughly. This will cool down the roux, stop it from browning any further, and flavor it at the same time.

Now you're ready to make gumbo!

The first thing you have to do is strain and de-fat your stocks. Remember, you have two—chicken and sausage. And to get the best results out of this gumbo, you should use all the chicken stock (which should come out to be about 6 to 8 cups after the reduction) *but* just enough of the sausage stock to give you the flavor of sausage (maybe 2 cups). *Don't overpower the gumbo with sausage! You just want a hint of it!*

So now bring the combined stocks to a rolling boil in a large pot and begin stirring in the roux a little at a time. You want to give the stock "body" but you don't want it thick. When the gumbo stock is the consistency you desire, toss in the mushrooms, the chicken meat, and the sausage pieces and stir everything together well. At this point you "taste" for seasoning and flavor—add salt if you need it, add more pepper if there wasn't enough in the sausage, and add some more sausage stock if you want to.

Then bring the entire pot of gumbo to a slow simmer and let it cook— *covered*—for another hour until all the flavors marry into a succulent and rich New Orleans Cajun delicacy!

All that's left is to ladle the gumbo over a bowl of hot steamed rice and serve it with a tall stack of crispy saltine crackers or a big piece of hot, buttered, fresh-baked French bread.

Mes amis … dat's Cajun, yeah!

Louisiana Lagniappe Gumbo

So who says you can only have shrimp in gumbo? Or crabs in gumbo? Or okra in gumbo? Or chicken and sausage in gumbo? You know what? You can make gumbo with anything you want to! That's what lagniappe is—*a little something extra!* Try this lagniappe gumbo and tell me it ain't the best-tasting stuff!

¼ cup vegetable oil
⅓ cup all-purpose flour
2 medium onions, coarsely diced
3 ribs celery, coarsely diced
1 lb. smoked sausage, cut in pieces
1 can tomato sauce, 16-oz. size
4 qt. bottled water
4 bay leaves
4 cloves garlic, finely minced
⅛ tsp. thyme
3 tbsp. Kitchen Bouquet

¼ cup sundried shrimp
1½ cups chicken stock
3 lb. frozen sliced okra
3 tbsp. extra-virgin olive oil
6 gumbo crabs, halved
Salt and black pepper to taste
3 lb. peeled salad shrimp
1 lb. claw crabmeat
¼ cup fresh-chopped parsley
1 lb. long-grain rice, cooked
1 box saltine crackers, buttered

As the old expression goes … "First you make a roux!" So in a 10-quart gumbo or stockpot, the first thing you do is mix together the oil and the flour and cook it over medium-high heat—*stirring constantly!*—until the flour turns a rich peanut-butter color. Then when you got it just the right shade, turn off the fire, drop in the onions and the celery, and let the vegetables cool the roux down (which is how you stop the flour from browning any further).

Next, remove the roux from the stockpot with a spoon and set it aside for awhile. Then in the same stockpot fry down the cut sausage over medium-high heat until the pieces just begin to brown slightly. At this point, you can begin putting your gumbo together. Here's what you do.

First, pour the tomato sauce into the stockpot over the smoked sausage—*but do this very slowly and very carefully.* Remember the pot is hot and there should be sausage drippings sizzling on the bottom—you don't want them to splatter. Then pour in the water and stir the entire mixture thoroughly. Now stir in the bay leaves, the garlic, the thyme, and the Kitchen Bouquet and bring the gumbo stock to a slow boil.

Meanwhile—*and here's the trick to making this gumbo taste unbelievably shrimpy!*—put the sundried shrimp and the chicken stock into a food processor. Then, using the steel cutter blade, puree the shrimp until they are silky smooth and almost creamy. Then thoroughly stir the shrimp puree into the gumbo stock and cook the entire mixture for about 15 minutes at a "slow bubble."

In the meantime, toss the sliced okra with the olive oil and place it in a steamer. Then after about 10 minutes of *steaming* over high heat (nope, you don't fry your okra for this gumbo!), gently drop the okra into the gumbo pot, along with the crabs, and begin spooning in your roux about a half-cup at a time.

Gotta caution you here: you absolutely *must* allow the gumbo to continue to cook over medium heat as you add the roux. Remember—you're gonna get some thickening from the okra as it cooks, and only after the roux cooks for 5 to 10 minutes will it swell and thicken. So be sure to let your gumbo cook about 10 minutes each time you add more roux—otherwise it's gonna turn out gritty and extremely pasty.

Now, when you get the stock just the right consistency (which is somewhere between a thick stew and a plain soup), turn the fire down to low, put the lid on the pot, and let the whole thing simmer for 45 minutes.

Then 15 minutes before you're ready to eat, with the fire still on low, add your salt and black pepper to taste and gently stir in the salad shrimp, the claw crabmeat, and the parsley.

I suggest you serve this gumbo piping hot over a bowl of steamed rice alongside a stack of buttered saltine crackers! Y'all ... it's hard to beat!

Chef's Note: *By not frying the okra, as is done in the traditional way of making gumbo, you're keeping it firm and green instead of turning it into a yukky, gooey military gray. But more importantly, by steaming it you're using okra specifically the way it is supposed to be used*—as a thickener!

Just for the record, you add the salad shrimp and the claw crabmeat at the end of the cooking process so that they don't overcook and fall apart.

Lagniappe Meat and Vegetable Gumbo

This is one of those "throw everything in the pot" recipes. I mean, if you plan to take time out and do a little relaxing, you don't want to waste any of it by being tied up in the kitchen cooking. Yet you still want to eat well! So with that in mind, I created Lagniappe Meat and Vegetable Gumbo. You take beef, chicken, pork, and sausage (or anything else you got left over in the fridge), blend it with lush fresh vegetables, smother it in a rich chicken stock, and serve it over steamed rice. I promise you, this stuff will get rave reviews—and you can eat whenever you're ready!

¼ cup Crisco oil
⅓ cup all-purpose flour
3 small onions, quartered
4 ribs celery, coarsely chopped
1 bell pepper, coarsely chopped
½ lb. fresh mushrooms, quartered
1 can whole-kernel corn, drained
1 lb. snow peas
4 carrots, peeled and chunked
2 jars baby corn, drained
3 cans Campbell's Chicken Broth

1 can Campbell's Cream of
  Asparagus Soup
2 tbsp. Kitchen Bouquet
1 skinned chicken breast, cubed
1 lb. country smoked sausage,
  chunked
1 lb. pork fillet, cubed
1 lb. beef stew, cubed
Salt and black pepper to taste
6 cups steamed white rice

First, take a heavy 6-quart Dutch oven, pour in the oil, stir in the flour, and make a light-brown roux. *Hint:* I suggest you cook the mixture over medium heat, stirring it constantly, so that it doesn't stick and it doesn't burn.

When the roux is ready, drop in the onions, celery, bell pepper, and mushrooms and mix everything together thoroughly. By adding the vegetables to the roux—*even over medium heat*—you will lower the temperature of the flour and cause it to stop browning, which is exactly what you want to happen. The process will also serve to soften the vegetables and slightly cook them.

Next, pour in the kernel corn, the peas, the carrots, the baby corn, the chicken broth, the asparagus soup, and the Kitchen Bouquet and stir the mixture until it becomes smooth and uniform. At this point, increase the heat to medium-high and bring all the ingredients to a slow bubble. When this happens, drop in the chicken, sausage, pork, and beef and stir everything together again.

Now reduce the fire to low and *simmer* the pot of gumbo for about an hour, stirring occasionally. Remember, you want to let the moisture tenderize the meats, so all this has to happen over a low fire. After about an hour, taste the gravy and adjust for salt and black pepper. Then put the lid back on the pot and continue to simmer for another 30 minutes. Just for the record, the consistency should not be thick, but it shouldn't be watery either. About halfway in between is just right!

When you're ready to eat, spoon the rice directly into the gumbo pot and gently mix it into the meat and vegetables. When it's piping hot, ladle it out into soup bowls and serve it with a big chunk of hot buttered French bread, alongside a frosty glass of iced tea.

It sticks to your ribs, it's tasty, and it's healthful.

Corn and Sausage Fricassee

Take fresh corn right off the cob, stew it down with spicy Rotel tomatoes and a mess of country smoked sausage, serve it with poached broccoli and flavored rice … and you're gonna have a hard time pushing away from the table.

4 strips slab bacon, diced	4 tbsp. chicken base
½ cup chopped onions	1 lb. smoked sausage
4 ears corn on the cob	4 cups fresh broccoli florets (not
1 can Rotel tomatoes with chilies	frozen)
2 qt. water	2 cups long-grain rice

This is one of those recipes you do in sequence … and in *only two pots*. Just follow my directions step by step and it will be the easiest dish you ever prepared!

First, take a 3½-quart saucepan, put it on the stove over medium heat, drop in the bacon pieces, and sauté them until they begin to render out the drippings. Then toss in the diced onions and cook them in the bacon drippings until they soften (they don't have to brown).

While this is going on, take a sharp knife and cut the kernels of corn off the cobs. Be sure you also scrape the cobs with the blade of the knife to get the "corn milk" out of the cob stalks.

Now add the sliced-off kernels and the "milk" to the pot with the bacon and onions and stir everything together well. Then pour in the can of Rotel tomatoes (liquid and all!) and mix everything once more. At this point, cover the pot, turn the fire down to low, and stew (*fricassee* means to stew) the corn with the tomatoes for about 30 minutes.

Meanwhile, in a heavy 4-quart Dutch oven, bring the 2 quarts of water to a rolling boil. Then spoon in the chicken base, stir it around until it is completely dissolved, and lower the fire to medium.

At this point, cut the sausage into 3-inch lengths and drop them in. *Note:* you don't want them to boil rapidly; just a "slow bubble" will do. After cooking about 30 minutes (with the lid on the pot), the sausage pieces should be very tender. Go ahead and take them out of the water with a pair of tongs and push them down into the stewing corn. Cover the pot again—*fire still set at low*—and continue to fricassee the corn.

Next, bring the water you used to cook the sausage back to a rolling boil. Then gently drop the broccoli florets into the pot. Now immediately turn off the fire, cover the pot, and poach the florets for about 4 minutes (or until they are just tender—you still want them a little crunchy when they come out of the pot; the residual heat will finish cooking them to perfection).

When the broccoli is done, take a slotted spoon, remove the florets from the stock, and place them in a 10-by-14 Pyrex baking dish. Cover the dish tightly with plastic wrap and set it aside momentarily.

Finally, in a fine-mesh colander, wash the rice to remove all the excess starch. Then, bring the same stock you used to boil the sausage and poach the broccoli back to a rolling boil and thoroughly stir in the rice.

Now here's the trick. Before you put the water back on the fire, you're going to have to pour off all but about an inch covering the rice. Let me put it another way—if you can take your index finger, put it into the pot, touch the rice with the tip of your finger, and have the water level come up to the first joint of your finger … it's perfect!

Then all you do is cover the pot tightly, reduce the fire to *very low,* and cook the rice until it absorbs all the water—which should take about 12 to 14 minutes. Actually, the rice is really absorbing the flavored stock—all the richness from the sausage as well as the broccoli. I do suggest, however, that about every 4 minutes or so, you uncover the pot, take a fork, fluff up the rice, and make sure it isn't sticking to the bottom of the pot.

Then when you're ready to eat, dish up the hot rice, ladle a big helping of the corn fricassee and a couple of pieces of the sausage over the top, and serve it alongside the flavored broccoli. As they say in back-a-town New Orleans … dem's some fine groceries, y'all!

Chef's Note:

1—Depending upon the kind of chicken base you use, it may take more or less base dissolved in the water to give you the correct flavoring for the stock. Ideally, you want it flavored to the point of saying to yourself, "Yep—that would make a great chicken soup!"

2—For added intensity, you might want to substitute a flavored rice (like basmati or jasmine) for the long-grain variety. It gives the dish a whole new dimension.

3—By the way, because of the intense flavoring of the stock, this dish doesn't need any additional salt and pepper.

CHAPTER 4

Meats

Filets and Rib Eyes … Steakhouse Quality in Your Kitchen!

If you've always complained that you can never get the steaks you grill at home to taste as good as the ones you buy at a steakhouse, I might be able to help you!

First of all, you need to start with the very best beef you can buy! The stuff you get packaged in shrink-wrap and Cryo-Vac at your neighborhood supermarket carries absolutely no guarantees other than "it came from a cow." And there is no way you can tell if a steak is going to be tender or tough just by looking at it. What's more, unless you have a direct line to stockyards in Kansas or the beef purveyors in Chicago you probably can't readily get Kansas or Chicago prime beef.

So what do you do?

You look for and buy only "prime beef"—it's the highest grade you can find. But because it is in such demand, it's often very hard to find. So, your next best bet is *Certified Angus Beef!* Lately it's been getting excellent distribution for the home consumer almost nationwide.

I've had the opportunity to work with the Angus growers and cook the steaks they produce for over ten years. And with the Certified Angus brand you're assured—without guessing—that you have the right amount of aging, marbling texture, and palatability to make it tasty and tender regardless of how you prepare it for the table.

Certified Angus quality used to be limited exclusively to the finest restaurants. But now, you can serve beef of that grade in your *own kitchen!* And usually at a very affordable price!

BUT WHAT ABOUT NUTRITION?

If you're worried about cholesterol, the research indicates that Certified Angus Beef contains less cholesterol than skinless chicken! In fact, shrimp have almost twice the cholesterol as Certified Angus Beef. Keep in mind, too, that the higher-quality Certified Angus has no more cholesterol than the lower-graded beef.

And calories?

Well, a good steak for example has only 57 calories per ounce compared to 70 calories found in each ounce of fried chicken. And each ounce supplies a large share of essential nutrients for those calories. What's more, Certified Angus is highly digestible—96 percent to be exact. That's more digestible than vegetables!

And as far as fat is concerned, 3 ounces of properly cooked Certified Angus contains only about 9 grams of fat … and over *half* of that is unsaturated.

STEAKS ON THE GRILL

This is the secret to cooking your steaks to succulence!

N'Awlins Marinade:

1 cup Crisco oil	⅛ tsp. thyme
½ cup Jack Daniels Black Label Whiskey	½ tsp. garlic powder
	1 tsp. sweet basil
1 tsp. tarragon or red wine vinegar	½ tsp. rosemary
2 tbsp. finely chopped green onions	1 tsp. black pepper
2 tsp. finely chopped parsley	½ tsp. Worcestershire sauce

Mix well. Cover the steaks—either filets mignons, rib eyes, or porter-houses—with the marinade and set them in the refrigerator for at least 3 hours. Then fire up the gas or charcoal grill and preheat it for at least 15 minutes.

When you're ready to cook, take the steaks out of the marinade, pat them dry with paper towels, dredge them in melted butter, and place them on the grill *no more than 3 inches* above the heat source. The whiskey will evaporate during cooking, leaving the meat with a rich charcoal flavor. The trick is to cook the meat *on one side only* (don't keep flipping it over!) until you see red juices seeping through the uncooked side.

Then remove the steaks from the grill, dredge them again in the melted butter, and place them back on the grill—this time flip-side down. All that's left is to cook them to the doneness you desire (but never more than *medium*). Medium-well or well-done steaks render out too much of the natural juices, resulting in a dry, tough, chewy piece of meat.

Oh—here's a gourmet hint: don't be reluctant to dredge the steaks in the melted butter anytime you see the surface starting to dry. The only thing you have to watch for are "flare-ups"—the grill will flame when the butter begins to burn. Just keep a bowl of water handy and sprinkle on a few drops occasionally to control the burn.

Before you remove the steaks from the grill, season them with salt and pepper (or Frank Davis Beef Seasoning) and flip them over once or twice to "melt" in the seasonings.

OTHER PREPARATION HINTS

—You *can* cook steaks while they are still frozen without losing taste or texture. Here's how you do it:

On the grill—instead of cooking 3 inches above the coals, cook 5 to 6 inches above the coals for the first half of the cooking time. Then continue as I've described above.

Broiling in the oven—instead of broiling 1 to 2 inches from the heat, cook 3 to 4 inches away from the heat.

Pan broiling—instead of cooking at medium temperature, sear the meat quickly in a *very hot skillet* before the surface of the meat has a chance to thaw. Slow thawing keeps the meat from browning. After searing, then reduce the heat to medium low.

Pan frying—first sear the meat in a very hot skillet to prevent slow thawing. Then add a thin layer of oil and cook till done. I also suggest you turn a frozen steak more often than you would an unfrozen one.

—Do not salt your beef before cooking. Salt has a tendency to toughen the meat and release succulent juices. Sprinkle on the salt only after the surface has been cooked.

—Do not pierce your steaks during cooking. A meat fork will reduce the juiciness. Use a spatula or tongs to handle meat on the grill or in the skillet.

—Always serve beef on a warm platter. The platter helps to hold in juices and give richer flavors to the beef.

TIPS ON DEFROSTING AND STORING

—Defrost your steaks only in the refrigerator. Never thaw them out at room temperature or by immersing them in water. It takes about 12 hours for a one-inch steak to defrost in the refrigerator.

—In the refrigerator, steaks will keep their flavor and freshness for up to 3 days. Just be sure you do not wrap the beef too tightly—it has to "breathe."

—In the freezer, high-quality beef—double wrapped in freezer paper or heavy plastic film—will stay fresh and full flavored for up to 6 months.

Perfectly Grilled Steaks
(With Jack Daniels Marinade and Creamy Baked Potatoes)

If you've always wondered how to cook steaks perfectly every time, here's the recipe you've been waiting for. And I've piqued the flavor by marinating them in a special sauce made with Jack Daniels Black Label Whiskey to get a subtle smokey taste in the meat when it's grilled. Tell you what ... try it and see if it's not the best you've ever come across!

1 cup extra-virgin olive oil	½ tsp. cumin
1 cup Italian salad dressing	⅛ tsp. thyme
½ cup Jack Daniels Black Label Whiskey	1 tsp. salt
½ cup onion flakes	1 tsp. black pepper
1 tsp. garlic powder	4 tbsp. Worcestershire sauce
2 tsp. sweet basil	6 choice or prime rib eyes (1 inch thick)
½ tsp. crushed rosemary	

First, make your marinade. To do that, take a large plastic or glass mixing bowl and, with a wire whip, mix together all the liquids and seasonings I've listed above. Be sure to take a few extra minutes to blend everything really well—you want the marinade uniformly mixed. Ideally, it should sit on the countertop for at least 2 hours so that all the flavors marry before you use them on the steaks ... but if you're in a hurry, you can use it right away.

Now take a glass or plastic pan *(do not use metal!)* and ladle some of the marinade on the bottom. Then place your steaks on the marinade in the pan. When this is done, pour the remainder of the marinade over the steaks, cover the pan with plastic wrap, and put the steaks into the refrigerator for at least an hour before you cook them. Again, for the ultimate in flavor, you should marinate the steaks overnight.

Then, when you're ready to cook, fire up the grill on high and lower the grating as close to the coals as possible. If you aren't able to raise and lower the grating, pass your hand over the coals to find the hottest spot—*that's where you want to start the steaks!* Here's how you cook them:

1—As soon as the steaks hit the grill, slide them back and forth gently to keep them from sticking to the grating.

2—Cook them *completely* one side at a time. Do not keep turning them over and over again. This just slings the juices out of the steaks and gives you a dry piece of meat. Cooking them one side at a time sears the steaks and locks the juices inside.

3—When the first side is done, flip the steak over with a spatula (not a meat fork—it makes holes in the steaks and allows the succulent juices to escape). Then immediately brush or drizzle on about a tablespoon of margarine—it helps the steak to char-brown and adds a richer flavor. Now equally cook the other side to the same doneness and drizzle it, too, with margarine when you remove it from the grill.

4—The one thing you don't want to do is overcook your steaks. And remember—*no steak should ever be cooked well done!* Well-done meat means that absolutely all the natural juices have been cooked out, leaving it dry, stringy, chewy, and unpalatable.

The juiciest steak is one that is *rare*—which means only the outside is cooked. *Medium rare* means the middle of the steak is still pink but slightly cool. *Medium* gives you a slightly pink middle but one that is warm. *Medium well* leaves you with very little pink in the middle, and it's right on the verge of being too dry.

The one thing you ought to know is that the "red" in a steak is not blood—it's the color of the meat pigment. This might help you decide not to overcook the next steak you toss on the grill!

Finally, you should always serve your steaks the moment they come off the grill. And I suggest you always serve them on heated plates. Most steaks are too small a cut of meat to retain the proper serving temperature in the time it takes to eat them.

Chef's Note:

1—Even if you don't drink alcoholic beverages, you can make and use this marinade, because once the steak hits the hot grill the whiskey will evaporate, leaving the meat with only a subtle charcoal flavor.

2—The best way to tell whether a steak is rare, medium, or well done while you're cooking it is to press it with your fingers while it's cooking. If it feels soft and spongy, it's rare. If it gives you a slight resistance, it's medium. And if it feels firm to the touch, you just overcooked it!

3—The best way to cook perfect baked potatoes is to wash them thoroughly, pat them dry, rub them down with vegetable oil, wrap them tightly in aluminum foil, and bake them for 1 hour at 500 degrees. It makes them tender and creamy.

N'Awlins Beef and Onions

Using either a black cast-iron skillet or Dutch oven, heat 3 tablespoons of a good-quality margarine almost to the point of smoking and quickly stir-fry 2 large yellow onions that you've sliced into rings. Now cook the onions until they turn a rich golden brown—this brings out the natural sugars in the onions and makes them sweet.

Then remove the onions from the pot, reduce the heat to medium, and—in the onion juices—drop in your steaks. You want to cook them until juices rise from the uncooked side. At this point, lightly brush the uncooked side with melted margarine and turn the steaks over. Continue cooking them to the degree of doneness you like—flipping them over several times to get a charred effect. *Make sure you remove whatever melted fat accumulates in the pan!*

When the steaks are just about done, remove them from the pan and season them with salt and pepper (or Frank Davis Beef Seasoning). Then wipe the pan dry with paper towels, place a layer of onions on the bottom of the pan, lay the steaks on the onions, and cover them with the remaining onions. Then let the steaks and onions "simmer" gently for about 5 minutes for the flavors to blend. Finally, serve the steaks and onions together on a warm platter.

N'Awlins Spicy London Broil
(With Shallot Butter)

Charred and crusty on the outside, tender and juicy on the inside, and quick and easy to prepare with just enough spice to make it Naturally N'Awlins—that's my London broil! And when you serve it topped with shallot butter … ummmmmmmmm!

1 can warm Dixie Beer (12 oz.)	3 bay leaves, crushed
¼ cup Crisco oil	3 cloves garlic, minced
1 bunch green onions, thinly sliced	2 tsp. red pepper flakes
2 tbsp. lemon juice	¼ cup soy sauce
2 tbsp. Worcestershire sauce	2 lb. London broil steak, trimmed
4 tbsp. dark brown sugar	lean
1 tbsp. Louisiana hot sauce	Fresh ground black pepper to taste

First, take a large plastic or Pyrex container (*do not use metal!*) and mix together thoroughly all the ingredients for the marinade—in other words, everything except the meat and the fresh-ground black pepper. Then drop the steak into the mixture, baste it well, and stash it (covered) in the refrigerator overnight.

I suggest that you turn it in the marinade every couple of hours to make sure it picks up the seasonings evenly.

Then, about 2 hours before you plan to serve it, remove the steak from the marinade, drain it, and pat it dry with a couple of paper towels. While you're preparing the meat, you should also set the oven to *"broil"* and pre-heat it.

At this point, put the steak in a shallow baking pan and slide it into the oven so that it rests about 4 inches under the broiler element. At that level, sear the meat for about 5 minutes on each side. Then lower the steak to about 6 inches below the broiler and finish cooking it for about 15 minutes on each side for medium rare.

Remember, hot meat right from the oven doesn't carve very well, so you should allow it to rest on the countertop for about 15 minutes before you slice it—*and I suggest you slice it across the grain on a 45-degree bias.*

Shallot Butter:

While the steak is broiling, take 1 pound of butter, place it in a bowl, allow it to come to room temperature, and cream it until it is smooth. Then make your shallot butter seasoning as follows:

½ cup dry burgundy wine	1 tbsp. paprika
½ cup minced green onions	2 tbsp. Louisiana Hot Sauce
4 cloves fresh garlic, minced	Salt and black pepper to taste
¼ cup minced parsley	

In a 2-quart saucepan mix together the wine, the green onions, and the garlic and simmer over a low fire until most of the wine has evaporated (which should take about 20 minutes). Then remove the pot from the fire and allow the mixture to cool. While it's cooling, whip the parsley, the paprika, and the hot sauce into the softened butter until uniformly blended. Finally, whip in the wine-shallot-garlic mixture until smooth and creamy and season with salt and pepper to taste.

When you're ready to eat, place several slices of the London broil on heated dinner plates, top them generously with a couple of scoops of the shallot butter, sprinkle on some fresh-ground black pepper, and serve with my Sour-Cream Potato Salad and French Market Spinach.

M'frien, this meal will straighten out the bend in the Mississippi River!

Chef's Note: *Go ahead and double the recipe for the shallot butter and keep some extra around for other dishes. Just place the unused portions in waxed paper, roll them into tube shapes, and chill them in the refrigerator until thoroughly set. Then when you need a nice topping for an entrée that's light on natural sauce (or if you want a special spread for French bread), just slice off as much shallot butter as you need and melt it over the dish. Ummmmmmmm!*

By the way, you can do this London broil on the outside grill as well as in the oven. Simply sear the steak close to the flame on high heat *for 5 minutes on each side ... then finish it off* on medium heat *for 15 minutes on each side. It will give you a London broil that's medium rare.*

Mardi Gras Roasted Steaks and Potatoes

Every Mardi Gras you spend the entire day in the streets, partying, watching parades, downing chili dogs and greasy cold fried chicken. But once you get back home, you want a real meal, something good, something wholesome ... yet something you can fix easily without a whole lot of hassle. I got it for you! And it's all done in just one pot!

1 can Pam cooking spray	**5 New York strip steaks (1½ inches**
1 lb. lean bacon	**thick)**
2 large onions, sliced in rings	**2 tsp. Frank Davis Meat Seasoning**
1 tsp. Frank Davis Vegetable	**3 tbsp. cornstarch + ¼ cup**
Seasoning	**chicken broth (optional)**
6-8 medium red potatoes, cut in	**½ cup red wine (optional)**
half crosswise	

The first thing you do is preheat your oven to 400 degrees. Then, take a 6-quart cast-iron Dutch oven or heavy aluminum oval roaster and liberally spray it with the Pam.

Now, lay the pound of bacon in single strips on the bottom of the pan and place the onion slices on top of the bacon. At this point, go ahead and sprinkle half of the vegetable seasoning over the onions.

Next, place the raw potatoes—cut side down—on top of the onion rings so that they're packed tightly together. Then sprinkle the rest of the vegetable seasoning on the potatoes, sprinkle the steaks on both sides with the meat seasoning, and place them on top of the potatoes. You'll get them in—you might have to wedge them together a little, but they'll fit.

Now cover the pot tightly, slide it into the oven, and bake the steaks and potatoes for an hour and a half. Trust me! They won't overcook ... and they won't be greasy!

See, the dry heat forces the bacon drippings into the potatoes to start them cooking. Meanwhile, the onion juices provide just enough moisture to soften the potatoes and begin rendering out steak drippings. Ninety minutes later, the entire dish is done—the meat will be tender enough to slice with a fork, the potatoes will be just right, and the gravy in the bottom of the pan will make a great *au jus*. (You can tighten it up with the chicken broth/cornstarch mixture if you want it thicker.)

I do suggest you check the pot occasionally, say, after an hour or so. You want to make sure you keep about an inch of liquid in the bottom of the pot to prevent the meat from drying out. If your oven thermostat is working properly, the dish should come out perfectly and you shouldn't have to add more liquid—but if the oven is cooking hotter than indicated simply pour in a little red wine as it's needed.

What you do is cook the dish on Lundi Gras (the Monday before Mardi Gras) and stash it away in the refrigerator until Tuesday—*Mardi Gras*. Then when you get back from a day on the streets, put the pot in the oven at 350 degrees as soon as you walk in the house, take off your costume, sort through your beads and throws, and take a hot shower. Then when you're ready to sit down to supper, just set out a couple of plates and spoon out a hot nutritious meal … one that's fit for both *Rex* and *Zulu*!

Chef's Note: *To garnish the steaks and potatoes with the Mardi Gras colors, use purple cabbage and green and yellow bell peppers.*

Sirloin Beef Tips with Mushrooms and Wine Sauce

Whether it's for an elegant, candlelit, sit-down dinner or just a regular ol' weekend meal for the immediate family, this is one dish that everyone who tastes it will want again and again. And once you see how easy it is to prepare, I promise you that's how often you'll probably fix it.

¼ stick butter
2 cups diced onions
½ cup sliced green onions
2 cups sliced mushrooms
4 lb. sirloin tip roast, cut in 1-inch cubes
⅓ cup all-purpose flour
2 cups hearty Burgundy

3 cups beef stock
6 cloves garlic, minced
½ tsp. dry mustard
½ tsp. ground cumin
4 tbsp. Worcestershire sauce
¼ cup minced parsley
Salt and black pepper to taste

In a 5-quart cast-iron Dutch oven, melt the butter until it sizzles—*but don't let it burn!* Then toss in the onions, green onions, and mushrooms and quickly stir-fry them over high heat until the onions turn a rich caramel color (which should take about 10 minutes or so). When they're done, remove the vegetables from the pot and set them aside in a baking pan.

Next, drop in the beef tips a few at a time and quickly brown them over high heat. When they've all been seared, set them aside, too, in the same pan as the seasoning vegetables.

Now reduce the heat to medium, sprinkle the flour into the Dutch oven, and cook it very lightly for a minute or two to absorb the excess oils. Then stir in the wine and the beef stock, increase the heat to high once more, and deglaze the pot.

At this point put the beef—plus all of the vegetables—back into the Dutch oven, mix everything together well, cover the pot, and simmer the meat for about 30 minutes.

Meanwhile, preheat your oven to 350 degrees. Then after the allotted simmering time, stir in the garlic, the mustard, the cumin, and the Worcestershire sauce. And when everything is thoroughly mixed, cover the pot, place it in the oven, and bake the dish for 2 hours.

About 15 minutes before you're ready to eat, remove the pot from the oven, stir in the parsley, and season the sauce to taste with salt and pepper. I suggest you keep the beef tips in the oven on "warm" until you're ready to serve them.

Chef's Note: *This dish is best served piping hot over a mixture of long-grain and wild rice, accompanied by my Baked Broccoli-Cauliflower-Carrot Casserole, and topped off with a big chunk of fresh-baked French bread.*

For full, robust flavor, substitute my Frank Davis "Strictly N'Awlins" Beef Seasoning for the salt, pepper, and cumin listed in the ingredients.

N'Awlins Pepper Steak

Want a tasty, light, summertime dish that won't leave you bloated and uncomfortable (unless you eat four helpings!)? Well, try this New Orleans version of Chinese pepper steak. You'll probably end up cooking it all year round!

4 tbsp. peanut oil
2 beef round steaks, cut in thin
   strips
1 large green bell pepper, sliced
1 large yellow bell pepper, sliced
1 large red bell pepper, sliced
1 medium yellow onion, coarsely
   chopped

3 ribs celery, bias cut
4 cloves garlic, finely chopped
2 cups concentrated beef stock
½ cup Chablis Blanc wine
¼ cup soy sauce
¼ cup chopped pimientos
3 tbsp. cornstarch + ½ cup water
Salt and white pepper to taste

First, take a 12-inch heavy aluminum skillet, heat half of the peanut oil to high, and quickly fry the stripped beef until it browns. Then remove the meat from the pan and set it aside for awhile.

Next, using the same skillet, heat the remaining oil to high and sauté the bell peppers, the onions, and the celery until they soften (this should take about 5 minutes). Then when the vegetables are just about ready, stir in the garlic and cook it for about a minute (but don't let it burn!).

At this point, put the beef back into the skillet with the vegetables, stir in the stock, the wine, and the soy sauce, and mix everything together thoroughly. Then when the liquid comes to a boil, quickly reduce the heat to low, cover the pan, and "simmer" all the ingredients until the meat and the vegetables become tender (which should take about 30-40 minutes if you bought a good grade of round steak). By the way, you should be able to pierce the meat easily with a fork when the dish is done.

About 10 minutes before you're ready to eat, toss in the pimientos and bring the liquid back to a boil. Then slowly begin adding the cornstarch and water mixture (*and you need to stir constantly!*). This converts the liquids into a thick brown sauce.

All that's left is to season the dish to taste with salt and white pepper ... and chow down!

Chef's Note: *I recommend you serve N'Awlins Pepper Steak with a bowl of steamed buttered rice and a side order of Oriental Fried Cabbage. Ummmmmmmm!*

Be careful when adding salt to this dish. Most good soy sauces are salty in themselves. You may have enough for your taste without having to add extra.

Crescent City Stroganoff

Eat beef stroganoff most places and you get egg noodles and beef stew with a little sour-cream gravy over the top. But that's not what you get when you eat stroganoff in the Crescent City. Our stroganoff is rich with onions and beef stock and mushrooms and wine. Here's the recipe!

2 lb. lean beef round	3 tbsp. margarine
1 cup finely diced onions	3 tbsp. vegetable oil
¼ cup olive oil	2 cups sliced fresh mushrooms
3 tbsp. Worcestershire sauce	2 cups beef stock
1 tsp. salt	½ cup white wine
½ tsp. white pepper	4 tbsp. all-purpose flour
¼ cup white wine	1 cup sour cream
2 tsp. Frank Davis Beef Seasoning	¼ cup thinly sliced green onions
1 lb. extra-wide egg noodles	

First, take the beef round and thinly slice it on a bias—which means you cut the raw roast into strips on a 45-degree angle to make it tender. Then place the strips in a glass or plastic bowl and mix in the diced onions, olive oil, Worcestershire sauce, salt, white pepper, wine, and beef seasoning. When everything is thoroughly combined, cover it with plastic wrap and refrigerate it for at least 2 hours to marinate.

Meanwhile, cook the egg noodles for 6 minutes uncovered in a pot of rapidly boiling water (to which you've added about a teaspoon of salt and a tablespoon of oil). When they're "al dente," drain them in a colander and—*while they're still hot*—toss and coat them thoroughly with the margarine to keep them from sticking together. Then set them aside.

When you're ready to cook, take a heavy 4-quart Dutch oven, pour in the vegetable oil, and sauté the mushrooms over high heat until they begin to brown slightly. Then drop the marinated beef into the same pot with the mushrooms and sear the strips until they brown.

At this point, pour in the beef stock and the ½ cup of wine and bring the mixture to a boil. Then immediately reduce the temperature to low, cover the pot tightly, and "simmer" the beef for about an hour until it becomes supertender.

When it's done, thoroughly whip the flour into the sour cream and stir it into the beef gravy in the Dutch oven. I suggest you continue to stir the gravy for about 5 minutes over low heat until the cream and flour thickens and turns silky smooth. Oh—if the mixture becomes too thick to your liking, simply add either a little extra beef stock or wine.

When you're ready to eat, combine the beef mixture and the noodles in the Dutch oven, toss for another minute or two to heat the noodles, and serve piping hot alongside a plate of buttered steamed broccoli and a crisp green salad.

All that's left is to garnish with the thinly sliced green onions, complement it all with a chilled glass of wine, and you've got one elegant stroganoff like none other you've ever tasted.

Chef's Note:

1—For this dish, I recommend you use a good Gewurztraminer wine. It's semi-dry, delicately fruited, and has a spicy floral bouquet, just what you need for a beef stroganoff. And by the way, you should serve this same wine with the meal.

2—A couple of cans of beef broth make a good stock to use in this stroganoff recipe. Just don't use bouillon cubes—they are much too salty!

3—If you don't have Frank Davis Beef Seasoning in your pantry, you can substitute a sprinkling of salt, black pepper, white pepper, cayenne, onion powder, garlic powder, cumin, and paprika in its place. But premixed seasonings are easier to use and they give your dishes more consistent results. If you can't find them where you shop, give me a call. The toll-free number is 1-800-742-4231.

Real Italian Meatballs

Just about everybody cooks meatballs and spaghetti! And just about everybody's meatballs and spaghetti tastes different! Well, a few years back I spent several weeks touring Italy … but I spent a great deal of that time in Italian kitchens. So if you want a recipe for meatballs and spaghetti the way the Italians fix and eat it, here it is!

3 lb. lean ground beef
1 lb. lean ground pork
1 cup finely chopped onions
4 cloves garlic, finely chopped
1 cup Italian seasoned bread
    crumbs
½ cup whole milk

2 whole eggs, well beaten
2 tsp. Frank Davis Italian Seasoning
½ tsp. oregano
1 tsp. sweet basil
2 tsp. salt
1 tsp. black pepper

First, take a large bowl that will give you a lot of mixing room and thoroughly blend together the beef and the pork. Remember, it's that subtle hint of pork that gives an Italian gravy its distinctive flavor. Then, *in order,* start adding the rest of the ingredients one at a time ... *mixing well between each addition.* The trick is to get a pasty, uniform consistency—not gluey, but not wet either.

When the meat mixture is sticky, moisten your hands and begin rolling meatballs—a little bigger than a golf ball is a good size. It also helps if you moisten your hands between each one.

When they're rolled, place them in a shallow baking pan, slide them into a preheated oven at 400 degrees, and bake them for about 20 minutes or until lightly browned. This seals in natural juices, cooks off excess fat, and helps to hold the meatballs together in the gravy. But don't overcook them! Overcooking makes for tough meatballs.

After they're brown, take them from the oven and let them cool slightly—this keeps them from falling apart. Then take a slotted spoon (so that the excess drippings stay in the pan) and place the meatballs in a pot of rich Italian gravy—but make sure that each one of them is submerged. Now bring the gravy to a "near boil" ... and then immediately reduce the heat to *simmer* and cook the meatballs *slowly* for about 2-3 hours until tender.

When you're ready to eat, spoon a couple of meatballs and a couple ladles full of the gravy over your pasta—and I still think #4 spaghetti goes best with meatballs!—sprinkle on Romano cheese, break out the garlic bread and the red wine, and think Italian!

Chef's Note: *The Italian seasoning I use in this recipe is a subtle blend of rich Sicilian herbs and spices. If you can't find it in the stores where you shop, you can order it direct by calling 1-800-742-4231.*

Italian Meatballs and Spaghetti
(In Sicilian Tomato Sugo)

Wait till you try making my meatballs and spaghetti! This is so Italian, with every bite you'll hear mandolins playing "O Solo Mio" in the background! And the taste is buono!

The Meatballs:

2 lb. lean ground beef	1 cup whole milk
1 lb. lean ground pork	2 tsp. salt
2 medium onions, finely diced	1 tsp. black pepper
4 cloves garlic, finely minced	1 tsp. basil
2 whole eggs, beaten	1 tsp. Italian seasoning
1 cup coarse-ground bread crumbs	

The Tomato Gravy (Sugo):

¼ cup extra-virgin olive oil
1 medium onion, finely chopped
6 cloves garlic, finely minced
2 small cans tomato paste
6 tomato-paste cans filled with
   water

2 tsp. sweet basil
1 tsp. Italian seasoning
2 bay leaves
Salt and black pepper to taste
2 lb. #4 spaghetti
2 cups grated Romano cheese

First you make your meatballs. Here are the steps.

In a large mixing bowl combine the ground beef and the ground pork until the two are uniformly blended. Then drop in the remaining ingredients and, *with your hands,* work everything together until you end up with a smooth meat mixture.

Now, keeping your hands wet so that the mixture doesn't stick to your fingers, begin rolling out the meatballs (you want them to be slightly larger than a golf ball). As each one is shaped, place it on a lightly greased shallow baking sheet.

When they're all made, place them into a 400-degree oven and bake them—turning them once—for about 15 to 20 minutes, or until the meat begins to firm and brown slightly. This does two things—it helps hold your meatballs together while they're cooking in the gravy, but more importantly it renders out most of the excess fat from the meat and keeps your gravy from being greasy.

While the meatballs are baking, it's time to make your tomato gravy. If you follow these directions to the letter, it will be some of the best you've ever had!

In a heavy 5-quart Dutch oven, heat the olive oil to medium high. Then drop in the chopped onions and the garlic and—stirring constantly—lightly sauté them together until they just soften (it is not necessary to brown the onions and you don't want the garlic to burn); about 2 to 3 minutes should do it.

When the onions and garlic are uniformly blended, add the tomato paste to the pot and rapidly stir it into the mix. Remember—*you don't have to fry the tomato paste to make a good red gravy:* if you accidentally fry the paste too long, you will increase the acidity of the tomatoes and the gravy will be strong, harsh, and bitter. You want it to come out light and sweet. So just cook it a minute or two until the paste, onions, garlic, and olive oil are mixed well.

At this point, add the water to the tomato paste and stir again until the mixture is silky smooth. Keep in mind that the secret to making a gravy the right consistency is to use *3 cans of water for every 1 can of tomato paste* you use.

When the sauce is thoroughly mixed, add the basil, the Italian seasoning, and the bay leaves and season the gravy with salt and black pepper to your taste.

Now you're ready to drop in the meatballs—*but just the meatballs: throw the pan drippings away!* Gently place the meatballs into the pot with a spoon or a pair of tongs, being careful not to break them apart, and position them so that they're completely covered with the gravy. All that's left now is to cover the pot and cook at a "simmer" for about 2 hours.

When you're ready to eat, cook the spaghetti in about a gallon and a half of rapidly boiling, lightly salted water until it's *al dente* (firm yet tender, but not soft). When it's ready, drain it thoroughly *(don't rinse it!)*, toss it with about a cup or two of the tomato gravy to keep the pieces from sticking together, sprinkle it liberally with the Romano cheese, and serve it piping hot with the meatballs!

I don't care where you've eaten meatballs and spaghetti before ... this is gonna be your all-time favorite!

Chef's Note:

1—For perfect spaghetti that doesn't stick together, cook it uncovered, stir it almost constantly, add about 3 or 4 tablespoons of olive oil to the water while it's boiling, and season the water with about 3 teaspoons of salt. Then when the spaghetti is done, drain it thoroughly in a pasta colander, immediately put it back into the pot you boiled it in, coat it lightly with some of the hot tomato gravy, and serve it piping hot.

2—Oh—just for the record ... you don't add sugar *to an authentic Italian gravy. Prepare it properly and it will be light and naturally sweet.*

Holiday Baked Barbecue Burgers

Served very simply with baked beans and potato salad for such occasions as the Fourth of July, Labor Day, or any day, this gourmet hamburger is rich, full-bodied, and succulent enough for royalty. And it's easy to make!

2 lb. lean ground chuck
1 cup fresh plain bread crumbs
1 cup finely chopped onions
½ cup finely chopped celery
¼ cup finely minced parsley
3 whole eggs, beaten
½ cup whole milk
1 tsp. Liquid Smoke
3 tbsp. Worcestershire sauce

½ cup barbecue sauce
1 tsp. salt
½ tsp. black pepper
⅛ tsp. cayenne pepper
1 cup shredded sharp cheddar
   cheese
2 cups hickory-flavored barbecue
   sauce

In a large bowl, use your hands to mix the ground meat, bread crumbs, onions, celery, and parsley until uniformly blended. Then pour in the beaten eggs and the whole milk and work everything together thoroughly.

At this point, season the mixture with the Liquid Smoke, the Worcestershire, the barbecue sauce, the salt, and the pepper. Then sprinkle on the shredded cheese and mix everything well again.

Now, form the meat into slightly oversized hamburgers—*remember they're gonna shrink a little when they cook*—and place them on a lightly greased baking sheet or cookie pan. Then slide them into a 450-degree preheated oven and bake them for about 10 minutes on each side.

When the baking time is over, remove the burgers from the oven, drain off the drippings into a large measuring cup, and place the burgers back in the baking pan. Then pour off the beef fat that floats on the surface of the drippings and mix the remaining au jus with the 2 cups of barbecue sauce.

Now move one of your oven racks to the highest position possible and set your oven to *broil*. Then while the element is heating up, take a pastry brush and liberally douse the baked burgers *(both sides)* with the barbecue-sauce mixture.

All that's left is to run the pan of hamburgers under the broiler for about 3 minutes or so on both sides (or until the surface of the meat turns slightly charred).

And when you're ready to eat, just place a burger on a slightly toasted bun, dress it with lettuce, tomatoes, dill pickles, mayonnaise, mustard, ketchup, or whatever else your heart desires … and have yourself a happy holiday!

Nothing—but nothing!—beats these homemade hamburgers!

N'Awlins Pot-Roasted Chuck Roast

Either slow-simmered on top of the stove or slow-baked in the oven, this is one of the tastiest roasts you're ever going to eat! I promise it will be your family's favorite!

2 tbsp. vegetable oil	¼ cup finely chopped bell pepper
4 lb. boneless chuck roast, trimmed	1 cup sliced mushrooms
8 cloves fresh garlic	4 cups beef stock or canned
2 tsp. Frank Davis Beef Seasoning	bouillon
½ cup vegetable oil	⅔ cup port wine
½ cup all-purpose flour	4 carrots, peeled and chunked
1 cup finely chopped onions	½ cup heavy cream
¾ cup finely chopped celery	Salt and black pepper to taste

First, take an *empty,* heavy, cast-iron Dutch oven and heat it over a medium-high flame for about 3 minutes. Then pour in the 2 tablespoons of vegetable oil and let it get hot.

Meanwhile, plug the chuck roast with the garlic and liberally sprinkle on the beef seasoning, rubbing it in all over. Then put the roast in the Dutch oven and brown it thoroughly in the vegetable oil to seal in the juices. When it's fully *seared,* remove the meat from the pot temporarily and set it aside.

At this point, with the heat still on medium high, pour the remaining vegetable oil into the Dutch oven and let it get hot. Then gradually sprinkle in the flour and, with a wire whip, cook the oil-flour mixture into a dark brown roux (which should take about 15 minutes over medium-high heat). *Remember to keep stirring the mixture constantly so that the flour does not burn.*

When the roux turns a "chocolate color," quickly drop in the onions, celery, bell pepper, and mushrooms and remove the pot from the fire. (The procedure serves to cool down the roux, keeps it from browning any further, and slightly cooks the vegetables.)

Immediately, pour in the beef stock and the port wine (very carefully since it could splatter!) and stir the mixture until it turns smooth. Then put the pot back on the fire on high, bring the gravy to a boil, and put the carrots and the browned roast in the gravy. Now reduce the heat to simmer and cook the roast—*covered*—for about 2½ hours or until fully tender.

About 15 minutes before serving, remove the meat from the gravy and skim off any excess beef fat that floats on the surface. Then stir in the heavy cream, bring the gravy back to a *slow boil,* and reseason the mixture with salt and pepper to taste. Remember, you want to cook the gravy only until it becomes rich and silky (about 8 to 10 minutes).

When you're ready to eat, slice the meat into serving-size pieces, place them on a platter, and cover with the gravy. The roast goes great with cheesy potatoes, noodles, or rice, accompanied by a crisp, tossed green salad and a lot of French bread for sopping.

Chef's Note: *To make the pot roast completely greaseless, remove the meat after cooking, place the gravy into a large bowl, and chill it in the refrigerator until the beef fat congeals on the surface. Then remove the fat, discard it, and reheat the remaining gravy (au jus) to a slow boil. If you'd like it thicker than it is, just stir in a little cornstarch mixed with cold water while the gravy is boiling. Just before serving, drop in the sliced beef and simmer it for about 10 minutes. You'll be surprised how many calories you'll trim away just by doing this!*

Cooking Variation: *Instead of slow-simmering the roast on top of the stove, after combining all the ingredients place the entire Dutch oven into a 325-degree oven and let it bake—covered—for about 2 hours. Then remove the pot, skim off the excess beef fat, and serve as described above.*

N'Awlins Pot Roast-n-Onions

This is one of those recipes yo' momma used to fix—a big, juicy, boneless chuck roast smothered down in caramelized onions till its own juices turn into a rich thick sauce, then sliced in chunks and spooned out over rice with carrots and broccoli! Oh, y'all … this is real N'Awlins!

2 tsp. salt
¼ tsp. white pepper
¼ tsp. black pepper
¼ tsp. cayenne pepper
5 lb. boneless chuck roast
½ cup peanut oil
2 large onions, sliced in rings
4 cloves garlic, finely minced

½ bell pepper, coarsely chopped
1 rib celery, finely chopped
½ lb. mushrooms, sliced
2 cups heavy beef stock (from bone
    reduction)
3 bay leaves
1 tsp. sweet basil
6 peeled carrots, coarsely diced

First, salt and pepper the roast and set it aside for a moment. Then heat your Dutch oven for 2 to 3 minutes over a medium flame and pour in the peanut oil. When the oil *just begins* to smoke, drop in the onions and "caramelize" them (in other words, fry them until they turn a pretty golden brown). At this point, toss in the garlic, bell pepper, celery, and mushrooms and fry them along with the onions until they wilt (about 4 minutes should do it).

Next, remove all the seasoning vegetables from the pot and quickly sear the roast on all sides. Then when the roast is seared, put the seasoning vegetables back into the pot, pour in the beef stock, and add all the remaining ingredients—including the carrots.

Now, bring the liquid to a rolling boil! *But* as soon as it boils, reduce the heat to low, put the lid on the pot, and "simmer" the roast until it wants to fall apart (about 2½ hours). *Oh—and you don't have to peek in the pot every 5 minutes! Let it cook!*

Meanwhile, boil some rice, slice some broccoli florets, and turn some French bread into garlic toast. Then butter and parsley the rice and steam the broccoli (and either cover it with a cheese sauce or drop the florets into the roast gravy about 3 minutes before you serve the meat).

Then when the roast is tender, remove it from the Dutch oven and carve it into slices. But before you serve the gravy, strain out the vegetable seasonings, bring the strained gravy back to a boil in the Dutch oven, add a couple tablespoons of cornstarch dissolved in cold water, and thicken your gravy to the desired consistency.

Serve the roast and gravy generously over a bed of fluffy rice, alongside a cold mixed salad, and you got "pure Crescent City."

Chef's Note: *You'll find that the roast will carve easier if you let it cool for about 5 minutes after you remove it from the hot Dutch oven.*

Down-Home N'Awlins Rump Roast

Looking for a perfect crisp-on-the-outside, juicy-on-the-inside, full-flavored roast? Well, that's just what you get when you fix this roast for your family! And it's probably the easiest one you've ever done! Try it and see!

1 boneless rump roast, 3 lb. average	**2 large onions**
2 tsp. salt	**2 tsp. margarine**
2 tsp. black pepper	**2 cups beef stock**
5 cloves fresh garlic	

Start off by preheating your oven to 500 degrees.

Now place the roast on the countertop and liberally season it with the salt and pepper. Then slice each pod of garlic in half lengthwise, poke holes in the roast with a pointed knife, and push a piece of garlic down into each hole. When this is done, set the roast aside for a moment so that the seasonings seep in.

Next, peel the onions and slice them into half rings. Then take the margarine, grease a baking pan large enough to hold the roast, and scatter the onions over the bottom of the pan.

When you're ready to start cooking, insert a meat thermometer into the thickest part of the roast. Then put the roast—fat side up!—on top of the sliced onions. This does two things. First, as the onions cook they flavor the meat. But most importantly, the onions serve as a trivet to keep the roast from soaking in the drippings that are being rendered out during baking.

Now, slide the roast—*uncovered*—into the oven. But watch it very carefully. You want to cook it at 500 degrees only until the fat begins to turn a light brown color (which should take only about 15 minutes). After it browns, turn the oven down to 325 degrees and continue cooking the roast until the thermometer reaches 150 degrees (which should take about 2 hours and give you a roast that's medium rare).

Keep in mind that once you remove the roast from the oven, it will continue to cook for another 20-25 minutes on the countertop as it "sets." So you need to figure that into your cooking time! Otherwise, a roast that you cook until it's *medium* will actually turn out to be almost *well done* after it "sets." And if you cook it until it's well done (170 degrees), after it "sets" you'll have shoe leather!

One little trick! About 20 minutes before you remove the roast from the oven, pour the beef stock into the baking pan and stir it well into the browned onions and the pan drippings. This is called *au jus*—baste the roast with it several times.

When you're ready to eat, cut the roast in thin slices against the grain and spoon on a little of the au jus.

Chef's Note: *N'Awlins rump roast goes great with steamed rice, baked potatoes, and even pasta. And a marinated artichoke salad on the side really tops off the meal!*

While it's common in homestyle cooking to bake a roast for so many minutes to the pound, this is never an accurate method and rarely gives you consistency time after time. To do it right, and to improve your talents in the kitchen, I recommend you make an investment in a good-quality meat thermometer (Taylor/Sybron makes an accurate yet inexpensive one that's available at most kitchen shops). The thermometer should be inserted into the thickest part of the meat to a point where the tip of the thermometer is ¾ inch past the center of the roast, but not in contact with bone, fat, or gristle. And you can bet that when the thermometer registers the correct baking temperature, your roast is done ... and it's done right!

And for a real "roast," don't cook it in a covered pan, a baking bag, or wrapped in foil. Roasting means cooked with dry heat, *so that the outer surface of the meat turns crispy to seal in the natural juices. If you wrap or cover the meat, you end up creating a moist steamy effect that renders out natural juices and produces a tasteless piece of meat!*

A list of all of the internal baking temperatures for beef, veal, venison, ham, pork, chicken, turkey, duck, and goose appears in the back this cookbook. My Frank Davis Cooks Naturally N'Awlins *cookbook also has a chart on page 250 for baking temperatures and times.*

Melt-in-Your-Mouth Barbecued Brisket

I don't know why it is, but New Orleanians just love their brisket! But unlike most briskets that are boiled, I do this one on the outdoor grill so that all the great flavor stays locked inside the meat. It's the real N'Awlins way, y'all!

1 prime beef brisket, 3 to 4 lb. average	½ tsp. basil
6 cloves garlic	¼ tsp. cayenne pepper
Water to cover	1 tsp. salt
½ tsp. black peppercorns	2 tsp. Worcestershire sauce
2 whole bay leaves	1 large yellow onion, thinly sliced
1 cup prepared barbecue sauce	4 carrots, peeled and halved
½ tsp. rosemary	¼ cup heavy cream
	4 tbsp. horseradish

You want to start off by *plugging* the brisket—just take a paring knife, make six small holes evenly across the beef, and shove the garlic pods deep into the holes. Then place the brisket down inside a 6-quart Dutch oven and add just enough water to barely cover it.

Then to the water, add the peppercorns, bay leaves, and one-quarter of the barbecue sauce. Now bring the water to a boil, but immediately reduce the heat to low so that you *poach* the brisket in the liquid until it turns a "cooked grey." It is important to skim the floating fat scum from the liquid as it cooks (which should take just about 15 minutes).

When the meat has cooked for the allotted time, remove it from the pot and set it aside to cool. You also want to save the poaching liquid.

Then after the brisket has cooled enough to handle it, place it in the center of a piece of extra-heavy aluminum foil and add to it the rosemary, basil, cayenne, and salt. At this point you want to brush on the Worcestershire and the remaining barbecue sauce. Then lay the sliced onions evenly over the top of the beef and place the carrots around the sides.

Now wrap the brisket tightly in the foil and place it either outdoors on the barbecue grill (set at low with the lid closed) or in an oven (set at 300 degrees). You want to cook the brisket about 25 minutes to the pound.

In the meantime, reduce your poaching liquid in a saucepan on top of the stove to half of its original volume—this will concentrate the beef flavor. Then add the heavy cream and cook it until the stock thickens slightly. When you get it the consistency you want, stir in the horseradish and cook it for about a minute or two.

When the brisket is tender, add the juices trapped inside the aluminum foil to the horseradish sauce you made in the pan, stir everything together well, simmer for another 3 minutes, and serve it over your sliced beef.

With smothered cabbage, a few creamer potatoes (see index for Pommes Petites), and some garlic bread on the side for soppin', you got yo'sef a mouth-watering meal that won't quit!

Chef's Note: *You'll have an easier time slicing the brisket if you allow it to cool slightly before you serve it. If you try to cut it right out of the foil while it's hot, it tends to fall apart—that's how tender it will be! I also suggest that you slice it across the grain for extra tenderness.*

Baked Brisket in Jack Daniels Sauce

Most briskets are served boiled with a little bit of horseradish on the side. But this one is done in the oven—wrapped in foil—so that it produces a rich flavorful gravy that comes from a special Old Number 7 marinade you're gonna make. Wait till you try this! It's Naturally N'Awlins, y'all!

The Marinade:

1 cup extra-virgin olive oil	1 tsp. garlic powder
½ cup Jack Daniels Black Label Whiskey	1 tsp. sweet basil
	½ tsp. cumin
1 tsp. tarragon or red wine vinegar	½ tsp. rosemary
½ cup finely chopped green onions	1 tsp. black pepper
⅛ tsp. thyme	1 tbsp. Worcestershire sauce

In a large plastic or glass container (no metal!), mix together well all the ingredients. Then cover the container with a sheet of plastic wrap and set it aside for at least 3 hours at room temperature before you use it. In the meantime, begin preparing your brisket.

The Brisket:

1 trimmed beef brisket, 4 lb. average	1 tsp. black peppercorns
	½ cup heavy cream
8 cloves fresh garlic	1 cup prepared roux or 3 tbsp. cornstarch in water
1 large yellow onion, coarsely diced	
6 carrots, peeled and halved	Salt and black pepper to taste
1 cup beef stock	4 tbsp. Creole mustard
1 cup marinade mix	4 tbsp. horseradish
4 bay leaves	

First, plug the brisket with the garlic. Then place it in the plastic container with the marinade you made and allow it to rest in the mixture for at least 2 hours (but preferably overnight!). If you marinate the meat for 2 hours, do it at room temperature; if you marinate overnight, cover it and put it in the refrigerator.

Next, when the marination is done, line a baking pan with heavy-duty aluminum foil and place the marinated brisket in the pan. Then sprinkle on the diced onions, arrange the carrots around the side of the meat, ladle on the stock and the marinade mix, and add the bay leaves and peppercorns. Then fold over the foil to tightly seal it around the brisket and place the pan in a preheated 350-degree oven. At this point, you want to bake it for at least 2 hours (depending upon the grade of beef, it could take 3).

After the meat is tender, remove it from the baking pan and place it on a cutting board to cool. You'll notice that a large quantity of fat rendered out of the beef is floating on the surface of the gravy. Pour off the gravy (along with the fat) into a large measuring cup. Then place the cup into your refrigerator for about an hour. The temperature will cause the fat to congeal and you can lift it off the surface of the gravy, making the gravy virtually greaseless.

Oh—while the gravy is in the refrigerator, thinly slice the beef across the grain into pieces about a half-inch thick and cover them to keep them from drying out.

When you're ready to eat, pour the defatted gravy into a skillet and bring it to a boil. Then slowly add the heavy cream and cook it for about 5 minutes until it turns smooth. To thicken it to the consistency you desire, stir in a little roux or cornstarch mixed with water while the sauce is bubbling. Then season to taste with salt and pepper.

All that's left is to place the sliced brisket into the sauce to heat it. Then serve it with dirty rice or parsleyed potatoes, a crisp green salad, the carrots you cooked with the beef, and a garnish made by mixing together the Creole mustard and the horseradish. Ummmmmmmm!

Chef's Note: *All the alcohol will evaporate out of the marinade as the brisket cooks, leaving only the charcoal essence of the whiskey behind for flavoring. For a more concentrated Jack Daniels taste, simply save about a half-cup or so of the marinating mixture and add it to the sauce as you finish it.*

How to Make Your Own Corned Beef

Lots of folks skip over making their own corned beef because they think it's difficult ... but it really isn't. Follow these instructions and see just how simple it really is!

5 lb. choice top round roast
Water to cover beef by 3 inches
Salt (see recipe directions)
1 raw egg in the shell
2 onions, coarsely chopped
6 cloves garlic, smashed
12 whole black peppercorns
6 whole cloves

3 bay leaves
2 tsp. Frank Davis Beef Seasoning
½ tsp. thyme
½ lemon, sliced
1 tsp. Tabasco sauce
¼ cup granulated sugar
1 tsp. Frank Davis Liquid Crabboil

Start with a *nonmetallic* pot (crock, glass, enamel, plastic, or porcelain) and place the beef roast in it. Then measure out enough water to cover the meat by 3 inches. Now, *take the water back out!*

Next, cut the beef into chunks about 4 inches thick and set them aside for a moment—the reason you cut the meat is you want the "corning solution" to penetrate all the pieces thoroughly.

Then, using the same nonmetallic pot, refill it with the predetermined amount of water and begin adding the salt. Now this is important! Begin stirring in and dissolving salt until you can get the raw egg in the shell to begin to float. See, when the egg starts floating, you know you've got enough salt to produce "corned" beef. It's that simple!

Incidentally—just for the record—you don't need saltpeter (sodium nitrate) to make corned beef. It's just an unnecessary chemical used primarily to turn the beef red—I suggest you leave it out!

Now, bring the water to a boil and toss in the onions, garlic, peppercorns, cloves, bay leaves, beef seasoning, thyme, lemon, Tabasco, sugar, and crabboil. Then let the stock boil for about 10 minutes uncovered.

At this point, turn the fire off, add the beef, weight it down with a large dinner plate or soupbowl so that it doesn't float, and set the pot aside until the pickling stock comes to room temperature. Then cover it and place it in the refrigerator for *15 days*—remember, it takes a full 15 days to "corn" the meat in the pickling stock. And I suggest you turn the meat and stir the mixture every other day.

When you're ready to cook the beef, take it from the pickling stock and soak it for about 2 hours in cool fresh water to remove any excess salt (I'd change the water a few times). Then drain the meat and cook it according to my N'Awlins Corned Beef and Cabbage recipe.

Chef's Note: *Not only beef but wild game can be corned this way (deer, antelope, rabbit, etc.) using the same recipe. And if you want to freeze some of the meat, you can. Just transfer it directly from the pickling stock to a Ziploc bag, add about a cup of the stock to the meat, squeeze out all the air from the bag, and drop it in the freezer!*

N'Awlins Corned Beef and Cabbage

Not only on St. Patrick's Day, but any day this is a great low-calorie main dish that your family will relish whether they're Irish or not! You got to do this one real soon!

5 lb. corned beef
Water to cover
1½ oz. whole pickling spice (garni)
½ tsp. Frank Davis Liquid Crabboil
2 medium heads cabbage,
    quartered

1 large onion, sliced
6 carrots, peeled and chunked
8 medium Irish potatoes, peeled

Place the beef in a 10-quart stockpot, cover it with water, and bring the water to a boil. Then while the heat is coming up, wrap the pickling spice in a bouquet garni (which is a double thickness of cheesecloth tied at the top to make a pouch), and add it to the pot, along with the crabboil.

When the water comes to a boil, cook the meat until all the foam is released (about 5 minutes)—*and remember to skim the foam off the meat.* Then reduce the fire to a *simmer,* cover the pot, and cook the beef for about an hour (or until it turns tender).

Then, when the meat is cooked, toss in the quartered cabbages, the onion, the carrots, and the Irish potatoes and let everything simmer for another 30 to 45 minutes till done.

When you're ready to eat, put the beef on a large serving tray, cut it into thin slices against the grain, and lay the vegetables around it.

Of course, to spice up the beef I also suggest you serve this classic recipe with my Creamed Horseradish Sauce.

Chef's Note: *This dish is cooked the same way whether you make your own corned beef or buy one from your supermarket. But if you buy a corned beef prewrapped, I do suggest you allow it to soak in cool water for about an hour to remove excess salt before you cook it.*

Creamed Chipped Beef on Toast

When you ate it for breakfast in the army, you called it SOS! But this version is a far cry from the recipe your mess sergeant used at Fort Polk! In fact, if they had used this recipe to make SOS ... I just might have reenlisted!

Oil
2 lb. boneless rump roast
Salt and black pepper to taste
1 stick butter
⅓ cup all-purpose flour
5 cups whole milk

1 tsp. onion powder
¼ tsp. garlic powder
½ cup water
8 slices buttered toast
8 hard-boiled eggs
2 tbsp. finely minced parsley

First, take a shallow baking pan, grease it lightly with a drop of oil, and place the roast that has been thoroughly seasoned with salt and pepper into it. Then, with the oven set at 350 degrees, bake the beef (uncovered) for about 2 hours or until it comes out medium well. When it's done, set it aside and let it cool to room temperature. *Remember, you have to cook it long enough so that it crumbles when you slice it—that's how you eat "chipped" beef.*

While the roast is baking, take a heavy skillet and a wire whisk and, over medium heat, combine half the butter and most of the flour into a light roux. But don't let it brown: you just want it silky smooth. And when it's ready, let it cool too.

At this point, remove the roast from the baking pan, cut it into thin slices across the grain of the meat, and crumble it into small "chips."

Then pour the whole milk into a 4½-quart Dutch oven, drop in the beef chips, increase the heat to medium high, and stir everything together until the mixture is uniform and it starts to bubble slightly. Meanwhile, season the milk stock with the onion and garlic powder, along with extra salt and black pepper if you desire.

Now begin adding the butter roux, a spoonful at a time, stirring it thoroughly into the hot milk stock. Keep an eye on it at this point, though, because as the temperature of the roux increases ... the milk stock will thicken. When it reaches the consistency of soupy oatmeal, stir in the rest of the butter, reduce the heat to low, cover the pot, and let the SOS simmer for about 30 minutes so that the milk picks up all the beef flavor. By the way, you will have to stir the pot periodically to keep the milk from sticking to the bottom.

Oh—remember those baked-on drippings the beef left in the pan after it roasted? Well, take the half-cup of water, heat it to boiling, and use it to deglaze the pan, scraping loose all the drippings. Then pour those drippings into the creamed beef to increase the flavor.

And when you're ready to eat, place two slices of toast cut on a diagonal on a heated plate, spoon a generous helping of creamed beef over the bread, lay of couple of sliced eggs on the beef, sprinkle once more with salt and black pepper to taste, and garnish with a smidgeon of fresh parsley.

I promise … it's a great way to face reveille!

Chef's Note: *If you prepare the dish as I've described above, you have authentic army-style SOS. But for a tasty variation, try this. Finely chop a small yellow onion and about a half-pound of mushrooms. Then sauté them in butter until fully wilted, and stir them into the milk stock when you add the chipped beef. The taste increases considerably!*

The best SOS is made from well-done, crumbled-up roast. But in a pinch, you can also use extra-lean ground beef. I suggest you first fry it down in a pan with about a half-cup of finely chopped onions. Then use the rendered beef fat to make your roux. After that, it's simply a matter of following the recipe as I've described above.

Oh—like red beans, gumbo, and jambalaya … SOS is always better the next day. So if you want the best blend of flavor you can get, fix it today and serve it tomorrow!

Italian Breaded Calf's Liver
(Fegato e Italiano)

Order fried liver in New Orleans and you'll probably get beef liver dusted in flour, fried, and smothered down in a rich onion gravy. If you like liver, it's wonderful! But if you want a much milder liver taste that's subtle yet delicately flavored you got to try this recipe. It's my favorite!

1 lb. calf liver, thinly sliced	**1 tsp. Italian seasoning**
2 cups seasoned all-purpose flour	**1 tsp. veal seasoning**
6 eggs + 2 cups whole milk, beaten	**1 tsp. oregano**
4 cups coarse French bread crumbs	**1 tsp. garlic powder**
1½ cups Pecorino Romano cheese	**Peanut oil for frying**
½ cup freshly minced parsley	

The most important thing to remember about doing this recipe is that the liver slices must be handled individually, one at a time. In other words, take each slice all the way through the preparation stage before you begin working on the next slice. If you try to do the slices in batches, the final results won't give you the crispy texture you want in this dish. With that in mind, then …

1—First, lightly dust the liver in the seasoned flour.

2—Then dip it quickly in the eggwash.

3—Then roll it in the seasoned bread crumbs until every part is thoroughly coated.

4—Then set it on a platter for 2 minutes to "rest" so that the eggwash and the crumbs can form a binding.

Meanwhile, in a heavy 12-inch skillet heat the peanut oil to 350 degrees. Then, with a meat fork, gently place the slices of liver into the oil and fry them on both sides until they turn golden brown and crunchy-crispy. It should only take a minute or two ... so don't overcook them or they'll dry out.

When they're done, remove them from the skillet with the fork and place them on a warming platter on several layers of paper towels so that they'll drain. Done properly, each slice of liver should be totally greaseless and supertender.

I suggest you eat them piping hot right out of the skillet, sprinkled lightly with a little more Romano cheese for garnish! Served with cheesy mashed potatoes and baked Italian creamed green beans ... this is one meal hard to beat even if you hate liver!

Chef's Note:

1—To make the seasoned bread crumb mixture, thoroughly blend together in a large bowl the crumbs, parsley, Italian seasoning, veal seasoning, oregano, garlic powder, and Romano cheese. If you don't have veal seasoning on hand, just leave it out.

2—To make seasoned flour, simply take all-purpose flour and add salt and black pepper to taste.

3—If you want a superb coating and a great-tasting way of fixing fried food, use this same recipe for veal cutlets, flattened chicken breasts, thinly sliced round steak, and filleted catfish—especially filleted catfish. I promise you rave reviews from your dinner guests like you've never gotten before!

French Quarter Grillades

One of the classic old Creole dishes of New Orleans, grillades are made with veal that's been slow-cooked till succulent and tender in a veal stock and lightly flavored with tomatoes. And yes, it's served with grits!

2 tbsp. butter
1 tbsp. Crisco oil
2 lb. veal round, cut into 2-inch
  squares
2 tsp. salt
1 tsp. black pepper
¼ tsp. cayenne pepper
1 cup all-purpose flour for dredging

5 cloves garlic, finely chopped
1½ cups finely chopped onions
¾ cup finely chopped celery
½ cup finely chopped bell pepper
1 lb. fresh tomatoes, finely chopped
1½ cups veal or chicken stock
4 tbsp. prepared roux

First, in a heavy 12-inch skillet, mix the butter and the Crisco oil together and bring it up to medium heat on the stove.

In the meantime, sprinkle the pieces of veal with the salt, black pepper, and cayenne, rubbing the seasonings well into the meat with your fingers. Then vigorously dredge the veal in the flour and thoroughly brown it in the butter/oil mixture. When it's "just cooked" (which takes about a minute or so on each side), remove it from the skillet and set it on paper towels to drain. *(Take special care not to overcook the meat or it will tend to dry out.)*

At this point, using the drippings in the pan, sauté the garlic, onions, celery, and bell pepper until they become soft and tender.

Finally, put the meat back into the pot, stir in the chopped tomatoes and the veal stock, and simmer the dish *covered* for about an hour or until the veal is tender.

About 10 minutes before you're ready to eat, thicken the sauce in the skillet by stirring in the roux a little at a time. Then serve your grillades piping hot … over hot buttered grits.

Chef's Note: *If you want to cut back on the amount of fat in your diet, instead of using a prepared roux to thicken the sauce stir in a little cornstarch and water mixed together and cook it at a low boil for about a minute or so. About 3 heaping tablespoons of cornstarch in ¼ cup of water should be more than you need.*

Grits and grillades (pronounced gree-yards) is a classic old Cajun and Creole breakfast which tastes best when served with 2 eggs fried over-easy.

Frank's and A.J.'s Sicilian Veal Parmesan

It's one of the most classic dishes in Italian cuisine! But there are as many recipe variations as there are dialects of Italian. This one follows the "homestyle" version and it's so good, A. J. Tusa even serves it that way in his New Orleans restaurant, Anthony's Pasta House!

The Tomato Gravy (Sugo):

¼ cup extra-virgin olive oil
1 medium onion, finely chopped
6 cloves garlic, finely minced
2 small cans tomato paste
6 tomato-paste cans filled with
　water

2 tsp. sweet basil
1 tsp. Frank Davis Sicilian
　Seasoning
2 bay leaves
Salt and black pepper to taste

The Veal Cutlets:

3 cups seasoned bread stuffing mix
⅔ cup grated Pecorino Romano
　cheese
2 tsp. Frank Davis Sicilian
　Seasoning
1 tsp. granulated garlic
1 tsp. oregano
½ cup finely chopped parsley
2 tsp. black pepper
Peanut oil for deep frying

2 veal round steaks or 6 cutlets,
　thinly sliced
2 cups all-purpose seasoned flour
2 cups eggwash (2 cups whole milk
　+ 6 eggs)
4 cups shredded mozzarella cheese
1 cup grated Parmesan cheese
¼ cup grated Pecorino Romano
　cheese

First, make your red gravy. Here's how you do it.

In a heavy 5-quart Dutch oven, heat the olive oil to medium high. Then drop in the chopped onions and the garlic and—stirring constantly—lightly sauté them together until they just soften (it is not necessary to brown the onions and you don't want the garlic to burn); about 2 to 3 minutes should do it.

When the onions and garlic are uniformly blended, add the tomato paste to the pot and rapidly stir it into the mix. Remember—*you don't have to fry the tomato paste to make a good red gravy:* if you accidentally fry the paste too long, you will increase the acidity of the tomatoes and the gravy will be strong, harsh, and bitter. You want it to come out light and sweet. So just cook it a minute or two until the paste, onions, garlic, and olive oil are mixed well.

At this point, add the water to the tomato paste and stir again until the mixture is silky smooth. Keep in mind that the secret to making a gravy the right consistency is to use *3 cans of water for every 1 can of tomato paste* you use.

When the sauce is thoroughly mixed, add the basil, the Sicilian seasoning, and the bay leaves and season the gravy with salt and black pepper to your taste. All that's left now is to cover the pot and cook the sugo at a "simmer" for about an hour. It's a good idea to occasionally stir the gravy to keep it from sticking on the bottom of the pot and to keep the ingredients uniformly blended.

Now you're ready to prepare the veal. Here's how.

First, take a large bowl and mix together all the ingredients for the frozia bread crumbs—crumbs, cheese, Sicilian seasoning, garlic, oregano, parsley, and black pepper. In fact, for a superrich flavor, you should mix the crumbs and let them "set" for at least 2 hours before you use them so that the flavors can marry. Better yet, let them set overnight!

When you're ready to cook, preheat your peanut oil to exactly 350 degrees (I suggest you use a thermometer so that you get it just right—remember, you're going to be cooking veal coated with bread crumbs, so if you fry it too hot the crumbs will brown long before the veal is cooked).

While the oil is coming up to heat, pound out the veal between two sheets of plastic wrap until the pieces are about ¼ inch thick, dredge them in the seasoned flour, dunk them in the eggwash, and roll them in the seasoned frozia crumbs.

Now—*and this is the most important part of the whole recipe!*—let the cutlets rest on a piece of waxed paper for 2 minutes so that the frozia mix can "fix to the veal." If you try to fry without letting the cutlets rest, the crumbs will fall off in the hot oil.

Then when the oil is at the right temperature, begin dropping in the cutlets one at a time until you fill the frypan (but don't overcrowd them—you want to give them room to fry).

You'll find that it takes only a few minutes for the frozia coating to turn a rich golden brown color and take on a crispy, crispy texture. When this happens … they're done! Don't overcook 'em! Lift them out of the oil with a set of tongs and place them on several layers of paper towels to drain.

Now there are two ways to serve Veal Parmesan.

1—When the veal and the gravy are both ready, take a Pyrex baking pan (9 by 11 inches should do fine) and pour a small amount of the gravy in the bottom of the pan. Then place a layer of the veal on top of the gravy and pour a little more gravy on top of the veal. Then sprinkle on a layer of the shredded mozzarella and a little of the Parmesan. Repeat the process with another layer of veal, gravy, mozzarella, and Parmesan. Then cover the dish and bake it at 350 degrees for about 45 minutes so that the flavors marry and the cheeses melt. When it's ready, serve the Veal Parmesan over piping hot pasta topped off with a sprinkling of Romano cheese.

2—About 30 minutes before you're ready to eat, cook the spaghetti in about a gallon and a half of rapidly boiling, lightly salted water until it's *al dente* (firm yet tender, but not soft). When it's ready, drain it thoroughly *(don't rinse it!)*, toss it with about a cup of the tomato gravy to keep the pieces from sticking together, and dish out a serving of pasta on an oval plate. Then place one of the cutlets on top of the pasta, layer on some of the sugo and a handful of the mozzarella and Parmesan cheeses, and run the plate under the broiler for 5 minutes or so until the cheeses melt and the veal is bubbly. Then sprinkle the dish liberally with more Parmesan cheese and serve it piping hot right from the oven, garnished with a little Romano and accompanied by a cold Italian olive salad.

Chef's Note:

1—Don't use Italian seasoned bread crumbs—they're too fine and won't give you the crispiness you want. Buy a bag of stuffing mix (it's coarse-ground bread, usually French bread), crumble it just a little with your hands, and use it to create the batter coating for your cutlets. There is no substitute!

2—The Sicilian seasoning I use in this recipe can be ordered by calling 1-800-742-4231.

3—Because you can use this same frozia bread crumb mix for frying not only veal but fish, shrimp, oysters, zucchini, cauliflower, broccoli, liver, and eggplant, I suggest you double the recipe and keep what you don't use in the freezer.

4—Seasoned flour is all-purpose flour to which you've added salt and black pepper to taste.

Real Cajun Boudin

There was a time when I was growing up when you could buy boudin in two varieties—*red and white*. The red boudin was more commonly referred to as "blood sausage," but you can't get it anymore because the government won't let it be sold. The white boudin, however, is as popular as ever. And if you always wanted to make your own, here's the recipe!

4 lb. lean pork butt	2 tsp. black pepper
1 lb. pork liver	1 tsp. white pepper
4 bay leaves	1 tbsp. Frank Davis Pork Seasoning
1 cup finely chopped parsley	½ tsp. ground sage
6 medium onions, finely chopped	3 cloves garlic, finely chopped
½ bell pepper, finely chopped	2 bunches green onions, thinly
1 cup finely chopped celery	sliced
2 tbsp. salt	8 cups cooked rice
2 tsp. cayenne pepper	

First, cut the pork butt and the pork liver into pieces small enough for grinding. Then add all of the ingredients *(except the green onions and rice)* to a 12-quart stockpot, cover with water, and boil over a medium-high fire until the meats are tender (about an hour and a half should do it). Be sure to skim off all the "scum" that forms on the pork stock.

While the meats are cooking, boil the rice; but keep in mind that you want it *"just barely cooked."* If you even slightly overcook it, it will turn mushy inside the boudin casings.

When the meats are done, drain them in a colander (but save the stock). Then meticulously remove and discard any excess fat from the pork and grind the pork and the liver (along with the green onions) through the ³⁄₁₆ plate of a grinder. If you don't have a grinder, chop the meat and the green onions to a fine consistency in your food processor.

While you're preparing the meats, put the meat stock back into the pot, turn the fire up to high, and reduce it to one half of its original volume. Remember that a stock reduction concentrates the intensity of the flavor, thereby intensifying the flavor of whatever it's added to.

At this point, place the cooked rice into a large mixing bowl and *gently fold* in the seasoned meats until the mixture is uniform (which is why you don't want to overcook the rice). If, while you're mixing the rice and meat together, the mixture becomes too dry, simply moisten it with some of the stock—*keep in mind that your boudin should be pasty, but not mushy and wet.*

Finally, adjust the seasoning by adding salt and pepper to taste and stuff the mixture into natural sausage casings *while it's still warm.*

To serve the boudin, you can steam it, bake it uncovered in a 350-degree oven, quickly toast it over a barbecue pit, or microwave it until it's piping hot.

The only thing left to do is enjoy being Cajun ... whether you're Cajun or not!

Chef's Note: *Good boudin has only a slight hint of liver in it. Be careful not to mix in too much (even if it means cutting back on what's called for in this recipe to suit your taste).*

Your rice will be perfect for boudin if you rapidly boil it in a full gallon of salted water for exactly 13 minutes, then drain it in a colander and rinse off the excess starch with lukewarm water.

You can order the pork seasoning I use in this recipe by calling 1-800-742-4231.

How to Make Your Own Sausages

Whether it's pork sausage, hot sausage, or Italian sausage, there's something special about making your own from scratch. And it's really not that difficult to make if you have a good recipe. These, y'all, are good recipes! Try 'em and see!

New Orleans Pork Sausage:

4 lb. lean pork butt	**1 tsp. thyme**
2 lb. ground pork fat	**2 tsp. brown sugar**
2 tsp. salt	**2 medium onions, finely chopped**
2 tsp. black pepper	**6 cloves garlic, finely minced**
2 tsp. cayenne pepper	**1 bunch green onion tops**
2 tbsp. Frank Davis Pork Seasoning	**1 qt. water**
2 tsp. sage	

First, cut the pork butt into chunks small enough to fit into the grinder. Then mix the pork pieces uniformly with the pork fat.

Next, using the ³⁄₁₆ grinding plate, run the meat and the fat through the grinder once, depositing the finished product into a large mixing bowl.

At this point, sprinkle all the seasonings (including the onions, garlic, and green onion tops) over the meat and, with your hands, mix everything together well. In fact, to get the seasoning blend just right, I suggest you even *knead* the meat as you would dough. Then when you figure it's mixed well, add just enough water to give the bulk sausage a smooth consistency *... and mix it again!*

When it's ready, form the sausage mix into patties or stuff it into natural casings. I recommend you double-wrap the patties or links in 1-pound packages and freeze what you don't intend to use right away.

Chef's Note: *If you decide to make patties instead of links, be sure you place small pieces of waxed paper between each patty to keep them from freezing together.*

The pork seasoning I use in this recipe can be ordered direct by calling 1-800-742-4231.

New Orleans Hot Sausage:

5 lb. lean beef chuck roast	2 tbsp. parsley flakes
3 lb. pork butt plus fat	½ tsp. celery seed
2 tbsp. black pepper	1 tsp. ground ginger
2 tbsp. red pepper	2 tsp. Frank Davis Beef Seasoning
2 tbsp. white pepper	½ tsp. ground nutmeg
4 tbsp. granulated onion	3 tbsp. salt
2 tbsp. granulated garlic	1 qt. water

First, cut the beef roast and the pork butt into chunks small enough to fit into your grinder. Then, using the ³⁄₁₆ grinding plate, run the beef through the grinder once. Then change to the ⅜ plate (or a coarse plate) and regrind the chuck along with the pork pieces, depositing the finished product into a large mixing bowl.

At this point, sprinkle all the seasonings over the meat and, with your hands, mix everything together well. In fact, to get the seasoning blend just right, I suggest you even *knead* the meat as you would dough. Then when you figure it is mixed well, add just enough water to give the bulk sausage a smooth consistency ... *and mix it again!*

When it's ready, form the sausage mix into patties or stuff it into natural casings. I recommend you double-wrap the patties or links in 1-pound packages and freeze what you don't intend to use right away.

Chef's Note: *If you decide to make patties instead of links, be sure you place small pieces of waxed paper between each patty to keep them from freezing together.*

For hot sausage, the mixture should always be a 70/30 beef to pork ratio.

The beef seasoning I use in this recipe can be ordered direct by calling 1-800-742-4231.

New Orleans Sicilian Sausage (Italian):

5 lb. lean chuck roast	2 tsp. caraway seed
2 lb. pork butt with fat	3 tbsp. sweet basil
2 tbsp. granulated onion	2 tsp. oregano
2 tbsp. granulated garlic	3 tbsp. salt
2 tsp. savory	2 tsp. crushed red pepper
2 tsp. thyme	1 tbsp. black pepper
1 tbsp. sugar	2 tbsp. parsley flakes
2 tbsp. fennel seed	1 qt. water
2 tbsp. Frank Davis Sicilian Seasoning	

First, cut the beef roast and the pork butt into chunks small enough to fit into your grinder. Then, using the ³/₁₆ grinding plate, run the beef through the grinder once. Then change to the ³/₈ plate (or a coarse plate) and regrind the chuck along with the pork pieces, depositing the finished product into a large mixing bowl.

At this point, sprinkle all the seasonings over the meat and, with your hands, mix everything together well. In fact, to get the seasoning blend just right, I suggest you even *knead* the meat as you would dough. Then when you figure it's mixed well, add just enough water to give the bulk sausage a smooth consistency ... *and mix it again!*

When it's ready, form the sausage mix into patties or stuff it into natural casings. I recommend you double-wrap the patties or links in 1-pound packages and freeze what you don't intend to use right away.

Chef's Note: *If you decide to make patties instead of links, be sure you place small pieces of waxed paper between each patty to keep them from freezing together.*

For Italian sausage, the mixture should always be an 80/20 beef to pork ratio.

The Sicilian seasoning I use in this recipe can be ordered direct by calling 1-800-742-4231.

Italian Sausage and Pasta in Red Gravy

It's hard to beat a big pot of Italian sausages simmering in a rich tomato gravy. But if you've always avoided fixing 'em for your family because you're convinced that you just can't make a good gravy ... well, get ready! I'm gonna teach you exactly how to do it—authentically Italian!

2 lb. Italian sausage	**2 tsp. sweet basil**
1 cup tap water	**1 tsp. Italian seasoning**
¼ cup extra-virgin olive oil	**2 bay leaves**
1 medium onion, chopped	**Salt and black pepper to taste**
6 cloves garlic, minced	**2 lb. mostaccioli or ziti pasta**
2 small cans tomato paste	**1 cup grated Romano cheese**
6 tomato-paste cans filled with water	

First, place the Italian sausages in a 10-by-14 baking pan. Then prick a few holes in each sausage casing, pour the cup of water over the top, and bake at 350 degrees for about 20 to 25 minutes, turning occasionally. This reduces the amount of fat you'll get when the sausages are cooked in the gravy and it tenderizes the sausage casings.

Now, in a heavy 5-quart Dutch oven, heat the olive oil to medium high. Then drop in the chopped onions and the garlic and—stirring constantly—lightly sauté them together until they just soften (it is not necessary to brown the onions and you don't want the garlic to burn); about 2 to 3 minutes should do it.

When the onions and garlic are uniformly blended, add the tomato paste to the pot and rapidly stir it into the mix. It's an old wives' tale that you have to fry the tomato paste to make a good red gravy: if you accidentally fry the paste too long, you will increase the acidity of the tomatoes and the gravy will be strong, harsh, and bitter. You want it to come out light and sweet. So just cook it a minute or two until the paste, onions, garlic, and olive oil are mixed well.

At this point, add the water to the tomato paste and stir again until the mixture is silky smooth. Remember that the secret to making a gravy the right consistency is to use *3 cans of water for every 1 can of tomato paste* you use.

When the sauce is thoroughly mixed, add the basil, the Italian seasoning, and the bay leaves and season the gravy with salt and black pepper to your taste. Then drop in the sausage links, toss them around so that they're completely coated with the gravy, cover the pot, and simmer over a *low* fire for about 2 hours.

When you're ready to eat, cook the pasta in about a gallon and a half of rapidly boiling, lightly salted water until it's *al dente* (firm yet tender, but not soft). When it's ready, drain it thoroughly *(don't rinse it!)*, toss it with about a cup or two of the tomato gravy to keep the pieces from sticking together, sprinkle it liberally with the Romano cheese, and serve it piping hot with the sausages.

Mama mia! That's Italian!

Chef's Note:

1—For perfect pasta that doesn't stick together, cook it uncovered, stir it almost constantly, add about 3 or 4 tablespoons of olive oil to the water while it's boiling, and season the water with about 3 teaspoons of salt. Then when the pasta is done, drain it thoroughly in a colander and coat it lightly with a little extra olive oil while it's still hot.

2—When you remove the sausages from the baking pan, go ahead and discard the sausage drippings. While it contains a lot of flavor, it also contains too much grease to be put in your gravy.

3—I've said it before; I'll say it again—you don't add sugar *to an authentic Italian gravy. If you prepare it properly, it will be light and naturally sweet.*

Cochon à l'Orange
(Orange-Glazed Pork Chops)

Take eight tender, center-cut pork chops, glaze them with a succulent orange juice and liqueur sauce, and serve them with cheesy pasta and my Sicilian Green Bean and Olive Salad and you got one of the finest meals you'll ever sit down to!

8 center-cut pork chops (about ¾ inch thick)
2 tbsp. Frank Davis Pork Seasoning
½ tsp. ginger
2 tbsp. butter

1 cup chicken stock
¼ cup orange liqueur
½ cup thinly sliced green onions
4 tbsp. minced parsley

First, lay out the pork chops on a sheet of waxed paper, lightly sprinkle them with the pork seasoning and the ginger, and rub the seasonings well into the meat with your hands. Then, in a heavy 12-inch skillet, melt down the butter, quickly brown the chops on both sides, and prop them up on end in a baking pan. Incidentally, a wire baking rack works great for this because you can drop the chops between the wires.

Then mix together well the chicken stock, orange liqueur, and green onions and pour the mixture into the bottom of the baking pan. Remember, you want to keep the chops out of the liquid—you just want to use the liquid to moisten the meat as it bakes.

At this point, cover the pan tightly with aluminum foil, set the oven at 350 degrees, and bake the pork chops for an hour. Then remove them from the oven and allow them to cool; and while they're cooling, make your glaze.

Glaze:

½ stick butter
½ cup brown sugar
2 tsp. Worcestershire sauce
2 tbsp. orange zest
½ cup orange liqueur
1 can frozen orange juice (10-oz. size)

2 cups orange marmalade
3 tbsp. apple cider vinegar
2 tbsp. cornstarch
¼ cup chicken stock

Take a 4-quart saucepan, melt the butter, stir in the brown sugar, and cook over medium heat—*stirring constantly*—until the sugar and butter form a smooth paste (which should take about 4 minutes). Then begin adding the remainder of the ingredients (except the cornstarch and chicken stock) one at a time ... *stirring continuously*. And don't forget to stir in the pan drippings you got when the pork chops were baking!

When the sauce is smooth and shiny, reduce the heat and simmer it gently—*uncovered*—for about 5 minutes so that all the flavors blend thoroughly. Then, while the mixture is cooking, beat the cornstarch and the chicken stock together and slowly add it to the bubbling sauce—*again stirring all the while*—until the glaze reaches the thickness you desire. For best results it should be the consistency of honey.

At this point, take a pastry brush and paint each pork chop—still in the meat rack!—so that it is thoroughly coated with the glaze. Then slide the pan back into the oven at 350 degrees and continue to bake—this time *uncovered*—for about 30 minutes or until the chops turn sugary and shiny. I suggest that you brush additional glaze onto the meat several times during the final baking process to enrich the flavor.

When you're ready to eat, gently remove the chops from the wire rack, serve them piping hot, and top them with a little extra glaze and a sprinkling of green onions and fresh minced parsley. The chops go well with cheesy pasta and my Sicilian Green Bean and Olive Salad.

Oh—and I bet you can't eat just one!

Chef's Note: *Be careful not to overcook the pork or it will dry out. And watch the glaze as it bakes—too high a heat in the oven will cause the sugar to burn.*

Frank Davis Pork Seasoning can be ordered by direct mail by calling 1-800-742-4231.

N'Awlins Pork Roll Frittata

There are scrambled eggs ... and then there are scrambled eggs! But this scrambled egg breakfast dish, served with a lean-cut pork roll, defies verbal description. It's one of those dishes you just got to taste for yourself. Oh—and if you learn only one dish to prepare for breakfast guests ... make it this one! It's quick, it's easy, and it's mouth-watering!

1 tsp. salt
½ tsp. black pepper
1 lean pork fillet
¼ cup ketchup
¼ cup clover honey
1 tsp. Spanish paprika
Pinch cinnamon
1 tsp. Worcestershire sauce
½ tsp. ground ginger
10 whole eggs
⅓ cup light cream

¼ cup grated Parmesan cheese
2 cups finely chopped spinach
½ cup finely chopped parsley
1 small white onion, finely chopped
1 bunch green onions, finely chopped
1 clove garlic, finely minced
2 tbsp. margarine
½ tsp. salt
½ tsp. black pepper

Start off by salting and peppering the pork fillet (you want to forcefully rub it into the meat with both hands). Then slice the fillet crosswise every half-inch or so, but be careful not to slice it all the way through—remember, your objective is to "fan" it out. Then mix together all the pork seasoning ingredients—ketchup, honey, paprika, cinnamon, Worcestershire, and ginger—and spread it evenly over the fillet with a pastry brush.

Next, fan out the roll, pin the edges with toothpicks so that the roll cooks evenly and retains its "fanned" shape, and place it on a broiler pan in a preheated 400-degree oven. Now cook it until it's tender (which should take about 35 to 40 minutes). *Be careful not to overcook it or it'll dry out!*

When the roast is done, set it aside in a warm oven and start on the eggs.

You'll need a large bowl and you want to beat the eggs with a wire whip until well blended. Now toss in all the other ingredients except the margarine, salt, and black pepper and mix everything together well.

In a heavy skillet, melt the margarine, pour in the egg mixture, add the salt and pepper, and cook over medium-low heat. When you see the bottom and sides of the eggs cooking, keep rolling the sides and bottom over on itself so that the eggs cook evenly. *Remember, the eggs should not be cooked dry—you want them moist and shiny!*

Then, when you're ready to eat, place the roast on a heated platter and spoon the eggs around the pork. The only thing left is to serve the dish with hot buttered English muffins and currant jelly!

Chef's Note: *Because pork fillets are extremely tender, they cook relatively quickly. For perfect results, I recommend you bake it to an internal temperature of 160 degrees. It will come out moist and juicy. All you need is a meat thermometer.*

To intensify the flavor of the pork, you can sprinkle on about a teaspoon of Frank Davis Pork Seasoning. If it's not available where you shop, order it direct by calling 1-800-742-4231.

N'Awlins Panéed Pork Chops

If you want to treat your family to one of the classiest old New Orleans meals, fix them Panéed Pork Chops, Frank's N'Awlins Baked Macaroni, and my Famous Eleven-Minute Cauliflower (see *Frank Davis Cooks Naturally N'Awlins* for the side-dish recipes). This is so good, you'll be fixing it more than once a week!

8 pork chops (trimmed ¾ inch thick)	1 cup whole milk
3 tsp. Frank Davis Pork Seasoning	3 cups seasoned coarse-ground bread crumbs
3 whole eggs	Peanut oil for frying

First, lay out the pork chops on a sheet of waxed paper and sprinkle them on both sides with the pork seasoning. Then set them aside for a moment.

Meanwhile, combine the eggs and the milk in a large mixing bowl and beat them with a wire whip until frothy.

Now—*one at a time!*—dip the pork chops into the eggwash mixture and immediately roll them in the seasoned bread crumbs, making sure they are coated thoroughly.

But do not fry them right away!

After you coat them, place them on a clean sheet of waxed paper and let them "set" for at least 5 minutes. This step allows the eggwash and the crumbs to bind together, thereby preventing the coating from falling off in the pan when you fry the chops. If you don't allow enough "setting time," the coating will flake off in the hot oil.

When you're ready to cook, pour enough oil to completely cover the chops into a cast-iron or heavy-aluminum 12-inch skillet and heat it to medium high. Then fry 3-4 chops at a time until they turn a golden brown. Oh—and be sure you turn them over only once. This keeps the bread coating from fracturing, absorbing oil, and falling off in the pan.

When they're done, place them on a few sheets of paper towel to drain … then serve them immediately. You'll find that pork chops prepared this way will be tender and juicy on the inside, crispy on the outside, and totally greaseless!

Chef's Note: *Remember that the perfect eggwash mixture is always 3 eggs plus 1 cup of milk. Never, ever vary those proportions … or the coating will fall off of whatever you're cooking.*

In the old days, you had to fry the life out of pork—a slight hint of pink was verboten. *Today, the National Pork Council says that because pork is a cleaner form of meat it can be fried less with no danger of contracting food-borne diseases. That means juicier cuts and more succulent flavor.*

One more note! If you don't have my preblended pork seasoning on hand (which really makes all the difference in the world when you prepare panéed pork or pork roast) you can substitute plain salt and black pepper in this recipe. But remember, you can order my spicy pork seasoning simply by calling 1-800-742-4231.

Crispy Piglets with Smothered Kraut and Taters

It has to be the ultimate taste in deep frying—big, juicy pork steaks, sprinkled with spicy seasoning and fried to a crispy succulence, served with smothered shredded cabbage and oven-roasted potatoes! This is *"Strictly N'Awlins, y'all!"*

The Taters:

3 lb. raw Irish potatoes
½ cup extra-virgin olive oil
2 tbsp. vegetable seasoning

⅔ cup freshly grated Parmesan cheese

First, preheat your oven to 450 degrees.

Then, without peeling them, wash the potatoes thoroughly under cold running water, making sure you remove all the soil completely ('cuz you're going to roast them with the skins on). Now at this point, dry them and cut them into quarters.

Next, place the olive oil and the vegetable seasoning in a large mixing bowl and, with a wire whip, blend them to a creamy, smooth consistency. Then drop in the potato pieces and toss them until each and every piece is thoroughly coated with the seasoning mix.

All that's left is to transfer the potatoes to a large, shallow baking pan and roast them *(uncovered)* for about 45 minutes or until they are toasty brown. I do suggest that to get an evenly roasted, evenly seasoned effect, you stir the potatoes several times with a slotted spoon during the baking process.

Five minutes before you're ready to eat, sprinkle on the grated Parmesan cheese and toss them one more time. Then serve them piping hot right from the oven. Incidentally, this dish goes great with almost any entrée … not just pork!

The Kraut:

1 small head cabbage	**2 small red delicious apples, diced**
¼ cup olive oil	**½ cup bottled bacon bits**
1 small onion, coarsely diced	**2 tbsp. vegetable or pork seasoning**

Start off by cutting the cabbage into quarters and removing the "knots" at the base of the head. Then shred each section to the consistency of coleslaw and set it aside for a moment.

Now take the olive oil, the onions, and the apples and drop them into a heavy 1-inch aluminum skillet. Then quickly fry down the mixture over high heat until the onions begin to brown and the apples soften slightly (this should take about 6 minutes or so). *Remember to stir continually during the cooking process.*

Next, add the shredded cabbage to the skillet and fold it into the apples and onions, making sure that all the cabbage is coated with the mixture. At this point, put a steamer lid on the pot, reduce the fire to medium, and let the cabbage smother for about 3 minutes—stirring occasionally. Don't worry about the little bit of cabbage that slightly chars on the bottom of the skillet. This is *caramelization* (natural acids turning to sugar) and it's supposed to happen.

Now take the lid off the pot again, drop in the bacon bits and the vegetable seasoning (one at a time, stirring between the additions), and *stir, stir, stir!* The seasonings have to coat all the cabbage shreds well; otherwise the dish will lack uniformity. And when you are satisfied that you've blended everything together as best you can, put the lid back on the pot, reduce the heat to low, and let the cabbage cook for about 20 minutes (stirring occasionally) until it turns tender, but crispy.

Just before you plan to serve the dish, adjust your salt content. Remember, there's going to be salt in the vegetable seasoning and it has to cook into the cabbage before you can determine its potency. So add whatever salt you use ... last!

By the way, when the cabbage is ready, place it in a Pyrex baking dish, cover it tightly with a sheet of aluminum foil, and keep it warm in the oven until your *Crispy Piglets* are done!

The Crispy Piglets:

8 center-cut pork steaks, 1 inch thick
½ gal. peanut oil for frying

4 tsp. pork seasoning
Hot pepper jelly for garnish

First, take the pork and a sharp knife and *"score"* each side of each steak in a crosscut pattern about one-quarter way through. This allows the pork to deep fry quickly without drying it out!

Meanwhile, heat the peanut oil to 350 degrees in a heavy cast-iron or aluminum skillet. Then while the oil is heating, sprinkle the pork seasoning on the steaks and rub it into the meat briskly with your hands.

Then, when you're ready to eat, drop the steaks into the hot oil and fry them—totally submerged!—until they turn a rich golden brown. Be careful not to overcook them! If done properly, they'll be crispy on the outside and *unbelievably tender and juicy* on the inside.

When you remove them from the skillet, place them on a couple layers of paper towels for a minute or two so that any excess oil drains off. But here's a surprise! Contrary to what you might think … *they won't be greasy!* Because they don't have a batter or coating, the hot oil seals the meat, keeping the juices in and the oil out!

I suggest you serve them topped with the hot pepper jelly, alongside the smothered kraut and the oven potatoes for one of the best meals you'll ever have!

Chef's Note: *Don't use the imitation bacon bits! Hormel Real Bacon brand is what you want. It's available at most large supermarkets!*

A variation of the smothered fresh cabbage is to use bottled sauerkraut that's been thoroughly washed and drained. Just cook it the same way—the only difference is a "tart" taste rather than a sweet one that the diced apples impart.

I know your grandma told you to do it, but it is no longer necessary to cook the life out of pork just to make sure it's done! Pork we buy in the supermarket today, when it's cooked properly, should have a very light hint of pink on the inside when it's sliced. That's when it is at its ultimate best!

Spicy N'Awlins Fried Ribs
(With Gravy-Baked Potatoes and Cold Green-Bean Salad)

Everybody, but everybody, takes baby-back pork ribs, marinates them in some favorite spices, and tosses them on the barbecue grill. But have you ever thought about how tasty those same little ribs would be if they were spiced, double-dipped in an eggwash and flour, and deep fried nice and crispy? Well, I want you to know that until you fix these, you just don't know what finger-lickin' really means!

3 lb. trimmed baby-back pork ribs	**2 tbsp. dry mustard**
4 tbsp. salt	**6 eggs**
4 tbsp. black pepper	**2 cups milk**
4 tbsp. paprika	**4 cups vegetable oil for frying**
3 tbsp. onion powder	**3 cups all-purpose flour**
3 tbsp. garlic powder	**(unseasoned)**

First, be sure the silverskin on the back of the ribs is removed; otherwise the seasonings won't fully penetrate the pork during marination. Then have the butcher cut the slab lengthwise and separate the ribs into "singles." Try to buy only small ribs. Large ribs take too long to fry, thereby making the flour batter overbrowned before the pork fully cooks.

Now put all of the little "ribettes" into a large mixing bowl and generously sprinkle on the seasonings—salt, black pepper, paprika, onion powder, garlic powder, and dry mustard. Then tightly cover the ribs with plastic wrap and place them in the refrigerator to marinate for at least 3 hours.

When you're ready to cook, thoroughly mix together the 6 eggs and the 2 cups of milk to form an eggwash (you must use this proportion—anything less will not give you a crispy batter). And, using a deep-sided frypan, heat the vegetable oil to precisely 325 degrees (the best way to do this is with a fry thermometer—they're inexpensive and can be purchased at any kitchen shop).

Now take the ribs from the refrigerator, dip them first into the flour, then into the eggwash, then back into the flour. Then set them on a platter for about a minute or so to let the coating "rest." *Note:* I suggest you dip and coat at any one time only the number of ribs you can fry—if you do too many ahead, the coating will turn soggy and the batter will be tough rather than crunchy.

When the temperature of the oil is just right, drop in the ribs. Here's the formula: small bony ribs fry for about 4 minutes; medium meaty ribs fry for about 5-6 minutes; and larger meaty ribs fry for about 6-7 minutes. You want them cooked … but you don't want them overcooked or they'll be tough!

Then when they're crispy and golden brown, remove them from the oil, place them on paper towels to drain, and serve them piping hot alongside a dish of Gravy-Baked Potatoes and a Cold Green-Bean Salad! (Actually, you don't have to serve them with anything—that's how finger-lickin' good they are! Okay—maybe a frosty beer to wash 'em down! But that's it!)

Gravy-Baked Potatoes:

First, oil and wrap 4 medium-size baking potatoes with aluminum foil and bake them at 450 degrees for about an hour or so until they're done.

Now while they're cooling, take a heavy aluminum skillet and bring to a boil 4 cups of chicken stock. Then add to the stock ½ cup of thinly sliced green onions, ¼ cup of minced parsley, and about a teaspoon of Kitchen Bouquet.

At this point, cook the mixture at a slow boil until the sauce reduces to approximately ⅔ of its original volume—*this intensifies the flavor of the sauce.*

Now, season the mixture to taste with salt and black pepper. Then, while the sauce is still boiling, mix 2 tablespoons of cornstarch with ¼ cup of cold water and slowly stir it in a little at a time until the sauce thickens to the consistency you desire.

All that's left is to unwrap the potatoes, slice them in halves, and place them into a baking pan. Then liberally ladle the sauce over the potato halves, place the pan into a 300-degree oven, and heat them—uncovered—to piping hot.

This is a great low-fat, low-cholesterol, low-cal topping to put over baked potatoes. So the next time your doctor says baked potatoes are good for you as long as you don't heap them with butter, sour cream, shredded cheese, and bacon bits ... make this sauce! You don't have to eat plain old baked potatoes ever again!

Cold Green-Bean Salad:

Take 4 No. 303 cans of whole green beans and drain them in a colander. Then in a large bowl, mix together:

1 cup crumbled bacon bits	1 medium yellow onion, coarsely
5 slices chili peppers, finely diced	diced
½ cup extra-virgin olive oil	3 hard-boiled eggs, chopped
⅓ cup vinaigrette salad dressing	

Now place the drained beans in the bowl and *gently* toss them into the dressing until each one is thoroughly coated. At this point, season the salad with salt and black pepper to taste, cover with plastic wrap, place into the refrigerator to chill for about 2 hours, and serve as a side dish.

N'Awlins Oven-Baked Baby-Back Ribs
(With Clover Honey Barbecue Sauce)

They're succulent … and they're so tender the meat falls off the bone. And once they're glazed with the clover honey sauce, there's just no way you can stop eating them! Ummmmmmmm!

2 racks baby-back pork ribs
2 tsp. salt
2 tsp. black pepper
2 tsp. paprika
4 cups water
2 cups hickory-flavored barbecue
   sauce
1 cup clover honey

½ cup ketchup
2 tsp. Worcestershire sauce
2 tsp. dry mustard
1 tbsp. paprika
1 tsp. ground ginger
½ tsp. ground cinnamon
¼ tsp. allspice

First, preheat your oven or barbecue grill to 250 degrees.

Then, while the oven is heating, take a small knife and, beginning at the edge of the rib bones, loosen the silverskin from the back side of the rack of ribs and strip if off. It comes off relatively easily once you get it started. (If you leave the silverskin on, the ribs will be "chewy" once they're cooked.)

At this point, liberally sprinkle the ribs with salt, black pepper, and paprika and rub the seasonings well into the pork.

Now pour the water into a baking pan, place a wire rack on top of the pan, and place the ribs on the rack. Then slide the whole works into the oven—*uncovered*—and bake for at least an hour or so (or until the ribs begin to brown slightly).

Meanwhile, in a large bowl, thoroughly mix together all the ingredients for the barbecue sauce. In fact, for a deep, rich flavor you can make the sauce a day or two in advance, then let the fixin's "marry" in the refrigerator.

Now when the ribs have browned, remove them from the oven and "mop" them generously with the sauce while they are still piping hot! Then slide them back into the oven for about 20 minutes so that the honey can form a "glaze."

When you're ready to eat, take the ribs off the rack, cut them into individual pieces, and serve them with extra sauce on the side.

Y'all, they don't get more tender nor more tasty than this!

Chef's Note:

1—It is not necessary to parboil pork ribs before you cook them. If you parboil them, they lose a lot of flavor. By slow-roasting them on a rack over a pan of water, they not only tenderize but they become virtually greaseless! What happens is the steam from the waterpan rises to baste the ribs and keep them moist. It also renders out all the excess fat from the pork, keeps the pork drippings from flaring up in the hot pan, and makes cleanup a snap.

2—Never put barbecue sauce on pork ribs until they are almost done. All barbecue sauce contains some form of sugar, and sugar tends to burn and taste burnt when cooked in an active oven. Mop on your sauce at the end of the cooking process, just far enough in advance to allow the sugar to form a shiny glaze. The results are sweet and smokey ... just the way they should be to complement baby pork.

Shredded Pork with Szechwan Sauce

If you like good, richly flavored Chinese food made with quality ingredients that are delicately spiced to perfection, then you're going to love this Szechwan pork, especially when you serve it over a big plate of Pork Fried Rice!

1 lb. lean boneless pork, cut in thin strips	½ tsp. sugar
1 tsp. minced garlic	¼ tsp. sesame oil
4 tbsp. soy sauce	½ cup peanut oil
1 egg, slightly beaten	1 bell pepper, cut in thin strips
2 tbsp. cornstarch	2 celery ribs, bias cut
1 tbsp. rice wine	½ tsp. dried red pepper flakes
2 tbsp. rice wine vinegar	6 green onions, thinly sliced

First, mix together well in a small bowl the pork, ½ teaspoon of garlic, 2 tablespoons of soy sauce, the beaten egg, the cornstarch, and the rice wine. Then set the mixture aside and let it marinate for about 15 minutes—*this step serves to both flavor and tenderize the meat strips.*

Meanwhile, blend together in a large measuring cup the remaining soy sauce, vinegar, sugar, and sesame oil—*this is the flavor base for the Szechwan sauce.* Set it aside too.

At this point, pour the peanut oil into the wok and heat it to approximately 400 degrees. Then, drop in the marinated pork mixture and—tossing constantly—stir-fry the strips *uncovered* until the pork loses its pink color (this should take you about 2 to 3 minutes). Now, remove the meat from the wok with a Chinese strainer or a slotted spoon and set it aside.

Next, to keep the dish as fat free as possible, drain off all but 1 tablespoon of the peanut oil from the wok. Then reheat the wok to 350 degrees, collect all your ingredients, and get them ready to stir-fry. Once the wok is hot, drop in the bell pepper strips, celery, red pepper flakes, green onions, and the remaining ½ teaspoon of garlic. Listen for the sizzle and watch for the steam—it means you're frying at the right temperature. Now, with a couple of spatulas or chef's spoons, constantly toss the vegetables around the hot pan for about 30 seconds. Don't let them burn! They'll cook quickly!

Finally, return the cooked pork to the wok (along with the vinegar mixture), toss the meat strips and vegetables together until everything is uniformly blended, and stir-fry once more for another minute or two. If the sauce turns out a little on the thin side, stir in about a half-cup of chicken stock mixed with a tablespoon of cornstarch. If the sauce is a tad too thick for your taste, just thin it out with a small amount of plain chicken stock.

Shredded Pork with Szechwan Sauce is best when you serve it immediately; but leftovers (if there ever are any!) can be placed in a tightly covered container, refrigerated, and reheated the next day for lunch.

Chef's Note: *Total* preparation *time for Szechwan Pork is about 15 minutes— actual cooking time is about 5 minutes. The secret to preparing good Chinese food is to have all the ingredients measured out and laid out before you on the counter, ready to drop into the wok without interruption.*

By the way, you can buy Chinese rice wine and rice wine vinegar at all Oriental grocery stores, most gourmet shops, and any supermarket that has an international foods section. In a pinch, however, dry sherry and white wine vinegar are suitable substitutes.

CHAPTER 5

Poultry

Bacon-Tomato Chicken

If you like the combination flavor of bacon, lettuce, and tomato sandwiches, wait till you taste the zest that bacon and tomato give to simmered chicken. This is real family cooking at its best, especially when it's served with pasta.

2 lb. slab bacon	2 tbsp. all-purpose flour
2 young fryer chickens, skinned	2 tsp. Worcestershire sauce
2 tbsp. Frank Davis Sprinkling Spice	1 tbsp. chili pepper sauce
2 cups all-purpose flour	1 cup chicken broth
1 large onion, sliced	2 cups semidry white wine
5 large tomatoes	1 lb. ziti pasta, cooked al dente

First, take a heavy 12-inch skillet, place it on a low fire, and render out the slab bacon until it turns crisp. I suggest that you set the bacon strips aside on paper towels to drain after they cook to remove all the excess fat.

While the bacon is cooking, cut the chicken into serving-size pieces, season each piece with the sprinkling spice, and dredge them lightly in the 2 cups of all-purpose flour. Then in the same skillet you used to render the bacon, brown the chicken pieces in the leftover bacon drippings and set them aside on paper towels to drain as well. See, all you really want to do is *flavor* the chicken with the bacon—you don't want all of the fat in the dish.

At this point, take about 2 tablespoons of the bacon drippings and place them into a heavy 5-quart Dutch oven. Then, over high heat, fry the sliced onions just until they begin to brown slightly. While the onions are cooking, peel and seed the tomatoes and chop them into small chunks. Then add them to the frying onions.

When the onions wilt and the tomatoes soften, stir in the 2 tablespoons of flour, Worcestershire sauce, and chili pepper sauce. Then when the mixture is smooth, pour in the chicken broth and the white wine, toss in the crumbled bacon, and stir everything together well. Now bring the heat up to a slow boil, *but immediately reduce it* to low and simmer all of the ingredients together—uncovered—for about 5 to 10 minutes.

Finally, take the browned chicken and drop it into the Dutch oven, making sure that each piece is completely nestled into the gravy. Then tightly cover the pot and simmer the dish on low for about an hour. Be sure the heat is not too high because (1) you can't stir the pot or you'll break up the chicken pieces, and (2) if the heat is too high the chicken on the bottom of the pot will stick and burn.

When you're ready to eat, remove the chicken from the pot with a pair of tongs and place the pieces on a serving platter. Then take the ziti pasta, pour it into the gravy in the pot, thoroughly toss it over and over, and serve it piping hot in a large casserole dish.

Accompanied by a cold, crisp cucumber salad and a glass of chilled white wine (and soft drinks for the kids!), this meal is hard to beat any day of the week ... and three times on Sunday!

Chef's Note:

1—Almost any good white dry wine works in this recipe—Chenin Blanc, Chablis, Gewurztraminer, Grenache, Rhine—but I prefer to use a French Colombard. It's just fruity enough to complement the subtleness of the bacon and tomato.

2—If you can't find chili pepper sauce where you shop, you can substitute Szechwan sauce, Mexican picante sauce, or even a few dashes of Louisiana hot sauce in its place. You just want to pique the flavor of the bacon and chicken with a hint of pepper.

3—To make your own supply of my "sprinkling spice," mix together in your food processor 8 tbsp. salt, ½ tsp. black pepper, ½ tsp. cayenne, ½ tsp. white pepper, ¾ tsp. garlic salt, 2 tsp. onion powder, ⅛ tsp. garlic powder, and 2 tbsp. paprika. And whatever you got left over just store on your pantry shelf in a plastic container and "sprinkle" it on your steaks, pork chops, ribs, seafoods, and salads.

4—To peel fresh tomatoes, drop them into boiling water for about a minute or so (or until the skin begins to split). Then gently peel away the skin with a paring knife.

To seed the tomatoes, slice each one in half crosswise, place a half-tomato in your hand (sliced side down), and forcefully squeeze the seeds out into a bowl with your hands, leaving only the pulp remaining. It's really easy to do.

N'Awlins Marinated Chicken

Take four large, skinned chicken breasts, marinate them overnight in a savory mixture of beer, soy sauce, garlic, green onions, and the perfect blend of herbs and spices, and then bake them until they turn toasty and tender ... and you've got one of the best chicken dishes you ever tasted! Try this!

1 can warm Dixie beer (12 oz.)	4 cloves garlic, minced
¼ cup Crisco oil	2 tsp. red pepper flakes
6 green onions, thinly sliced	¼ cup soy sauce
2 tbsp. lemon juice	½ tbsp. whole cloves
2 tbsp. Worcestershire sauce	1 tbsp. Dijon mustard
4 tbsp. dark brown sugar	2 tsp. sweet basil
1 tbsp. Louisiana hot sauce	Salt and black pepper to taste
3 bay leaves, crushed	4 skinned chicken breasts

First, take a large plastic or Pyrex container *(do not use metal!)* and mix together thoroughly all the ingredients for the marinade—in other words, blend everything except the chicken. Then drop the individual breasts into the mixture, baste them well, and stash them *(covered)* in the refrigerator overnight.

Oh—I suggest that you turn the chicken in the marinade every couple of hours to make sure the pieces pick up the seasonings evenly.

Then, about an hour before you plan to eat, remove the chicken from the marinade, drain the pieces, pat them dry with a couple of paper towels, and place the pieces in a shallow baking pan. While you're preparing the breasts, go ahead and preheat your oven to 375 degrees.

When the temperature is right, slide the pan into the oven and bake the chicken—*uncovered*—for 25 minutes on each side until the breasts are moist and tender. *But here's the secret: about every 12 minutes are so, baste the chicken with a pastry brush liberally dipped into hickory-flavored butter* (the recipe follows). What you end up with are juicy, very slightly smokey-flavored chicken breasts that melt in your mouth!

I suggest you serve this chicken piping hot with baked beans and corn on the cob for a real summertime treat! Or let the pieces cool, cut them into chunks, and fold them into a crisp combination of lettuce, tomatoes, cucumbers, celery, and diced onions—*topped with a light vinaigrette*—for a delicious cold-chicken summer salad.

How to Make Hickory Butter:

Take 1 pound of butter, place it in a bowl, allow it to come to room temperature, and cream it until it is smooth. Then, in a 2-quart saucepan, combine:

½ cup minced green onions	1 tsp. sweet basil
4 cloves fresh garlic, minced	1 tbsp. paprika
¼ cup minced parsley	2 tbsp. Louisiana hot sauce
½ cup dry Burgundy wine	2 tsp. Liquid Smoke
1 tbsp. fresh lemon juice	Salt and black pepper to taste

Then simmer everything together until just about all of the wine has evaporated (which should take about 10 minutes). Now remove the pot from the fire and allow the mixture to cool.

When it reaches room temperature, stir the seasoning mix into the softened butter until uniformly blended. Then whip the butter until it turns smooth and creamy and season it to taste with salt and pepper.

Chef's Note: *If you can't find Dixie beer where you shop, a good 12-ounce can of a popular national brand will substitute nicely. Just don't use a "light" beer—and you need a full 12 ounces.*

Watch the chicken as it bakes. Depending upon the thermostat in your oven, you may have to shorten or lengthen your baking time—but do not overcook the chicken or it will come out dry and unappetizing.

Also be careful when using Liquid Smoke. A little bit works well as a flavor enhancer—too much can make the entire dish inedible.

Leftover flavored butter can be placed in waxed paper, rolled into tube shapes, chilled in the refrigerator, and dolloped into a variety of foods whenever you need a nice topping for an entrée that's light on natural sauce. Ummmmmmmm!

Country Potpie Pockets

You can take this recipe and make traditional Yankee potpies with it. But if you want something bordering on great … fry up some French bread pistolettes and stuff this filling into them. What you end up with is individual "Country Potpie Pockets"! Bubba, we're talking hard to beat, yeah!

8 chicken drumsticks
Water to cover
2 tbsp. mayonnaise
½ stick butter
1 cup finely chopped onions
½ cup finely chopped celery
¼ cup finely chopped bell pepper
3 cloves garlic, minced
3 tbsp. flour
1 cup whole milk
¼ cup heavy cream
1 cup concentrated chicken stock
1 large potato, diced

1 cup broccoli florets
2 carrots, diced
1 cup julienned tasso
1 lb. crawfish tails and fat
1 cup petit pois peas
1 tbsp. chicken base + ¼ cup water
½ tsp. white pepper
½ tsp. poultry seasoning
¾ cup diced pepper cheese
64-oz. bottle peanut oil for frying
24 Hearth Farms Brown-N-Serve
   pistolettes

First, place the drumsticks in a 5-quart Dutch oven or stockpot and pour in just enough water to cover them. Then bring the water to a gentle boil and cook the chicken legs for about an hour until they're tender. Oh—be sure to skim the foam off the pot as it cooks.

In the meantime, take a heavy 12-inch skillet, combine the mayonnaise and butter over medium heat, and sauté the onions, celery, bell pepper, and garlic until they become soft and tender. When the vegetables are done, sprinkle on the flour and cook it into the mixture for about 5 minutes. Then pour in the milk, the heavy cream, and the chicken stock and "simmer" the ingredients over low heat until the sauce turns smooth, silky, and slightly thickened.

When the drumsticks are cooked, remove them from the stockpot and let them cool *(but save the liquid!)*. Then put the liquid back into the pot, bring it back to a boil, drop in the potatoes, broccoli, and carrots, and lightly boil them until they soften ever so slightly.

Meanwhile, pick the meat off the drumsticks and coarsely chop it into chunks. Then drop the chicken meat into the sauce—along with the tasso and the crawfish tails and fat—and stir everything together until uniformly blended. Then add the poached potatoes, carrots, broccoli, and peas to the sauce and continue to cook the mixture over low heat for another 5 minutes. Oh—be gentle when you stir from here on; you don't want to smash the vegetables too much.

Now stir in the chicken base, white pepper, and poultry seasoning. Then drop in the pepper cheese chunks and stir them until they melt and become uniformly mixed into the sauce.

At this point, heat the peanut oil in a frypan and fry the pistolettes on both sides at 350 degrees until they are golden brown. Then place them on a couple of paper towels to drain (you want them greaseless).

Now with a sharp knife, cut a slit in the oval edge of the pistolette, push back some of the inside dough with the knife blade to make a pocket, and fill the hollow with the hot potpie stuffing. When they've all been stuffed, place them on a baking sheet, slide them into a preheated 325-degree oven, and bake them for 12 to 15 minutes until they're piping hot and supercrispy.

All that's left is to serve them right from the oven with a cold tossed salad topped with French dressing and an ice-cold frosty root beer.

Chef's Note: *If you'd like to take this recipe and make an old-tyme traditional potpie, first allow the stuffing to come to room temperature. Then take a Pet Ritz piecrust and prebake the bottom crust for 5 minutes at 350 degrees (to keep the bottom crust from puffing, place about a cup of dried red beans on top of the dough in the pie plate). Then remove the crust from the oven, pour out the beans (you can use them over and over again for baking), and allow it to cool slightly.*

Now spoon the stuffing into the bottom crust, lay on the top crust, cut 6 vent slits in the top, and bake the pie in a preheated 375-degree oven for 20 to 25 minutes until the piecrust is crisp and brown.

A variation to the ready-made piecrust is one made from crescent dinner rolls. Just take the dough straight from the can, unroll the perforated triangles, and lay them side by side on a lightly floured surface. Then pinch the edges of each triangle together to seal them, flatten them out with a rolling pin, and cut them into 1-inch strips.

Then spoon the cool filling into a buttered Pyrex piedish, lay the strips in woven-lattice fashion over the top, brush the strips with a little melted butter, and bake in a 375-degree oven for 20 minutes until the crust is golden brown and flaky.

If you can't find chicken base where you shop, you can substitute a couple of bouillon cubes dissolved in ¼ cup of water in its place. Just be careful to reduce the amount of salt you add to the recipe because bouillon cubes are usually very salty.

Chicken-Broccoli-Shrimp Casserole
(With Broccoli Cheese Sauce)

You could fix this entire dish from scratch, which means you would have to make a butter roux, do a heavy-cream reduction, shred and melt cheddar cheese, and simmer all of it into a rich sauce that would top sautéed chicken, shrimp, chopped eggs, and steamed broccoli. *Or ...* you can put the *same* dish together by shortcutting a bunch of steps and coming up with this! Which means you spend just a few minutes making a casserole and you spend the rest of the time savoring the flavor!

3 tbsp. margarine	2 cups tiny cooked shrimp
1 medium onion, coarsely chopped	1 tsp. black pepper
3 chicken breasts, diced	1 can Campbell's Broccoli Cheese Soup
1 pat butter	
6 cups steamed broccoli florets, al dente	1 can Campbell's Cheddar Cheese Soup
6 hard-boiled eggs, coarsely chopped	½ can Campbell's Chicken Broth
	Dash paprika for garnish

First, take a heavy 12-inch skillet, heat the margarine to sizzling, toss in the chopped onions, and sauté them until they soften. Then drop in the diced chicken and stir-fry the pieces until they're about half-cooked (you'll know because they'll turn white all over).

Meanwhile, lightly butter an 11-by-16 Pyrex casserole dish (that's what the pat of butter is for) and arrange the steamed broccoli evenly across the bottom of the dish. (Make a note here: just lightly steam the broccoli—don't overcook it! You want it tender-crisp, not done. It still has to bake in the sauce you're going to make.)

Now, in layers, evenly sprinkle the chopped eggs and the tiny shrimp over the broccoli (work it between the florets a little just to make it uniform) and sprinkle on the black pepper. When it's ready, preheat your oven to 400 degrees.

At this point, with the sautéed onions and chicken still on the fire, stir in the broccoli cheese soup and the cheddar cheese soup and stir them together until they begin to melt. Then pour in the chicken broth a little at a time—*stirring constantly!*—until you get just the consistency you desire ... which should be the thickness of a rich cheese sauce.

Then while the sauce is still hot and bubbly, ladle it evenly over the casserole ingredients and gently work it into the mixture with a fork. Then slide the dish into the oven and bake it—*uncovered*—for about 45 minutes or until it's piping hot!

All that's left is to spoon out a generous serving into a big soupbowl, garnish with paprika, and you're set for some of the best gourmet eating you've ever experienced! This stuff is *greeeaaatt!*

Old-Fashioned N'Awlins Batterless Chicken

When I was growing up, I remember my grandma frying chicken every Sunday ... but she never ever put any kind of coating or batter on it! She just fried the chicken—plain chicken!—until the skin got nice and crispy. Then, while it was still hot, she sprinkled it with a seasoning salt she had made. Well, Franko Duet cooks chicken for his restaurant down in Galliano the same way. He showed me exactly how he does it. If you want to taste something that's really good ... here's the recipe!

2-4 whole fryer chickens, 2 lb. average
1 gal. peanut oil
1 lb. thick-sliced slab bacon
6 tbsp. salt
½ tsp. black pepper
½ tsp. cayenne
½ tsp. white pepper
½ tsp. garlic salt
½ tsp. onion powder
¼ tsp. garlic powder
1 tsp. paprika

First, take the chickens—*whole and with the skin left on*—and wash them thoroughly inside and out. Be sure to remove all the little bits of debris from the body cavity, too. Remember, you're going to fry the chickens whole, so they have to be cleaned well.

Next, take a handful of superabsorbent paper towels and pat the chickens dry (especially on the inside). This is an important part of the whole process; because if the chickens are wet when you drop them into the deep fat, the moisture will cause the peanut oil to splatter.

At this point, you're ready to fry. *Nope—you don't season the chickens before you cook 'em.* You season them after they cook. I'll tell you how to do that in a minute.

In the meantime, put the full gallon of peanut oil into your deep fryer—you can use an electric model or a cast-iron pot. If you decide on the cast iron you need to use a frying thermometer. The oil has to be heated exactly to 375 degrees. (I know, chicken is usually fried at 325 ... but that's for chicken covered with a batter. See, the lower temperature allows the inside of the chicken to fully cook before the batter browns. You don't have that problem with *batterless* chicken—you want a higher temperature so that it will crisp up the skin.)

When you're ready to cook, drop in the slab bacon and deep fry it until it turns crispy—see, you need the bacon to flavor the oil, which flavors the chicken. Then when the bacon is done, remove it from the peanut oil, place it on a couple of paper towels so that it can drain, and snack on it while your chicken is cooking.

Then when the oil comes back to 375 degrees, gently ease the chickens into the deep fryer. Don't let the oil boil over the side! Don't let the steam rise up and burn your wrists! Slowly ease the chickens into the oil! Then deep fry for about 20 to 25 minutes, or until the skin is honey brown and crispy.

While the chickens are frying, mix your seasoning salt in your food processor. Simply add all the ingredients together and blend them for about 30 seconds or so.

Finally, when the chickens are cooked, generously sprinkle them all over with the seasoned salt, cut them into pieces with an electric knife, and serve it piping hot ... alongside a big scoop of potato salad and a frosty glass of iced tea.

This ... is good stuff!

Chef's Note:

1—If you can find "pork crackling" oil, deep fry your chickens in it instead of peanut oil. You can eliminate the bacon if you use crackling oil.

2—You can take the seasoning salt you have left, store it in an airtight container, and stash it on your pantry shelf. It's good not only for deep frying chicken, but for grilling as well—use it on steaks, pork chops, ribs, and seafood.

3—And if you're ever down in Galliano and you want to taste the dish the way it's supposed to be served, stop in at Franko's Chicken & Gossip Cafe *on Bayou Lafourche. It tastes just like the stuff Grandma usta make!*

N'Awlins Oven-Fried Chicken

If you'd like to seriously cut back on the fat intake in your diet, yet you don't want to give up great-tasting Southern dishes like homemade fried chicken ... hey, I got it! Just whip up some of my crispy *oven-fried chicken!* You get all the flavor, but only about 14 grams of fat!

2 cut-up fryer chickens, skinned	**4 cups crushed Rice Crispies**
6 whole eggs, well beaten	**2 cups crushed potato chips**
2 large onions, coarsely chopped	**2 tsp. all-purpose seasoning**
2 tsp. Louisiana hot sauce	**1 can butter-flavored Pam**
6 cups whole milk	

First, thoroughly wash the chicken under cold running water to remove all the excess fat and slime. Then set the pieces in a colander to drain.

Meanwhile, in a large bowl, completely blend together the eggs, onions, hot sauce, and whole milk. Then transfer the chicken to a large plastic or ceramic container and pour the milk marinade over the pieces, making certain that each piece is covered. Remember, it's this marinade that is going to flavor and tenderize your chicken through and through—so don't pass on the marinade. Now, refrigerate the chicken for at least 6 hours (but preferably overnight).

Next, you want to crush enough Rice Crispies cereal and potato chips to give you about a 6- to 8-cup mixture when they are blended together. Then add to the mixture 2 teaspoons of a good all-purpose seasoning and blend everything evenly.

When you're ready to cook, preheat your oven to 375 degrees. Then pour the coating mixture into a shallow cookie sheet, take the chicken pieces right out of the marinade, and roll them over and over in the mix, making certain that each piece is completely battered.

At this point, lightly spray the bottom of a low-sided baking sheet with the butter-flavored Pam. Then, as you coat the chicken, take a pair of tongs (so that you don't remove the batter with your sticky fingers) and place each piece on the sheet—*but don't let them touch!* When the sheet is full, spray another very light coating of Pam over the top of the chicken.

All that's left now is to slide the sheet into the oven and bake the chicken for about 50 minutes or so until crispy and golden brown. Oh—I suggest you serve my Oven-Fried Chicken with baked or creamed potatoes, a side dish of saucy green peas, and a tall frosty glass of root beer.

A meal like that's got New Orleans written all over it!

Chef's Note:

1—Since this is a relatively low-fat, low-cal recipe, just for the record one serving of the chicken alone (about 2 small pieces) will give you approximately 254 calories, 14 grams fat, 73 mg cholesterol, 180 mg sodium, 410 mg potassium, 25 grams protein, and 9 grams carbohydrates.

2—When I make this dish, I season the coating mixture with my "Sprinkling Spice." Instead of being just a seasoned salt, it's a balanced blend of salt, pepper, onion, garlic, thyme, oregano, basil, and other herbs and spices that enhance natural food flavors. You can either try making a mixture of your own or buy it already prepared (1-800-742-4231).

3—If for some reason you don't have time to soak the chicken in the milk-egg-onion marinade, simply wash the chicken pieces as directed above and pat them dry. Then spray each piece with the butter-flavored Pam, roll in the coating mixture, and bake as directed in the recipe. The Pam will allow the mixture to stick to the chicken, and the only difference will be a slightly lighter batter. Tricky, huh?

Cajun Fried Chicken

Ain't nothin' as good as home-fried chicken! Oh, sure—the fried-chicken joints serve a pretty good three-piece dinner, but season up a batch at home, marinated with fresh-chopped onion, evaporated milk, eggs, salt, and cayenne, and drop it into fresh hot corn oil in your grandma's old black cast-iron Dutch oven … and now you're eatin' real Southern style.

2 large frying chickens	2 tsp. cayenne pepper
1 cup evaporated milk	2 cups coarsely chopped onions
4 whole eggs	2 cups all-purpose flour
2 tsp. Louisiana hot sauce	1 large Ziploc plastic bag
4 tsp. salt	4 cups corn oil for frying

First, take the chickens and cut them into frying-size pieces (you can skin them if you want to, but I prefer the skin left on). Then wash them thoroughly, making sure you remove all the globular fat, mucus, and entrails that may not have been removed during processing. After you've washed them, set them aside in a colander to drain.

Meanwhile, in a mixing bowl whip together the evaporated milk, the eggs, and the Louisiana hot sauce.

Now sprinkle the chicken pieces liberally with salt and cayenne pepper and place them in a large glass or plastic mixing bowl. But here's the trick: between each layer of chicken place a layer of chopped onions. Then pour the milk and egg mixture over the chicken, work it well into all the pieces, cover the bowl, and allow the chicken to marinate *overnight!*

Don't look for shortcuts to this part of the recipe! If you want the best fried chicken you ever had you gotta let the pieces "soak" in the eggwash and onions overnight! Two hours don't get it! Six hours don't get it! *Overnight!*

Then when you're ready to cook, place the flour in a Ziploc bag, take the chicken directly from the marinade, drop the pieces (a few at a time) into the bag, and shake the closed bag vigorously to thoroughly coat the chicken. Then drop the pieces into hot corn oil and fry them at 350 degrees for 10-20 minutes (depending upon the size of the pieces) until the chicken is golden brown.

When they're cooked, drain them momentarily on several thicknesses of paper towels and serve them piping hot. The outside should be crunchy-crispy, the inside should be light and delicately tender from the onion marinade, and each piece should burst with natural juices!

Now you wanna talk "finger-licking"? *This* is it!

Chef's Note:

1—For the best results, you should fry your chicken in a well-seasoned, black cast-iron Dutch oven. It distributes the heat evenly, cooks the chicken uniformly, and doesn't give you "hot spots" that will burn the batter. Of course, if you don't have any cast iron, heavy club aluminum is a good second choice.

2—The only way to get perfect fried chicken is to be sure the temperature is perfect—350 degrees. And you can't guess at it! You need a thermometer! Clip it to the side of the Dutch oven so that the tip doesn't touch the bottom, and be sure it reaches 350 before you drop in the first piece of chicken. It's the only way you can guarantee that your fried chicken won't be greasy!

3—The trick to frying chicken is to fry pieces of the same size together. When you cut up your chicken, try to cut pieces the same thickness—i.e., split the breast so that it's the same size as the thigh and fry them in the same batch ... put the drumsticks in with the wings ... fry all the backbones together. It makes timing easy, since all of the pieces come out of the oil at the same time.

4—If you deep fry your chicken, there's no need to turn the pieces. But if you "pan fry" it, the oil should be deep enough to come at least halfway up the pieces, and each piece should be cooked equally on each side.

Cajun Deep-Fried Breast of Turkey

If this Thanksgiving you want your turkey, but you don't want to have to cook the whole thing ... I've got a great recipe for you. Go out and buy just the turkey breast, but instead of baking, roasting, or barbecueing it, spice it up with a lot of seasoning and deep fry it. It'll come out nice and juicy on the inside and crispy on the outside. If they would have thought about it, the Pilgrims would have done it! Here's how you do it!

6 tbsp. salt	3 tsp. paprika
1 tsp. black pepper	1 whole turkey breast, 6 lb. average
½ tsp. cayenne pepper	1 tsp. poultry seasoning
½ tsp. white pepper	2 feet butcher's twine
1 tsp. garlic powder	1 gal. peanut oil
3 tsp. onion powder	1 lb. thick-sliced slab bacon

First, take a large measuring cup and thoroughly blend together all the dry ingredients except the poultry seasoning to make a seasoned mix. In fact, I suggest you do this hours before you're ready to use it to give the flavors time to marry.

Then take the turkey breast—*with the skin left on*—and liberally sprinkle it all over with the poultry seasoning and about half the mix—try to get some under the loose portions of skin as well, but don't tear the skin loose where it fits tight to the meat. Now take your hands and rub the seasonings in well—I'm talking serious massage here!

Next tie up the breast with the butcher's twine in half hitches about every inch or so (this keeps the skin from shrinking away from the meat as the breast fries). Then take a sheet of plastic film, wrap the turkey breast tightly, and place it in your refrigerator for at least 4 hours.

When you're ready to cook, put the full gallon of peanut oil into your deep fryer—you can use an electric model or a cast-iron pot. If you decide on the cast iron you need to use a frying thermometer. The oil has to be heated exactly to 325 degrees.

Then when it's at the right temperature, drop in the slab bacon and deep fry it until it turns crispy—see, you want the bacon to flavor the oil, which flavors the turkey. When the bacon is done, remove it from the peanut oil.

Then when the oil comes back to 325 degrees, gently ease the turkey breast into the deep fryer. *I recommend you do this outside!* Don't let the oil boil over the side! Don't let the steam rise up and burn your wrists! *Slowly* ease the turkey into the oil! Then deep-fry for about 5 to 7 minutes to the pound (which is about 30 to 40 minutes for a 6-pound breast). It's done when the skin is honey brown and crispy.

Finally, when the turkey is cooked, generously sprinkle some of the remaining seasoned mix you made over the breast while it's still hot, and carve it with an electric knife just as you would a whole turkey.

Happy Thanksgiving, y'all!

Chef's Note:

1—Don't remove the skin from the turkey breast. It helps to seal in the natural juices as the turkey breast fries, and when it's cooked it'll come out nice and crispy.

2—If you attach a couple of pieces of extra twine to the wrappings around the breast, you can use them to lower the turkey into the hot oil and avoid burning your hands.

3—Take whatever seasoning mix you have left, store it in an airtight container, and stash it on your pantry shelf. It's good not only for deep frying turkey and chicken, but for grilling as well—use it on steaks, pork chops, ribs, and seafood.

Turkey Erky Lerky

This was originally a classic Italian dish named "Aglio e Olio" until New Orleans firemen took the basic recipe, gave it a Ninth Ward nickname, enhanced the ingredients list, and came up with "Erky Lerky." It's been concocted at almost every fire station in the Crescent City since the Vieux Carré burned down the first time, and there must be a hundred different variations of the same recipe. But this one's mine ... and I like it best! Try it and see what you think!

3 cups thinly sliced onions
2 cups diced celery
1 cup diced bell pepper
3 tsp. salt
3 tsp. black pepper
2½ lb. skinned turkey necks
⅓ cup olive oil
1 whole head garlic, minced

1 lb. pasta, boiled al dente
2 cups rich turkey or chicken stock
1 cup petit pois peas
½ cup thinly sliced black olives
3 tbsp. cornstarch + ½ cup water
1 cup grated Parmesan cheese
Parsley for garnish

First, take an 11-by-14 baking pan and layer the onions, celery, and bell pepper evenly over the bottom. Then salt and pepper the turkey necks generously and place them in a single layer over the seasoning vegetables.

At this point, slide the baking pan—uncovered—into a 400-degree oven and bake the turkey necks for 45 minutes until they are nicely browned. Then remove the pan from the oven, cover it tightly with heavy-duty aluminum foil, return it to the oven immediately, and continue to bake the necks for another hour until delicately tender.

Meanwhile, in a 12-inch heavy aluminum skillet, heat a couple of tablespoons of the olive oil to medium high and sauté a little of the chopped garlic until it just begins to brown. Make a note here that you should *stir the skillet constantly* to keep the garlic from burning. Remember—burned garlic tastes bitter!

Now drop in just enough pasta to fill the skillet (but not overfill!). Now stir-fry the pasta, olive oil, and garlic together until the mixture is *hot* (which should take 2 to 3 minutes). Then immediately transfer the garlic-pasta to a baking pan large enough to hold all of it (plus the turkey necks). Repeat the process again: more olive oil, more garlic, more pasta, until all the oil and garlic is used and the entire pound of pasta is hot. Then take the pan of garlic pasta, cover it with aluminum foil, and place it into a warming oven temporarily.

At this point take the roasted and baked turkey necks, remove the necks to a platter, and pour the drippings into a 5-quart saucepan. Then, over high heat, stir in the turkey stock, the peas, and the black olives and bring the sauce to a slow boil. Immediately stir in a little of the cornstarch mixed with *cold* water and thicken the sauce very slightly. Then drop in the necks, cover the pot, reduce the heat to low, and simmer for about 20 minutes.

Then when you're ready to eat, ladle on just enough sauce to moisten the pasta and gently fold in the turkey necks—and you really need to be gentle because they should be so tender they'll probably tend to fall apart. All that's left is to dish up a generous serving of your Erky Lerky, top it liberally with the Parmesan cheese, and garnish it with a sprinkling of parsley (and maybe a little fresh ground black pepper).

Oh—a good chilled white wine on the side will give your meal a nice crowning Italian touch … N'Awlins style!

Chef's Note:

1—All Erky Lerky is made with pasta, olive oil, garlic, and cheese. But other variations include Shrimp Erky Lerky, Crawfish Erky Lerky, Sausage Erky Lerky, Shrimp and Sausage Erky Lerky, Crawfish and Sausage Erky Lerky, Oysters and Bacon Erky Lerky, and Vegetarian Erky Lerky (you use broccoli, cauliflower, mushrooms, peas, and carrots instead of meat or seafood).

2—The trick is to use just the right amount of olive oil and sauce—you want the pasta moist, but you don't want it "swimming" … especially in oil! Essentially, though, it is a very tasty dish, and it can be made as light and healthy as you want it to be.

3—If you're short on turkey drippings, you can add about 2 cups of extra turkey or chicken stock to the baking pan, deglaze it, and use it as a base for your sauce.

4—If you want to whip up a batch of Erky Lerky in a hurry and you don't have time to peel an entire head of garlic, you can substitute garlic-flavored *olive oil for the fresh garlic. When you have time, however, use fresh garlic—it gives the dish a classic nutty flavor.*

CHAPTER 6

Seafoods

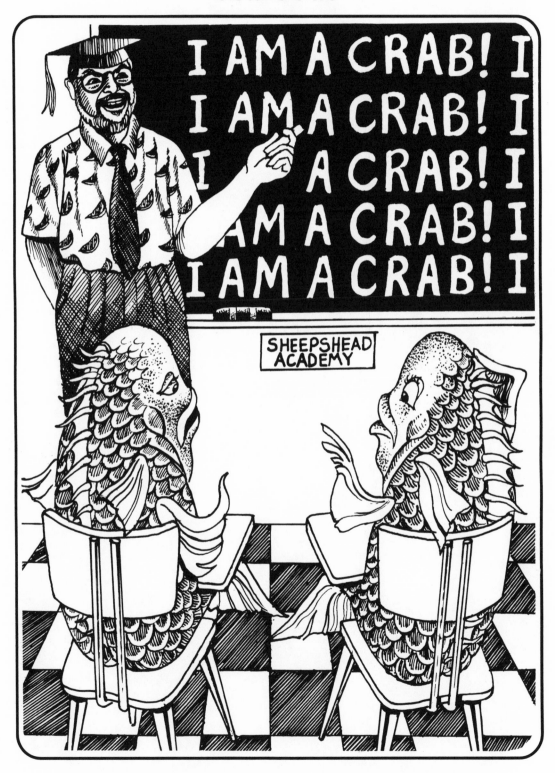

Frank's Famous Marinated Grilled Tuna

Folks call my office all the time and ask, "Frank, how do you cook fresh tuna?" Well, you can bake it, broil it, grill it, barbecue it, and smoke it. In fact, you can do anything but fry it—it's too oily to fry. But if you want a really super recipe, one I like best of all … fix it like this!

1 large bottle Wishbone Italian Salad Dressing	2 tbsp. Worcestershire sauce
½ cup extra-virgin olive oil	Dash Tabasco sauce
2 tbsp. garlic-flavored red wine vinegar	2 tsp. salt
	1 tsp. white pepper
¼ cup thinly sliced green onions	3 fresh limes
2 tbsp. finely minced parsley	3 lb. fresh blackfin or yellowfin tuna fillet

First, in an 11-by-14 Pyrex baking dish mix together the salad dressing, olive oil, vinegar, green onions, parsley, Worcestershire sauce, Tabasco, salt, and white pepper. Then stir into the mixture the juice of *one* of the limes.

I suggest you take a wire whip, blend all of these ingredients thoroughly, and allow the mixture to rest at room temperature for at least a couple of hours so that the flavors can marry uniformly.

Meanwhile, take the tuna fillet (the forward dorsal loin is the best part because it actually slices into steaks) and with a sharp knife remove the outer skin and every trace of the bloodline. Take your time and don't worry about wasting a little bit of the fish when you trim away the bloodline, because any of it that you leave on will give the tuna a strong taste rather than the mild sweet taste indicative of fresh tuna.

When the fillet has been trimmed, take a sharp knife and slice the fish into steaks about a half-inch thick. Then drop them into the marinade, cover them thoroughly, and allow them to rest in the refrigerator for at least 2 hours to pick up the seasonings. And just for the record, it's even better if you allow the tuna to marinate overnight.

Then when you're ready to eat, take the steaks from the marinade and place them on a hot grill that's been sprayed with either Pam or Vegelene to keep them from sticking. Tuna is a firm meat so you don't have to worry about it falling apart and dropping through the grating, but you do want to use a *spatula*—not a meat fork!—to turn the tuna over. And do it gently.

If you've sliced the fillet to the proper thickness, it will take you about 5 minutes on each side to fully cook your tuna steaks. *Please* … do not overcook them! Fresh tuna on the grill comes out looking and tasting not like fish, but like fine Provimi veal. It's succulent! It's delicate! It should not be cooked to the point of drying it out.

While the fish is grilling, thinly slice the remaining two limes and place them on a saucer. Then when you're ready to eat, serve the tuna topped with a slice of lime alongside a generous helping of mushroom-flavored rice and complemented with a cold crisp tomato and cucumber salad.

And, yep! Go ahead and crack open a good white wine!

Chef's Note:

1—If you don't have a grill, you can place a baking rack in a shallow baking pan, put the tuna steaks on top of the rack, and either broil the fish or bake it for about 20 minutes at 400 degrees. Be sure to cook on a rack—you don't want the tuna steaks soaking in the drippings.

2—When you place the steaks on your grill, cook them over high heat *close to the coals or lava rocks. And for at least half of the cooking time, close the top to the grill. It keeps the smokey flavor in the tuna as it cooks.*

Sicilian Redfish Frozia

It's the perfect natural combination—Cajun fried redfish with an authentic Sicilian flavor! Or to put it another way, it's some of the lightest yet crunchiest, best-tasting, juiciest fried redfish you every ate. Here's how you do it!

3 cups seasoned bread stuffing mix	2 tsp. black pepper
⅔ cup grated Pecorino Romano cheese	Peanut oil for deep frying
2 tsp. Frank Davis Sicilian Seasoning	2 redfish, filleted and cut into 2-inch pieces
1 tsp. granulated garlic	2 cups all-purpose seasoned flour
1 tsp. oregano	2 cups eggwash (2 cups whole milk + 6 eggs)
½ cup finely chopped parsley	½ cup extra-virgin olive oil

First, take a large bowl and mix together all the ingredients for the frozia bread crumbs—crumbs, cheese, Sicilian seasoning, garlic, oregano, parsley, and black pepper. In fact, for a superrich flavor, you should mix the crumbs and let them "set" for at least 2 hours before you use them so that the flavors can marry. Better yet, let them set overnight!

When you're ready to cook, preheat your peanut oil to exactly 350 degrees (I suggest you use a thermometer so that you get it just right—remember, you're going to be cooking large pieces of redfish fillets, and if you fry them too hot the crumbs will brown long before the fish is cooked).

While the oil is coming up to heat, dredge the redfish pieces in the seasoned flour, dunk them into the eggwash, and roll them in the seasoned frozia crumbs.

Now—*and this is the most important part of the whole recipe!*—let the fillets rest on a piece a waxed paper for 2 minutes so that the frozia mix can "fix to the fish." If you try to fry without letting the fillets rest, the crumbs will fall off in the hot oil.

Then when the oil is at the right temperature, begin dropping in the fillets one at a time until you fill the frypan (but don't overcrowd them—you want to give them room to fry).

You'll find that it takes only a few minutes for the frozia coating to turn a rich golden brown color and take on a crispy, crispy texture. When this happens ... they're done! Don't overcook 'em!

Now lift the fillets out of the oil with a set of tongs or with a strainer spoon and place them on several layers of paper towels to drain. *But ...* while they're still piping hot, brush them or drizzle them lightly with a little of the extra-virgin oil and sprinkle them with a little more Romano cheese.

All that's left is to serve them immediately, alongside a big scoop of New Orleans creamed potatoes and a chilled tossed green salad topped with Italian vinaigrette dressing.

Chef's Note:

1—Don't use Italian seasoned bread crumbs—they're too fine and won't give you the crispiness you want. Buy a bag of stuffing mix (it's coarse-ground bread, usually French bread), crumble it just a little with your hands, and use it to create the batter coating for your fillets. There is no substitute! "Coarse-ground bread-crumb mix" is what "frozia" means in Sicilian.

2—For extra zest and flavor, add 2 teaspoons of Frank Davis Seafood Seasoning to the frozia mix.

3—Because you can use this same frozia bread-crumb mix for frying not only fish but shrimp, oysters, zucchini, cauliflower, broccoli, and eggplant, I suggest you double the recipe and keep what you don't use in the freezer.

4—Seasoned flour is all-purpose flour to which you've added salt and black pepper to taste.

N'Awlins Baked Redfish with Lemon-Wine Butter Sauce

More often than not, when you sit down to eat baked redfish it's topped with a heavy Creole-style red gravy. Oh, it's good, but it's too close to court bouillon. I find it loses the intense natural flavors of the fish. Next time you get a nice red, try baking it this way. You won't be sorry, ... and you'll want to drink the sauce with a straw!

Pam cooking spray	2 lemons, thinly sliced
1 large yellow onion, diced	1 tbsp. paprika
2 ribs celery, diced	2 cups Sauvignon Blanc wine
½ cup thinly sliced green onions	½ stick sweetcream butter
4 medium tomatoes, finely diced	2 tsp. gravy flour
1 whole redfish, scaled and gutted (5-7 lb.)	Dash salt and pepper
2 tbsp. Frank Davis Seafood Seasoning	

First, preheat your oven to 350 degrees.

Then take a heavy, shallow baking pan, spray it with Pam (or another brand of nonstick spray to make cleanup easy), and evenly spread the chopped onions, the celery, the green onions, and the tomatoes over the bottom of the pan.

Meanwhile, take the redfish, wash it thoroughly (making sure all the blood along the backbone has been scrubbed away), and pat it dry inside and out with paper towels. Then liberally sprinkle on the seafood seasoning and rub it into the fish.

Now place the redfish on the vegetables in the baking pan. Then lay the lemon slices on top of the fish so that they slightly overlap, sprinkle everything lightly with paprika, slide the pan *uncovered* into the oven, and bake for about an hour or so.

When the fish is browned and tender, gently remove it from the baking pan (be careful—it will fall apart!) and set it aside on a warming tray. Then pour all the drippings into a heavy aluminum skillet and bring them to a rapid boil.

At this point, stir in the wine and cook the sauce over high heat until the liquids reduce to about one-half of their original volume—*this concentrates the flavor of the sauce.* Then pour the contents of the skillet into a fine-mesh strainer, force the liquid and the vegetable pulp through the mesh, and return the liquid to the skillet (you can discard the skins left in the strainer).

Now over a medium-high flame, heat the liquid until it begins to bubble slightly. Then cream in the butter by adding it to the hot liquid a little piece at a time. *Note: do not stir the pan—just swirl it in small circles to incorporate the butter into the sauce.*

Once the butter melts, you may find that the sauce is just the consistency you want—thin but rich. If it is too thin to your liking, however, sprinkle on a little of the gravy flour, whisk it into the sauce *lightly,* and continue to cook the flour and the sauce for about 3 minutes until it thickens and turns silky smooth.

When everything's ready, take a spatula, dish out a large portion of the baked redfish on a heated dinner plate, serve it alongside some of my N'Awlins-style potato salad, generously ladle the lemon-wine-butter sauce over the top of the fish, and season with salt and pepper.

Lawdy, Miss Clawdy! This is *some* good!

Chef's Note:

1—I use my "Strictly N'Awlins" Seafood Seasoning *when I bake redfish because the spices I need to flavor the fish are already preblended in the mix. But if you don't have any of the seafood seasoning on hand, you can substitute a light sprinkling of salt, black pepper, white pepper, paprika, garlic powder, and onion powder in its place.*

2—If you take time to trim away the dorsal fins of the redfish with a sharp filleting knife, the fish will serve a whole lot easier and you won't have to worry about biting into those little pin-bones when you're eating. Just a li'l trick!

You won't believe the flavor you get when you take tender, flaky catfish fillets, dip them into an eggwash, coat them with seasoned bread crumbs, sauté them in butter, and top them off with a creamy, spicy yogurt sauce. You gotta try it!

8 catfish fillets, cut in halves	**1 cup grated Romano cheese**
4 tbsp. lemon pepper	**1 cup Crisco oil**
3 whole eggs	**6 tbsp. real butter**
1 cup whole milk	
4 cups Italian seasoned bread	
crumbs	

First, wash the fillets under cold running water and set them on a sheet of freezer wrap or waxed paper. Then sprinkle each piece of fish liberally on both sides with the lemon pepper and rub it in thoroughly. Now let the fillets absorb the seasoning for about 15-20 minutes at room temperature.

Next, make your eggwash by combining the eggs and the milk in a large bowl and, with a wire whip, beating the two ingredients together until frothy. To make the coating mix, simply blend together the bread crumbs and the Romano cheese.

At this point, melt the oil and butter together over medium-low heat in a large heavy skillet—but be careful that you don't let it burn. When it is uniformly mixed, pour out all but a few tablespoons into a Pyrex measuring cup. You got to remember ... you're pan-sautéing—not deep frying!

Next, dip the fish fillets first into the eggwash then *immediately* into the breading mix. But do not panfry the fish right away! Set them once again on the countertop on a sheet of waxed paper and allow the coating mix to "cure" for about 20 minutes. What happens is ... the eggwash binds the gluten in the bread crumbs to the fish, and during the curing process the eggwash turns "sticky." Once the coating cures, it won't fall off the fish while it's panfrying. (By the way, this same *curing principle* works to keep the coating from falling off when you're frying shrimp, chicken, veal cutlets, and other meats.)

When you're ready to cook, turn the fire under the skillet up to medium high and fry the fish—several pieces at a time—in the butter-oil mixture until each piece turns a rich dark brown. When the skillet starts to dry out, just pour in a few more tablespoons of the oil-butter blend.

Then when the fish fillets are done, place them in a single layer on a shallow baking sheet and set them in a warming oven (about 200 degrees) to keep them crispy. Then when all your fish fillets have been panfried, make your sauce.

You'll need:

Pan drippings from the panfried fish
¼ cup all-purpose flour
4 tbsp. margarine (if needed)
4 cups fish or chicken stock

½ cup sliced green onions
¼ cup minced parsley
1½ cups nonfat yogurt
Salt and white pepper to taste

First, take the skillet you've been panfrying the fish in, toss the flour into the pan drippings (add the margarine if you don't have enough drippings), and make a very light roux. Then as soon as the roux is smooth, slowly pour in the stock and stir it until it becomes creamy (which should be about the consistency of melted ice cream). Then stir in the green onions and the parsley, reduce the heat to low, cover the skillet, and simmer the sauce for about 10 minutes.

After the allotted simmering time, gradually stir the yogurt into the mixture and season the resultant sauce with salt and white pepper to taste. Now cover the skillet again and simmer once more for another 10 minutes.

Then, when you're ready to eat, take the fish fillets out of the warming oven, ladle generous helpings of the sauce over them, and serve them piping hot … alongside creamed or fluted potatoes and accompanied by a cold lettuce and tomato salad topped with vinaigrette dressing.

You just won't believe the lowly li'l catfish could ever taste this good!

Chef's Note: *For a richer variation of this dish, substitute heavy cream for the yogurt and cook it over medium-high heat (uncovered) until the cream turns silky and smooth. Oooooh! This stuff could be a mortal sin!*

By the way, you can dip and coat the fish fillets up to 4 hours before you fry them and still have them turn out crunchy and crispy. Just keep them in the refrigerator until you panfry them.

Southern Smothered Catfish with Double-Butter Sauce

Take tender flaky catfish fillets, poach them in a special blend of spicy chicken stock and vermouth, and cream the resultant au naturel sauce with a double helping of seasoned butter, and you've got a meal nothing short of magnificent!

2 sticks butter
1 cup finely diced onions
½ cup finely diced celery
½ cup finely diced bell pepper
4 cloves garlic, finely minced
4 cups rich chicken stock
4 tbsp. dry vermouth
8 catfish fillets

Salt and black pepper to taste
3 tsp. Frank Davis Seafood
　Seasoning
6 drops yellow food coloring
2 tbsp. cornstarch + ½ cup water
¾ cup thinly sliced green onions
¼ cup minced parsley

First, take a 12-inch skillet, melt one-half stick of butter over medium heat, and sauté the onions, celery, bell pepper, and garlic until the vegetables soften *(but do not let the garlic burn)*.

Now slowly add the chicken stock and the vermouth to the vegetable-butter, bring the mixture to a boil, and cook it over medium-high heat for about 6 minutes so that the stock turns into a rich poaching liquid (court bouillon). *This is what will flavor your catfish fillets—so don't shorten this step!*

Next, drop the fillets into the poaching liquid, reduce the heat to medium, cover the skillet, and let the fish cook for about 5 minutes or so (or until they become tender and begin to flake). When they're done, take a spatula, *gently* remove them from the pan ('cuz you want to break them up as little as possible), set them on a shallow baking sheet, and place them in a warming oven.

At this point, bring the heat back up to high and reduce the court bouillon to one-half of its original volume—*this will further concentrate the rich fish flavor and form the base for the sauce.*

When the stock has reduced, take a sieve and strain out the seasoning vegetables. Then place the stock back into the pan over medium heat, stir in the remaining butter a little at a time, and season the mixture to taste with salt, pepper, and seafood seasoning.

All that's left is to stir in the food coloring and thicken the sauce by gradually adding just enough of the cornstarch and water mixture to reach the consistency you desire (it should be shiny and glossy and as thick as pancake batter).

Then, when you're ready to eat, place the fillets on heated dinner plates, ladle on a generous helping of the sauce, garnish with the green onions and parsley, and serve piping hot with Duchesse Potatoes and a crisp green salad.

Chef's Note: *If you can't get all the fillets into one pan, cook them in several batches ...* but in the same poaching liquid. *Each batch you cook will concentrate the stock further and make it richer!*

This dish is best when done with pond-raised catfish, because the taste is fresh, light, and delicate; but you can also substitute any lean, non-oily fish for the catfish and still come out with a great entrée.

N'Awlins Sheepshead Patties
(Mock Crabmeat Cakes)

When you want to fix Crabmeat Salad, Stuffed Crabs, Crabmeat Imperial, or Crabmeat Bisque, but the $10.50 per pound price tag for the real stuff gives you intense pain in the pocketbook ... go fishing for sheepshead. Prepared right, the fish is a perfect substitute for crabmeat. Try this recipe and see if you don't agree.

1 cup finely chopped onions	3 raw eggs
1 cup finely chopped green onions	Juice of ½ lemon
½ cup finely chopped celery	1 tsp. Frank Davis Seafood
½ cup finely chopped parsley	Seasoning
6 cloves garlic, minced	Salt and black pepper to taste
6 cups cooked, diced potatoes	2 cups seasoned bread crumbs
4 cups flaked cooked sheepshead	2 tbsp. Crisco oil
fillets (see Mock Crabmeat	2 tbsp. real butter
below)	

In a large bowl, combine the onions, green onions, celery, parsley, and garlic. Then thoroughly mix in the cooked potatoes—but take your time doing this because you want a uniform blend that still has small chunks of potatoes in it. You don't want to create a paste.

Next, gently fold in the flaked sheepshead fillets. It is especially important to "fold" rather than "mix" because you also want to avoid "shredding" the fish. Then when the consistency is uniform, fold in the raw eggs, the lemon juice, the seafood seasoning, and the salt and pepper to taste.

At this point, wet your hands and begin forming the patties—ideally, they should be about the size of large cookies.

When they're shaped, lightly dip them into the seasoned bread crumbs and set them aside on waxed paper to "cure" for about a half-hour. (Actually, you can make them as far as a day in advance and keep them in the refrigerator.)

Now when you're ready to eat, add a couple tablespoons of Crisco and a couple tablespoons of butter to a nonstick skillet, bring it to medium-high heat, and pan-sauté the patties on both sides until they turn a crunchy golden brown.

I suggest you serve the patties piping hot, topped with a rich Béchamel sauce flavored with green peas, and a crispy lettuce and tomato salad and Green Goddess dressing.

Chef's Note: *Béchamel sauce is a basic white sauce made with butter, flour, white onions, milk, salt, and white pepper. To enrich it, you can add concentrated chicken stock, garlic, green onions, parsley, and loads of extra butter.*

Mock Crabmeat
(From Poached Sheepshead)

So how do you convert a sheepshead into a bowl of mock crabmeat, you ask? And what's the procedure for poaching it to delicate succulence? Well, just follow these directions.

Clean the sheepshead with a *linoleum knife* by cutting just behind the head down to the rib cage. Then pull the point of the knife parallel to the lateral line of the fish, around the ribs, and down to the anal fin. Next, following the backbone as a guide, cut from the anal fin to the caudal fin (tail) of the fish.

Now spin the fish around so that the head is facing away from you and begin cutting (again using the backbone as guide) from the initial incision behind the head directly down the dorsal fin to the tip of the tail.

At this point, put the linoleum knife down and pick up your filleting knife. And using just the tip of the knife, begin stripping the flesh away from the backbone—lifting the fillet with your fingers as you cut. If you do it properly, the entire fillet should come right off the backbone. Turn the fish over and remove the fillet from the other side the same way.

Note: there is no need to scale, gut, or dehead the sheepshead, and you should never have to break open the belly cavity. This technique also works well for croakers, drums, redfish, and any other heavy-bodied fish.

But remember, to clean fish this way, you need both a filleting knife and a linoleum knife—no substitutes!

Now, to poach your fillets, take a stockpot and fill it with about a gallon of water. Then for every 3 pounds of sheepshead you plan to cook, add to the water 1 lemon cut into slices, 1 large onion, ½ cup of diced celery, ½ cup of sliced green onions, ¼ cup of diced bell pepper, ½ cup of milk, 2 tablespoons of liquid crabboil, 2 cloves of garlic, 1 teaspoon of salt, and ½ teaspoon of black pepper.

Next, bring the stock mixture to a rolling boil and let it continue to boil for about *10 minutes* to release all the flavors of the seasonings.

At this point, take a sharp knife and completely trim away all traces of the bloodline from the fillets. Then wrap the fillets in cheesecloth and drop them into the boiling seasoned stock. *As soon as the water comes back to a boil, remove the pot from the fire and let the fish "soak" in the stock for exactly 10 minutes.*

Finally, remove the poached fish from the stock, cut the cheesecloth, and place the pieces in a shallow bowl to cool. Then flake the meat with a fork and mix about a tablespoon of lemon juice into the flakes.

Now you're ready to use it in any dish calling for *crabmeat!* And if you don't tell anyone it's really a sheepshead … guess what?

Crispy Fried Sheepshead

All these years you've been throwing sheepshead back because you thought they were hard to handle and just weren't that great. Well, I've got a surprise for you! Try fixin' 'em like this next time you catch some. You'll see what I mean.

12 sheepshead fillets	4 lemons, quartered
64 oz. peanut oil	Tartar sauce
2 cups Frank Davis Fish Fry	1 or 2 dashes Louisiana hot sauce
Thinly sliced onions	

First, thoroughly wash the sheepshead fillets in cold running water. Then submerge them in an iced-water solution for at least 15 minutes. This chills the fish, which causes them to remain juicy inside when they're deep fried.

Meanwhile, in a heavy aluminum skillet, heat the peanut oil to 350 degrees. Then, without dipping the fillets in an eggwash, place them into the fish fry, toss them around so that every inch is covered with the mix, shake off the excess, and set them aside on a piece of waxed paper for 3 minutes so that the fish fry adheres to the fillets.

Then, when you're ready to eat, deep fry the fish in the peanut oil until each fillet is a crispy golden brown—which should take about 2 to 3 minutes for fillets averaging 4 to 6 ounces.

When they're done, drain them on several layers of paper towels, cover them with thinly sliced onions, and serve them piping hot with lemon wedges, tartar sauce, and a dash or two of Louisiana hot sauce.

Chef's Note:
1—Under no circumstances should you fry sheepshead (or any other kind of seafood, for that matter) without first soaking it in iced water. This is the secret for getting fish crispy on the outside yet *juicy on the inside. When the cold seafood hits the hot oil, the inside as well as the outside cooks. But because it's cold, the inside doesn't heat up as quickly as the outside. So what you end up with is a crispy outer coating without drying out the inside.*

2—Depending upon which name brand of fish fry you use, especially those composed primarily of fine corn flour or cream meal, you may have to dip the fish into an eggwash to keep the fish fry from falling off the fillets and to give you a crunchy coating. If you use my *fish fry, however,* do not use an eggwash on any seafood you cook. *The coating texture is naturally crunchy and blended not to fall off in the oil.*

3—This recipe and technique can be used on every form of seafood you fry!

Whole Fried Flounder

Take a small pan-size flounder, scale and clean it, crosscut both sides to the backbone, dip it in a rich eggwash, dust it in seasoned fish fry, and deep fry it whole until golden brown and crispy … and you've got a taste treat bar none!

2-4 whole pan-size flounders	**4 cups Frank Davis Fish Fry**
4 cups peanut oil	**3 lemons, sliced into wedges**
3 whole eggs	**Louisiana hot sauce**
1 cup whole milk	

First, scale and gut your flounders. This is best done with a paring knife since the short blade removes the tiny scales more effectively than a fish scaler—and you want to scrape away every single scale.

Then with a sharp utility knife, remove the head from the fish and thoroughly brush away the blood sac from against the backbone inside the flounder's belly cavity (I find that an old toothbrush does this best). Now wash the fish well under cold running water and pat it dry with paper towels.

Meanwhile, put the peanut oil in a large frypan and heat it to 350 degrees. Then, with a wire whip, mix together the eggs and the whole milk until frothy and pour the mixture out into a shallow baking pan.

When you're ready to cook, lay out the flounder on the countertop and with the utility knife make diagonal crosscuts on both sides of the fish about an inch apart. What you end up with is a series of diamond-shaped *hatchmarks* that should go all the way to the backbone. This allows the thick slabs of meat on both sides of the fish to fry through and through.

Now dip the flounder first into the eggwash then into the fish fry, making certain that the entire fish—including the cuts you've made—is coated with the fry. Then gently, *very gently,* so that you don't splatter the hot oil, lower the fish into the skillet "topside down" and fry for about 2 to 3 minutes. Then with a pair of tongs and a spatula, turn the fish over and fry it for another 2 to 3 minutes.

Depending upon the thickness of the fish, you may have to turn the flounder over more than once. What you want to end up with is a flaky, crispy-fried flounder that's golden brown. As a general rule of thumb, when you can see the backbone between the crosscuts … the fish is done!

All that's left is to remove the fish from the oil and drain them thoroughly on a couple of layers of paper towels. Then serve them piping hot, drizzled lightly with fresh lemon and a splash of Louisiana hot sauce.

Chef's Note:

1—Be careful not to overcrowd the fish in the oil or they won't fry nice and crispy. Rather than jam them closely together, it's better to fry them one at a time.

2—I recommend you use a frying thermometer to make sure the oil is right at 350 degrees. Frying hotter than 350 will cause the coating mixture to brown before the fish is cooked; frying cooler than 350 will cause the flounder to absorb oil, making it greasy and keeping it from becoming crispy.

3—While you can "whole fry" large flounders, those that average right about a pound or a little less always come out best.

N'Awlins Baked Flounder
(With Shrimp Stuffing)

Moist, tender, mouth-watering, and fit for a king—that's how this baked flounder lays on the palate! And it's extremely easy to fix—for your family or your next dinner party!

1 flounder (2 to 3 lb.), scaled and cleaned	½ cup fresh sliced mushrooms
Salt and black pepper to taste	1 lb. shrimp, peeled
2 tsp. seafood seasoning	¼ cup finely chopped parsley
1 stick real butter	Juice of 1 lemon
2 cups diced onions	2 cups fresh bread crumbs
1 cup diced celery	1 cup coarse French bread chunks
3 cloves garlic, minced	1 cup shrimp stock from heads and shells
¼ cup finely chopped bell pepper	1 raw egg

Start off by deboning the flounder. It's really not that difficult! All you need is a sharp fillet knife and a little bit of patience. Just cut down the center line of the flounder (the dark side) to the backbone. Then a little at a time, using the backbone as a guide, separate the meat from the bone.

Now turn the flounder over and, without breaking the skin, slide the knife between the backbone and the skin and separate the meat from the bone. All that's left is to take a pair of kitchen shears and cut out the backbone.

But if you don't feel adventuresome, just follow the procedure I gave you for the dark side of the fish and leave the backbone in. That works okay too!

After the fish is prepped, sprinkle it lightly with salt and pepper (plus a little dash of your favorite seafood seasoning), rub it down with a tablespoon or so of softened butter, and squeeze on a little lemon juice. Now set the fish aside until you make the stuffing.

In a skillet or small Dutch oven, melt down the butter until it begins to foam. Then toss in all of the seasoning vegetables (plus the mushrooms) and cook them over medium heat until they wilt—which should take about 6 to 8 minutes.

At this point, quickly stir in the shrimp—but cook them *only until they begin to turn pink*. Once they turn, add the parsley, lemon juice, bread crumbs, bread chunks, and shrimp stock. Then cook the entire mix for 3 more minutes to firm up the stuffing. *That's all there is to it! Just be careful you don't overcook the shrimp!*

Now take the pot off the burner, season with salt and pepper (and maybe a little more seafood seasoning), and quickly stir in the raw egg. You've got to do this very quickly; otherwise the egg is going to scramble! Now place the stuffing aside for a moment!

Meanwhile, set the oven to 375 degrees. Then take the shallow baking pan you're gonna bake the flounder in and put it in the oven to preheat it! (Incidentally, this is how you get the bottom of the flounder to cook as nicely as the top.)

When the dressing has cooled almost to room temperature, begin stuffing it into the fish ... but don't overstuff! You just want to pack it full.

Then carefully remove the hot baking pan from the oven and place the stuffed fish into it. Brush it liberally with melted butter, top it with several thin slices of fresh lemon, and bake the flounder for 25-30 minutes or until the stuffing browns and the fish is ready to burst open!

Chef's Note: *To make fresh bread crumbs, simply place several pieces of white sliced bread into your food processor and pulse-chop the slices with the cutting blade until you have a batch of light and fluffy, coarsely chopped crumbs. Fresh crumbs give you a lighter stuffing than fine-ground dry crumbs.*

When you pour in the seafood stock to make the stuffing, mix it in a little at a time so that you don't overwet the bread. Remember, you want it moist—not runny. You may or may not have to use it all.

I suggest you serve the stuffed flounder with buttered summer squash or zucchini, creamed spinach, breadsticks, and a bottle of nice white wine!

N'Awlins Shrimp Herbsaint

My buddy John Levy, when he was sous chef at Kabby's at the New Orleans Hilton, taught me how to put this dish together. And since the very first time that he blended the bell peppers, garlic, shrimp, and herbsaint, the dish has been one of my favorite shrimp recipes of all time!

3 lb. shrimp, peeled and deveined
   (shells and heads reserved)
Water to cover
1 stick + 4 tbsp. sweetcream butter
1½ cups sliced bell pepper
8 cloves fresh garlic, minced
½ cup heavy cream
½ cup heavy shrimp stock

2 tsp. paprika
4 tbsp. herbsaint
1 tbsp. lemon juice
3 tsp. seafood seasoning
1 loaf French bread
½ cup sliced green onions
¼ cup finely chopped parsley

First, in a heavy aluminum Dutch oven, gently boil the shrimp shells and heads (in just enough water to cover them) for about an hour to make your shrimp stock. Then strain out the shells and heads, set the stock aside, and allow it to cool.

Meanwhile, in a heavy 12-inch aluminum skillet, melt the stick of butter over high heat until it sizzles (*but don't let it burn!*). Then drop in the shrimp and, while stirring constantly with the heat reduced to medium high, cook them only until they turn pink—*about 2 or 3 minutes.* You will notice a creamy liquid forming in the pan: this is your sauce base.

When the shrimp are done take a strainer spoon, remove them from the liquid, and set both the liquid and the shrimp aside.

Now take the empty skillet again, heat the remaining 4 tablespoons of butter until it sizzles, and sauté the bell peppers until they begin to wilt. At that point, drop in the minced garlic and cook the mixture gently (making sure to stir constantly) until the garlic softens—*but do not let the garlic burn or it will become bitter!*

Now, add to the skillet the heavy cream, the shrimp stock, the paprika, and the liquid from the shrimp you sautéed earlier. Then turn the heat up to high and cook until the mixture is reduced to one-half of its volume and starts to thicken.

At this point, stir in the herbsaint and the lemon juice, cream in a little extra butter if you want the dish richer, and fold in the shrimp.

All that's left is to stir in the seafood seasoning (or sprinkle on some salt and white and cayenne pepper to taste). When you're ready to eat, serve open-face over a hearty slice of fresh-toasted French bread and garnish with green onions and parsley.

Chef's Note:

1—To get the best possible flavor from this dish, I recommend you use red, green, and yellow bell peppers *in combination.*

2—To do a low-cholesterol variation of this dish, simply substitute vegetable margarine for the butter and substitute 2 tablespoons of cornstarch blended into 1 cup of shrimp stock for the cream. Just stir the cornstarch mixture into the dish when you add the shrimp to thicken the resulting sauce.

3—Just like red beans, Shrimp Herbsaint gets better the next day. It will keep well in the refrigerator for a couple of days ... but I don't suggest you freeze it.

4—By the way, herbsaint is a licorice-flavored liqueur. But don't turn up your nose and go, "Ugh!" What it does to intensify the flavor of shrimp is unbelievable! Try it and see!

Shrimp Cocodrie

One of the tastiest shrimp dishes I ever ate is a secret concoction of Johnny Glover's, former state representative and operator of CoCo Marina in Cocodrie. But while Johnny absolutely refuses to give me the well-guarded recipe, I think I've just about figured out how he does it.

1 stick real butter	1 lemon, juiced and seeded
3 tbsp. bacon drippings	1 tbsp. Creole mustard
1 cup thinly sliced green onions	3 tbsp. Worcestershire sauce
½ cup finely chopped celery	2 tsp. Louisiana hot sauce
4 cloves garlic, finely chopped	4 lb. shrimp, peeled and deveined
½ cup white wine	½ cup cubed Velveeta cheese
1 cup reduced shrimp stock	1 4-oz. pkg. Philadelphia Cream
1 cup finely crumbled bacon	Cheese
2 large bottles Catalina French	½ cup finely chopped parsley
Dressing	Salt and cayenne pepper to taste

First, take a 12-inch skillet and sauté in the butter and bacon drippings (over medium heat) the onions, celery, and garlic until they soften—*but do not let the garlic burn.* Then pour in the wine and the shrimp stock, bring the heat to medium high, and cook until the alcohol is reduced and the seasoning vegetables blend into the stock—about 5 minutes or so.

Next, stir in the crumbled bacon and the dressing, reduce the heat to low, and simmer the mixture until the aroma of the vinegar is just about gone. Then gradually—one ingredient at a time—stir in the lemon juice, Creole mustard, Worcestershire, and hot sauce and mix everything until thoroughly blended. Continue to simmer for about another 5 minutes.

Meanwhile, place the shrimp into an 11-by-17 baking pan and set them aside momentarily. At this point, stir into the mixture in the skillet the two cheeses and dissolve them thoroughly. Then, when the sauce is creamy and smooth (with the consistency of melted ice cream), stir in the parsley and pour the mixture over the shrimp in the baking pan (you want to make certain the shrimp are almost covered with the sauce so that they bake evenly).

Now place the pan on the center rack of a 400-degree preheated oven and bake *uncovered* for about 8 to 10 minutes (or until the shrimp are pink and the sauce is hot and bubbly). *Be careful that you don't overcook the shrimp or they will turn tough and rubbery.*

Then, when the shrimp are just tender, add salt and cayenne pepper to taste, remove them from the oven, ladle them (plus a generous helping of the sauce) into a heated bowl, and serve them immediately with crispy French fries, an ice-cold tossed salad, and lots of fresh hot buttered French bread.

I can't begin to tell you how good this is!

Chef's Note: *Remember that a great deal of shrimp flavor in this dish comes from the rendering process as the shrimp bakes. The natural juices from the cooking shrimp go into the sauce, thin it out slightly, blend with the French dressing, and enhance the overall taste. Note that the shrimp in this recipe are well seasoned, but they are* not *exceptionally spicy. Feel free to add more hot sauce or cayenne to suit your taste.*

If you want to put baby new potatoes into the dish, just boil and peel them ahead of time and drop them into the sauce when you add the shrimp. The potatoes bake with the shrimp.

Note, too, that fresh 4-6-ounce redfish fillets can also be substituted for shrimp in this recipe to produce a dish I call "Redfish Cocodrie." Try it ... it's fantastic!

Shrimp Fried Rice

One of the most popular complementary dishes in Chinese cuisine, fried rice goes great with almost any entrée. And since it can be flavored with shrimp, ham, pork, beef, and just about anything else your heart desires ... it could really be a whole meal in itself. I know this recipe is!

3 tbsp. peanut oil
3 eggs, slightly beaten
¼ tsp. sesame oil
1 lb. shrimp, peeled and small-diced
½ cup small-diced carrots
½ tsp. white sugar
½ tsp. salt

6 green onions, sliced
½ cup thinly sliced celery
1 clove garlic, minced
3 cups cold cooked long-grain rice
¼ cup dark soy sauce
½ cup chicken stock (if needed)
1 cup cooked green peas
White pepper to taste

First, heat your wok to 400 degrees and add 1 tablespoon of the peanut oil. Then drop in the 3 eggs, let them set for a moment or two, and quickly scramble them. When they're cooked, remove them from the wok, place them in a small bowl, and set them aside.

Next, pour the remaining peanut oil plus the sesame oil into the wok, bring them up to heat, and toss in the shrimp, carrots, sugar, and salt and stir-fry the mixture until the shrimp just turns pink (about 1 minute should do it).

At this point, push as much of the shrimp up the slope of the wok as possible, making room on the bottom of the wok to stir-fry the vegetables. Then toss in the green onions, celery, and garlic, and stir-fry them for about 1 minute—*don't let the garlic burn or it will taste bitter!* When the vegetables are tender, push the diced shrimp down off the sides of the wok, stir it into the vegetables, and toss everything together well.

Next, drop in the cold rice and the soy sauce and stir-fry the mixture until well blended—about 2 or 3 minutes. If the rice appears too dry, moisten it slightly with a couple of tablespoons of chicken stock and a dash or two of sesame oil.

Then when the mixture is just right (hot and steamy), toss in the scrambled eggs and the green peas, season with the white pepper to taste, heat to serving temperature, and enjoy!

Chef's Note: *Fried rice* must *be made with cold rice. Rice that is just cooked or at room temperature will turn gummy when stir-fried in the wok. Incidentally, all fried rice may be prepared in advance, stored in a 2-quart casserole in the refrigerator, and heated uncovered in the oven at 350 degrees for about 1 hour before you're ready to serve.*

Just for the record, pork fried rice *is made using this same recipe. The only thing you do differently is shred a half-pound of pork and small-dice a half-pound of ham, drop them both into the wok, and stir-fry the meats for about 2-3 minutes or until the pork turns white.*

As with all Chinese cooking, success is achieved only if you make sure you have all the measured ingredients laid out in front of you on the countertop before *you begin to cook.*

Perfect N'Awlins Boiled Shrimp

Ain't nuttin' like a good N'Awlins shrimp boil! And this recipe gives you shrimp that are seasoned just right ... that peel so easily they almost fall out of their shells ... that never come out mushy ... in fact, that are perfect! And *you* can cook 'em like this every time—just follow the recipe.

2½ gal. water
3 medium onions, coarsely chopped
¾ head celery, coarsely chopped
3 large heads garlic, cut crosswise
4 whole lemons, sliced
6 whole bay leaves
1 bottle crabboil (8 oz. size)
1 lb. country smoked sausage, cut
   in pieces

1 heaping cup salt
2 tsp. cayenne pepper
2 lb. "B"-size creamer potatoes
4 ears fresh corn, quartered
5 lb. headless shrimp (26-30 count)
½ bag ice

First, take a heavy 20-quart stockpot and bring 2½ gallons of water to a rolling boil. Then drop in the onions, celery, garlic, lemon, bay leaves, crabboil, smoked sausage, salt, and cayenne pepper.

Now with the lid on the pot, *rapidly boil the mixture for at least 10 minutes to create a flavored seasoning stock.* This is one of the most important steps in fixing boiled seafood—the stock must be flavored before the seafood goes in!

At this point, follow the procedure to the letter:

1—Put the potatoes in the pot and boil them by themselves for 4 minutes. That gets the potatoes started.

2—Then put the corn in the pot with the potatoes and boil the corn and the potatoes together for 11 minutes. That will give you a total boiling time of 15 minutes, which is exactly the time it takes to have perfectly cooked corn and potatoes.

3—Meanwhile, thoroughly wash the shrimp until the water runs clear and remove any small crabs, fish, and grass that might have gotten mixed in with the catch. Then drop in the shrimp. The water will stop boiling! When it comes back to a rapid boil, time the shrimp for exactly 2 minutes. That's how long it takes to cook shrimp—*2 minutes!* Any longer than that and you're overcooking them, which means they will come out mushy, the shells will stick to the meat, and they'll be almost impossible to peel!

4—Then turn off the fire, take the pot off the hot burner ('cuz if you don't the shrimp will continue to cook from the secondary heat stored in the steel burner grate), and drop in about a half-bag of ice. The rapid cooling effect will force out the air trapped inside of the shells and cause the shrimp to sink into the flavored stock. And that's when they pick up the seasoning—not while they're boiling!

5—Now let the shrimp "soak" for about 15 to 30 minutes, depending upon how spicy you like the finished product. The longer they soak the more seasoning they get.

A few other notes here!

As you add the ingredients—potatoes, then corn, then shrimp—the water will stop boiling with each addition. So to time out everything right, you must wait for the water to come back to a full boil each time before you start timing.

When the shrimp are flavored just the way you want them, drain off the seasoned water, pile them—along with the corn, potatoes, and sausage—on several thicknesses of newspaper, and dig in! They're so good you really don't need a cocktail sauce to dip them in, but I would suggest you pop the top on a couple of cold brewskies just to make the meal complete ... and *Naturally N'Awlins.*

Chef's Note:

1—When I say a "head" of celery, I mean the whole celery; not just one "stalk." In this recipe, you use ¾ of the whole celery or about 6 ribs.

2—If you keep the lid on the pot while you're making your seasoning stock the water will come to a boil more quickly and the flavor will stay in the liquid.

3—You should learn to buy your shrimp by the count *(16-20, 21-25, 26-30, and so forth), not by size (small, medium, large, jumbo). Size is arbitrary; count is exact. A 26-30 count means 26 to 30 shrimp to the pound.*

4—Just for the record, no seafood—shrimp, crabs, or crawfish—can pick up seasoning while actively boiling. You gotta remember that while boiling is in progress, the heat causes air to be trapped inside the shells, thereby creating a barrier that keeps the flavored stock away from the meat. But when you drop in the ice and quickly reduce the temperature, air inside the shells contracts, and the contraction causes the shell segments and the bubbles to break, which allows the seasonings to seep inside the shells. Makes sense, huh?

So let's say you got a lot of shrimp to boil—30 pounds or more. First, cook up a big pot of highly seasoned flavored stock ... but don't cook your seafood in it. Just let it cool. In fact, go ahead and ice it down! Then put a second pot of plain water on the fire and bring it to a rolling boil. Then, in batches, boil all of your shrimp in the plain water—2 minutes per batch. And as each batch finishes, remove the shrimp from the water with a strainer and drop them into the iced flavored stock to soak. They'll come out so perfectly seasoned you won't convince anybody you did it this way! Now that's trickery!

And finally, never never put cooked shrimp back into the same container you used for the uncooked shrimp without first washing that container thoroughly with lots of extremely hot soapy water. That's how you get cholera!

Old N'Awlins Barbecued Shrimp

One of the Crescent City's all-time favorite dishes is "Barbecued Shrimp." And while it's really more oven baked than barbecued, and while there must be over a dozen variations as to how the recipe goes … I believe you'll feel that this one is right up there with the best of the best!

3 sticks margarine
¼ cup extra-virgin olive oil
2 tbsp. onion powder
2 tbsp. garlic powder
1 tsp. ground cloves
¾ tsp. cayenne pepper
3 tbsp. black pepper
3 tbsp. McCormick's Barbecue
  Spice

3 tsp. paprika
2 tsp. ground rosemary leaves
4 tbsp. Worcestershire sauce
1 lemon, juiced
2 bay leaves
1 can warm beer
2 tsp. salt
5 lb. large shrimp (heads on)

First, drop the margarine and the olive oil into a 12-inch heavy aluminum skillet and blend them together over medium-low heat (just make sure the mixture doesn't burn).

Then remove the skillet from the fire and—*adding one ingredient at a time*—stir in the onion powder, garlic powder, cloves, cayenne pepper, black pepper, barbecue spice, paprika, rosemary, Worcestershire, lemon juice, and bay leaves.

Now stir everything into the seasoning base really well. Then slowly add the beer and stir it into the mix until the foam disappears. At this point, stir in the salt, preheat your oven to 300 degrees, set the seasoning mixture aside to allow the flavors to marry, and place the shrimp in a large baking pan. Oh—be sure to use a pan large enough to give you room to stir the shrimp periodically as they bake.

When you're ready to cook—and this dish is best served right out of the oven—pour the mixture over the top of the shrimp, making sure you coat each shrimp really well. Then place the pan in the oven—uncovered—and bake for about 40 minutes, basting thoroughly every 10 minutes or so.

So how do you know when they're done? Easy!

When you see a slight air space appear along the back of the shrimp and you see the shell segments start to pull apart (actually, the shell pulls away from the meat), *they're ready to eat!*

I recommend you serve barbecued shrimp in soupbowls, piping hot with the shrimp swimming in the sauce, accompanied by a bottle of your favorite white wine and a big loaf of hot crisp French bread.

Chef's Note: Don't overcook 'em! *The shells will set and the shrimp will be hard to peel. If you plan to serve the shrimp as a dinner entrée, I recommend you serve them alongside either bronzed or creamed potatoes, Broccoli Cheese Casserole (see* Frank Davis Cooks Naturally N'Awlins*), and a crisp Italian salad. But most of all … you got to have a good supply of French bread to sop up the juices! It's the absolute best part of the whole recipe!*

One more thing: if you should have any of the basting sauce left over (which I seriously doubt will be the case!), it can be refrigerated in a small bowl and used as a topping for mashed potatoes, baked potatoes, or fried grits. It can also be used as a condiment for broiled oysters on the half-shell (a couple of teaspoons on each oyster), for brushing over redfish on the grill, or for whatever else tempts your palate. So go ahead and be creative!

Italian Shrimp Scampi

In Italy, a scampo (the plural is scampi) is not a shrimp at all—it's a small lobster (or a langoustine, as the Europeans prefer to call them). And the way Italians like to fix them is to broil them and baste them with garlic butter (in Northern Italy) or garlic and olive oil (in Southern Italy). But in America, we take this classic cooking method, apply it to shrimp instead of small lobsters, and call *the dish* "Scampi." So even though our dish more accurately should be called "shrimp prepared in the scampi style" … it really doesn't matter what you call it when it tastes this good!

2 lb. raw shrimp, peeled and deveined	**¼ cup extra-virgin olive oil**
½ tsp. salt	**¼ cup sweetcream butter**
½ tsp. black pepper	**3 tbsp. finely minced garlic**
¼ tsp. seafood seasoning	**3 bay leaves**
¼ tsp. Italian seasoning	**2 cups all-purpose flour, seasoned**
¼ tsp. garlic powder	**½ cup dry Italian white wine**
Peanut oil for frying	**½ fresh lemon, quartered in wedges**
	½ cup finely chopped parsley

First, wash the shrimp well in cold water and place them in a colander so that they drain thoroughly. Then put them in a bowl, sprinkle them with the salt, black pepper, seafood seasoning, Italian seasoning, and garlic powder, and toss everything together so that the herbs and spices fully coat the shrimp. Then cover the bowl with plastic wrap, put it in the refrigerator, and let the shrimp marinate for at least 3 to 4 hours.

When you're ready to cook, heat the peanut oil for deep frying to 375 degrees. Then mix together in a 12-inch skillet the olive oil and the butter and bring it to medium-high heat. When the butter foam disappears, toss in the minced garlic and the bay leaves and sauté until the garlic turns soft—*but do not let it brown or the butter sauce will be bitter.*

Meanwhile, take the marinated shrimp, dust them in the seasoned flour, and shake off as much excess as possible. At this point you want to let them rest on the countertop for a minute or two so that the coating will "cure." Then a handful at a time, drop the shrimp into the butter mix and cook them *only until they turn pink* (which should take about 4 to 5 minutes). When they're done, remove them from the pan with a slotted spoon, place them on a platter, and let them cool to room temperature. Continue to sauté the remaining shrimp in this manner until they are all cooked.

While the shrimp are cooling, pour the white wine into the pan, stir everything together until you get a uniform blend, and let the wine reduce to at least one-half of its original volume (remember, you're still cooking at medium-high heat). Then when the sauce is smooth, drop in the lemon wedges—*but don't squeeze them!*—and stir in the parsley.

When you're ready to eat, drop the sautéed shrimp by small handfuls into the hot peanut oil and deep fry them in batches for about 2 minutes until the outsides are crisp. This seals the juices inside the shrimp, keeps the inside tender, and gives the shrimp a nutty flavor.

When they're done, quickly return them to the scampi sauce and serve them sizzling hot, with lots of the sauce and several slices of fresh toasted French bread. Squeeze on the sautéed lemon wedges as you desire.

Chef's Note: *If you're doing more than 2 pounds of shrimp at a time, you will have to change the olive oil and garlic mixture several times so that the garlic doesn't burn. But don't toss it out! Pour each batch into a saucepan and blend it all together at the end to create the final sauce.*

Just in case you're wondering, the double-cooking technique (sautéing then deep frying) keeps the shrimp from drying out and losing all their juices. If you prefer not to deep fry, you can serve the shrimp directly from the sauté skillet ... but I sincerely recommend you "double cook" for real scampi.

For a richer Italian taste, deep fry the shrimp in pure olive oil instead of peanut oil.

Frank's Famous Shrimp Boiled in Margarine

Easier to prepare than boiling, lighter and more succulent than barbecuing, all the flavor and goodness of scampi, and finger-licking good hot or cold ... this shrimp dish will get you rave reviews. You're gonna love this—especially the part about sopping up the sauce with hot, fresh French bread! And believe it or not—*it's not oily!*

2 sticks margarine
1 cup coarsely chopped green
  onions
1 cup coarsely chopped bell peppers
1 cup coarsely chopped celery
1 cup coarsely chopped onions
8 cloves garlic, finely minced
5 lb. headless shrimp (21-25 count)

1 tbsp. salt
3 tbsp. Frank Davis Seafood
  Seasoning
3 tbsp. sweet basil
2 tbsp. paprika
⅔ cup white wine
Juice of 1 lemon
½ cup finely chopped parsley

Start by preheating an 8-quart, heavy aluminum or cast-iron Dutch oven over medium-high heat. Then toss in the margarine and melt it down until it starts bubbling and foaming.

Next, turn up the heat to high, add all of the chopped vegetable seasonings (except the parsley), and stir them rapidly—*and continually*—into the melted margarine for about 4 minutes. You will notice that as the ingredients cook, the yellow tint of the margarine will turn to a pale green color. *That's the vegetable margarine base.* It's what makes this dish so savory!

Now drop in the raw shrimp, along with the salt, Frank Davis Seafood Seasoning, sweet basil, paprika, wine, and lemon juice. And immediately stir everything together into the vegetable margarine mix so that every single shrimp is thoroughly coated. *I suggest you stir for at least 3 minutes.* Then once the shrimp are coated, cover the Dutch oven and cook—*still on high heat!*—for about 3 minutes or so.

The next time you uncover the pot, you will notice a sauce beginning to form—this is natural shrimp juice mixing with the vegetable margarine. Stir again … and when you have everything mixed, taste the sauce for seasoning and make whatever adjustments you want. Now, cover the pot once more and cook for another 3 minutes (or until you begin to see the shrimp meat breaking away from the shells). *Hint:* a slight air space will form along the dorsal (upper) part of the shrimp. That's your best indicator that they're done. *Don't overcook or the shells will stick and the shrimp will be hard to peel!*

Finally, remove the pot from the heat, put the cover back on, and let the shrimp "steep" for about 10 minutes in the sauce to pick up the full flavor of the seasonings before you serve them, garnished with parsley.

Chef's Note: *I suggest you serve the shrimp open-face over a 6-inch piece of French bread (which, of course, you ladle well with the sauce), alongside an authentic tossed Italian salad made with extra-virgin olive oil, tarragon vinegar, imported anchovies, and grated Romano cheese.*

Variation: *This dish may be prepared with heads-on as well as headless shrimp … but it should not be done with peeled shrimp. Peeled shrimp tend to become tough and rubbery when cooked this way.*

To serve this dish as an elegant dinner-party entrée, remove the shrimp from the sauce, peel them, and set them aside. Then strain the sauce, reheat it in a skillet to a gentle boil, and cream it with ½ stick butter (or cornstarch mixed with chicken stock) until it thickens, shines, and glazes.

When you're ready to eat, drop the peeled shrimp back into the hot sauce and serve them over creamed potatoes, rice, or pasta.

Shrimp-Stuffed N'Awlins Mirlitons

Every holiday season, one of the special dishes served in the Crescent City is "Shrimp-Stuffed Mirlitons." You can serve them with Thanksgiving turkey, Christmas capon, or New Year's pork; but whenever you serve them ... don't expect any to be left over. I recommend it as an appetizer or entrée!

6 medium-size mirlitons	1 tbsp. finely chopped parsley
4 tbsp. butter	¼ tsp. thyme
1 large onion, finely chopped	½ tsp. rosemary
3 green onions, finely sliced	1 tsp. salt
2 tbsp. finely chopped bell pepper	¼ tsp. cayenne pepper
½ cup finely chopped celery	½ tsp. black pepper
3 cloves garlic, finely chopped	2-4 cups seasoned coarse bread
½ cup coarsely chopped mush-	crumbs
rooms	1 egg, well beaten
2 lb. fresh shrimp, coarsely	1 cup buttered bread crumbs
chopped	

First, take your mirlitons and boil them in lightly salted water until a testing fork will pierce them all the way through (without using excessive force). Then remove them from the water and set them aside to cool.

Meanwhile, in a 5-quart Dutch oven, melt the butter over medium heat and sauté the onions, bell pepper, celery, garlic, and mushrooms until they are tender (which should take you about 5 minutes).

Next, slice the cooled mirlitons in half (lengthwise), remove the center seed pod, and throw it away. Then with a tablespoon, *gently* scrape out the mirliton pulp to within a quarter-inch of the outer skin ... but be careful not to break the outer skin. Now, with a sharp knife, dice up the pulp into small pieces.

At this point, turn up the fire under the Dutch oven to high and toss in the pulp. Stirring constantly for 10 to 15 minutes, cook the pulp and the vegetable seasonings together until a paste forms (it may be slightly watery, but don't worry about it). About three-quarters of the way through this portion of the cooking process, add the raw shrimp and stir them around. They will turn pink in about 2 minutes, which is exactly how you want them—*pink ... not cooked!*

Now, remove the pot from the fire and thoroughly stir in the spices and herbs—the parsley, thyme, rosemary, salt, and peppers. Be sure to blend them well into the pulp mix so that you have no "potent" spots. Then begin stirring in the dry bread crumbs a little at a time.

When all the dry crumbs are added, you should end up with a rather dry paste that tends to stick to the spoon. If it is still too moist, add a few extra crumbs, because if the mixture is too wet it will "run" during the baking process. If, on the other hand, your stuffing mix comes out too dry, simply moisten it to the proper consistency with a little canned chicken broth. Now, quickly stir in the egg to bind the mixture together.

Finally, spoon the stuffing into the cooled mirliton halves so that it forms rounded domes at the top (in other words, almost overstuff!). Then sprinkle the tops with the buttered bread crumbs, place the halves on a greased shallow cookie sheet, and bake them in a 300-degree oven for about 25 minutes or until the topping crumbs turn a toasty brown.

All that's left is to serve the mirlitons piping hot right from the oven!

Chef's Note: *For a little extra enhancement, liberally sprinkle the mirlitons with grated Pecorino Romano cheese when you serve them. Remember that mirlitons go great with creamed peas, buttered carrots, a crisp lettuce salad topped with French dressing, and a bottle of chilled Chenin Blanc wine.*

Classic New Orleans Shrimp Creole

Ever since the early days of the Crescent City, *Creole* food has always been aristocratic and considered highly elegant. But no Creole recipe has claimed as much fame as this one! From the most sophisticated restaurant to the neighborhood café, everybody makes "Shrimp Creole"! But the best you can get is the batch you whip up at home!

¼ cup Crisco oil	6 cans water
⅓ cup all-purpose flour	½ cup golden sherry
2 cups finely chopped onions	Juice of ½ lemon
½ cup finely sliced green onions	3 tbsp. Worcestershire sauce
½ cup finely diced celery	2 tbsp. Louisiana hot sauce
½ cup finely chopped bell pepper	2 tbsp. seafood seasoning
¼ cup finely minced parsley	2 tsp. salt (if needed to taste)
4 cloves garlic, finely minced	3 lb. medium shrimp, peeled
1 can tomato paste (12-oz. size)	6 cups cooked long-grain rice
1 can tomato sauce (12-oz. size)	

In a heavy 5-quart Dutch oven, heat the Crisco oil over a medium-high fire. Then, with a wire whisk, vigorously stir in the flour and continue to work it into the oil until it turns creamy smooth. What you're doing is making a light roux ... but be sure you cook it only until it just begins to turn a pale tan *(you don't want it to brown!)*.

Next, drop in the onions, green onions, celery, bell pepper, parsley, and garlic, stir them into the roux, reduce the heat to low, and cook the vegetables until they begin to soften (about 5 minutes or so should do it). Again, you will have to continue stirring the pot or the roux will burn.

Then when the mixture is uniform, stir in the tomato paste and the tomato sauce. And don't even think about not stirring the pot now! *If the tomatoes scorch ... the whole dish will become bitter!* So stir, stir, and stir again—for another 3 minutes or so.

At this point, increase the heat to high, pour in 5 cans of water and all the wine, and blend everything into a semithick sauce. Remember, you don't want the sauce to be too thin—it will naturally thin out when you add the shrimp. If, however, it seems a bit thick to you, go ahead and pour in the last can of water.

Now you're ready to season the sauce base, so stir in the lemon juice, Worcestershire, hot sauce, seafood seasoning, and salt if needed. Then reduce the fire to low, cover the Dutch oven with a tight-fitting lid, and simmer the sauce base for an hour, stirring occasionally. Then—and follow this closely—*exactly 10 minutes* before you're ready to eat, drop in the peeled shrimp and stir them well into the sauce base. If you cook the shrimp any longer than 10 minutes, they will shrink and turn mushy and gritty.

When you're ready to serve, spoon a generous helping of the Shrimp Creole over a plate of hot steamed rice and dish it up alongside some hot buttered French bread and a cold crisp salad covered with vinaigrette dressing.

Mes amis ... bon appétit!

Chef's Note: *When I say 6 "cans" of water, I mean to measure the water in the tomato-paste can. For Italian gravy, the correct mixture is 3 cans of water to 1 can of tomato paste. But for Creole, court bouillon, and sauce piquante, the correct mixture is 5 cans of water to 1 can of paste. That's because the roux is going to absorb a considerable amount of the water. The sixth can is kept aside just in case you need it.*

You may not need to add salt to the sauce, especially if you use a good-quality seafood seasoning. To be sure, I suggest you taste the sauce base before sprinkling in the salt.

I use my Frank Davis blend of seafood seasoning in this recipe for Shrimp Creole. But if you can't find it where you shop and you'd like to order it, simply call 1-800-742-4231.

All the flavor and spice of Shrimp Creole and Shrimp Stew, light on the diet, and extremely simple to prepare, this entire dish can be cooked in just a bit over *5 minutes!* If you like New Orleans foods but you don't have time to do a lot of cooking ... this is your dish!

4 tbsp. butter
4 tbsp. extra-virgin olive oil
½ cup finely chopped celery
½ cup finely chopped onions
¼ cup diced bell pepper
1 bunch green onions, thinly sliced
1 tbsp. all-purpose flour
4 medium-size Creole tomatoes, diced
3 cloves garlic, finely minced
1 small can diced green chilies

2 lb. shrimp, peeled
2 tsp. basil
2 tsp. seafood seasoning or salt to taste
½ cup minced parsley
2 tbsp. butter
6 cups cooked minishell pasta, al dente
1 cup finely grated Parmesan cheese

In a heavy 12-inch skillet, blend together the butter and the olive oil and heat it until it just begins to foam. Then immediately toss in the celery, onions, bell pepper, and green onions and stir-fry the mixture over high heat. Once the vegetables soften, quickly sprinkle on the flour and stir it evenly throughout the dish.

At this point, drop in the diced tomatoes—along with the garlic and chilies—and *stir constantly* until the tomatoes render out their juices and the liquid reduces to at least one-half of its original volume—this should only take you about 4 to 5 minutes.

Next, add the shrimp. And (again over high heat) continuously stir them until they *begin to turn pink.* But don't let them turn all the way—they'll cook too quickly and become tough. Just get them starting to turn!

Now, drop in the basil, the seafood seasoning, and the parsley and stir everything together once again to ensure that all the ingredients are uniformly mixed. Then cover the skillet and let the shrimp cook for about 3 minutes! When you take the lid off the pot again, the natural juices from the rendering shrimp will have formed a light but robust sauce.

Finally, stir in the remaining 2 tablespoons of butter and immediately serve the shrimp over hot pasta topped with a sprinkling of Parmesan cheese alongside a cold Creole tomato salad and a side basket of buttered French bread slices.

Shrimp, Ham, and Eggplant Casserole

New Orleanians have all kinds of ways of preparing eggplant. But if you want a special—yet fast and easy—casserole to serve at Thanksgiving, Christmas, New Year's, Mother's Day, or next Tuesday, try this spicy shrimp and ham dish!

½ cup extra-virgin olive oil
2 large eggplants, peeled and diced
   but uncooked
1 stick unsalted butter
2 lb. small or medium shrimp,
   peeled and deveined
½ cup coarsely chopped lean ham
1 cup finely chopped white onions
½ cup finely chopped celery

½ cup finely chopped shallots
2 tbsp. finely minced parsley
4 cloves garlic, finely minced
2 cups Italian seasoned bread
   crumbs
2 whole eggs, slightly beaten
4 tbsp. Pecorino Romano cheese
Salt and black pepper to taste

In a 12-inch heavy skillet, heat the olive oil and sauté the eggplants—stirring constantly—until they turn soft and tender. Then when they're cooked, put them in a large bowl (along with any excess olive oil) and set them aside for awhile.

Using the same skillet, melt the stick of butter over high heat (but watch that it doesn't burn!). Then toss in the shrimp, ham, onions, celery, shallots, parsley, and garlic and *cook only until the shrimp turn pink* (which should take no more than 3 or 4 minutes). Be careful that you don't overcook the shrimp—they'll turn rubbery!

Next, combine the "shrimp-ham-seasoning" mixture with the eggplants that you set aside. And I mean combine them well—you want to make sure the blend is uniform. Then when everything is together, begin stirring in your bread crumbs. You want to add just enough crumbs to absorb most of the moisture. Remember, you don't want the casserole dry, but you don't want it soggy either—keep it "wet."

When you think you got everything mixed just right, stir in the eggs and the Romano cheese, season with salt and pepper (or Frank Davis Sicilian Seasoning), and blend all the ingredients together one more time.

Finally, preheat your oven to 325 degrees, butter the sides and bottom of a Pyrex casserole dish, transfer your mix, and bake it—*uncovered*—for about 25 minutes.

Served piping hot, the casserole makes a great side dish for roasted chicken, grilled Italian sausage, baked meat loaf, or panéed pork chops. Now that I think of it ... it makes a great side dish for anything!

Fried Calamari Sicilia

I can't believe that just because they're squid, some folks won't eat calamari. They're one of the cleanest seafood forms in the ocean, they're easier than any other kind of seafood to prepare, and when they're fried according to this recipe there's nothing crispier or tastier!

2 lb. Monterey squid, fresh or frozen	2 tbsp. salt
	1 tbsp. black pepper
2 cups all-purpose flour	1 qt. vegetable oil for frying
1 tbsp. garlic powder	4 fresh lemons, sliced in halves
1 tbsp. onion powder	1 stick real butter, melted

First, take the squid and pull the head and tentacles off. Then with your fingers reach inside the body and remove the cuttlebone (there's only one of them and it looks like a transparent piece of thin plastic). It will pull right out.

Next, take a knife and slice off the tentacles just ahead of the eyes. Then hold the tentacles in your hand and, with your fingers, pop out the bony beak. It's easy to do! Throw the beak away and place the tentacles in a bowl.

Now under cold running water, slide your fingers back and forth over the body of the squid. This will loosen the purplish skin membrane. When it splits, just peel it off. It will all come off in one motion, leaving the body pure white. At this point, place the squid body on a cutting board and either slice it crosswise in rings (about ¼ inch thick) or slice it lengthwise in julienne strips.

When you're ready to fry, mix the flour, garlic powder, onion powder, salt, and pepper together. Then take a heavy 12-inch skillet, pour the vegetable oil into it, and heat it to 400 degrees. Then drop the *wet* calamari into the flour (and it must be wet so that the flour will stick to it) and coat all the pieces thoroughly. Now take a large-mesh strainer basket, place the coated calamari in it, and shake off the excess flour.

All that's left is to drop the squid pieces into the hot oil—*but drop them in a little at a time.* Putting in too many at once will cause the oil to plunge below frying temperature and your calamari won't fry crisp. Oh—and you need to know that at the right temperature, it'll only take about a minute or two for them to be golden brown and ready to eat.

When they're done, remove them from the skillet with a strainer spoon and spread them out on paper towels to drain. Then serve them on a warm platter, squeeze the lemon over the batch, and ladle on a stream of the melted butter.

This, y'all, is some good stuff!

Chef's Note:

1—I don't recommend you fry calamari in your electric deep fryer. Most of these devices never get hot enough to give you the crispness you want. And under no circumstances should you fill a deep-fryer basket with calamari and place the basket into the oil. Doing this will drop the cooking temperature so critically the squid will stop frying and do nothing but absorb oil!

2—If you're reluctant to cook calamari because of the psychology of what it is, I suggest you try your first taste as an appetizer in a good restaurant. Chef A. J. Tusa, who did this particular recipe with me on my television show, serves up a mean batch of the stuff at Anthony's Pasta House in the Riverwalk in New Orleans.

3—Oh—and for a little extra flavor, you can dip fried calamari either into a marinara sauce, a tomato-base seafood sauce, or a little extra melted butter. I also suggest you sprinkle your fried calamari with about a teaspoon or two of my "Strictly N'Awlins Seafood Seasoning."

N'Awlins Stuffed Crabs

This is a classic Louisiana recipe you don't often hear about anymore ... and I don't understand why! It's not difficult to prepare, it's one notch short of being gourmet, and it tastes superfantastic—especially if you make 'em using this recipe and real crab shells! Try 'em!

1 stick real butter
2 tbsp. margarine
1 large onion, finely chopped
½ cup finely chopped green onions
½ cup finely chopped celery
2 tbsp. finely chopped bell pepper
2 lb. fresh crabmeat (white or claw)
½ tsp. minced garlic
2 tbsp. finely chopped parsley
¼ cup light cream
⅛ tsp. thyme
1 cup seasoned coarse bread
  crumbs

1 tsp. Frank Davis Seafood
  Seasoning
Salt and black pepper to taste
¼ tsp. cayenne pepper
1 cup crab or chicken stock (if
  needed)
Crab shells
1 extra stick real butter, softened
Rock salt for baking the stuffed
  crabs

Take a 6-quart Dutch oven and melt down the butter and margarine over medium heat, blending it together well so that the butter doesn't burn. Then toss in the onions, green onions, celery, and bell pepper and sauté them "gently" until they soften.

Now add your crabmeat, garlic, parsley, cream, and thyme and fold it "very easily" into the softened vegetables—*make sure you don't break up the crabmeat any more than you have to!* Then, still over medium heat, cook the mixture for about 3 minutes.

At this point, go ahead and put in your bread crumbs, the seafood seasoning, salt, black pepper, and cayenne. And—once more!—stir ever so gently so that you don't shred the crabmeat! If the mix tends to be dry, add some of the crab or chicken stock. But remember, while you don't want the stuffing to be dry and crumbly, you don't want it runny and wet either. The ideal texture you're looking for is one that *just binds.*

Now take your crab shells (make sure they're cleaned well), liberally butter them on the inside, and begin stuffing them—you want to *overstuff* them slightly so that they come out rounded on the top. By the way, it's a lot easier to handle the stuffing after it has cooled to room temperature.

When the crabs are stuffed, sprinkle the tops lightly with a little more bread crumbs, dot with a dab of butter, and bake at 400 degrees in a shallow pan on a bed of rock salt until the tops are crusty brown (about 10-15 minutes).

Chef's Note: *Stuffed crabs go great with either potato salad or baked macaroni. I also suggest you serve them with chilled sliced tomatoes topped with Caesar dressing.*

Cajun Black-Pot Baked Crabs

I dearly love to sit down to about a dozen spicy boiled crabs and a frosty cold beer. But just recently, while I was fishing down in Larose, Phil Ledet told me about a dish his wife, Mary, makes with hard crabs that beats any boiled crabs I ever had. Well, I fixed 'em as soon as I got home … made a few changes to suit my taste … and I gotta admit, Phil's right—they beat any boiled crab I ever had!

2 doz. live crabs	⅓ cup golden sherry
1 bag crushed ice	4 tbsp. seafood seasoning
⅓ cup peanut oil	2 tsp. cayenne pepper
4 large onions, sliced in half-rings	8 cups cooked long-grain rice
6 cloves garlic, minced	

First, rinse the crabs thoroughly in cold running water to remove any debris from their shells. Then place them into a large plastic container—*a clean 5-gallon bucket will do*—and cover them with the crushed ice. (I find it's best if you alternate layers of crabs and ice—they'll chill more evenly that way.)

In the meantime, while the crabs are chilling, take a large 8-quart, cast-iron Dutch oven and place it on the fire. Then heat the peanut oil to hot, toss in all the onions, and fry them (stirring constantly) until they begin to clear. At that point, drop in the minced garlic, continue to stir, and fry the mixture until the onions soften. When they're ready, turn off the fire, remove the pot from the burner, and set it aside momentarily.

By this time, the crabs should be cold enough to prepare them for the dish. One at a time, take off the top shell and scoop out whatever fat is inside (you want to save this in a small measuring cup). Then with a paring knife, scrape away the gills (some folks call it the "dead man"), clean the inside chamber and, with a scissors, trim away the mouth parts and the legs. Then take a brush and thoroughly wash the cleaned crab—oh, be sure to remove the bottom flap. Finally, with a chef's knife, cut the crab into left and right halves.

When you've processed all 2 dozen, put the Dutch oven back on the burner, turn up the fire to high, and stir in the crab halves along with the crab fat. It is important to mix everything together well—you want the crabs and the onions uniformly distributed.

Now pour in the sherry and sprinkle in the seafood seasoning and the cayenne pepper. Then once again thoroughly mix everything, cover the pot, and turn the fire down to *low*. Note that your total cooking time is about 30 minutes, but you will have to stir the mixture 3 or 4 times during that period to evenly simmer the crabs (they're actually baking on top of the stove).

One note—*don't cover the pot tightly* or you will render out too much moisture from the onions and the crab halves and your crabs will actually be boiling. Instead, leave the lid slightly tilted. This will eliminate excess liquid … yet it will create just the right amount of extrarich gravy in the bottom of the pot.

When you're ready to eat, dish out 3 or 4 crab halves into a soupbowl, alongside a scoop or two of the rice, and generously ladle on the pot gravy. Incidentally, you eat this just like you eat a gumbo—a spoon for the rice and gravy and your fingers for picking the crabs.

Oh, yeah—and the dish is best when you serve it piping hot, right from the Dutch oven!

Chef's Note: *Be careful not to overcook the crabs. You should be aware that they will not be as firm as they would be were they boiled (they'll have more of a gumbo consistency). So if you overcook them even the slightest bit, they're gonna be mushy.*

The seafood seasoning I use in this recipe can be ordered by calling 1-800-742-4231.

Perfectly broiled soft-shells, basted in butter and lemon, and topped with a rich, succulent, classic meunière sauce! I promise that if you like trout fixed this way, you're gonna flip over the dish you'll create with soft-shell crabs!

The Crabs:

8 medium soft-shell crabs	2 tsp. cayenne pepper
4 cups cultured buttermilk	2 tsp. paprika
1 stick butter	Juice of 1 lemon
2 tsp. salt	

The Meunière Sauce:

1½ cups soft-shell pan drippings	2 tsp. paprika
2 tsp. minced garlic	2 tbsp. capers
3 sticks sweetcream butter	Salt and cayenne to taste
2 tbsp. all-purpose flour	½ cup finely chopped parsley
3 tbsp. Worcestershire sauce	1 lemon, thinly sliced
Juice of 2 lemons	

First, wash the crabs well under cold running water. Then, with a paring knife, remove from each crab the bottom flap, the eyes, the mouth, the sandbag, and the gills. Now, place the crabs in a shallow pan, pour the buttermilk over them, and let them marinate for about a half-hour.

Next, melt a stick of butter and pour it into a small baking dish. Then remove the crabs from the buttermilk and dip them into the dish with the melted butter (and be sure to coat them well—top, bottom, all over). When they are coated thoroughly, sprinkle them with salt, cayenne, and paprika and lay them topshell-side down in a baking pan so that they are barely touching each other.

Then squeeze a little lemon juice over each crab and slide the pan into the oven under the broiler. One important note here: *you have to cook the crabs about 6 inches from the broiler element; otherwise the legs will burn.* Incidentally, proper cooking time is about 12 minutes on the bottom side, and about 5 minutes more on the top side … and if your broiler is working properly, it might not be necessary to turn the crabs at all.

When the crabs are done, remove them from the pan with a spatula (but save the drippings!), arrange them on a serving platter, and place them in a warming oven right-side up. Then make your meunière sauce.

First, pour the pan drippings into a heavy skillet or saucepan, stir in the garlic, and bring the mixture to a boil. *But as soon as it boils,* reduce the heat to *low* and simmer the mixture for about 3 minutes or so. Then take the pan off the fire and set it aside momentarily.

At this point, take another skillet or saucepan, melt a half-stick of butter over high heat until it begins to brown, and quickly whisk in the flour, whipping it until it turns smooth. Immediately, take the skillet off the fire, pour in the pan drippings, and whisk everything together briskly until thoroughly blended (about 3 minutes).

Now put the skillet back on the fire, set the heat as low as it will go, and begin whisking in the remainder of the butter—a little at a time. When the sauce smooths and "creams," whisk in the Worcestershire, the lemon juice, the paprika, and the capers, and season to taste with salt and cayenne.

All that's left is to stir in the parsley, continue to cook over low heat (for about 4 minutes) until the sauce thickens slightly, and ladle generously over the soft-shell crabs.

I suggest you top each crab with a thin slice of lemon and serve it with a tomato salad with cucumber dressing and a baked potato garnished with butter, sour cream, and bacon bits.

Oh, yeah—and French bread to sop up the meunière!

Chef's Note:

1—The sandbag of the crab is located inside of its mouth and it can be pulled out with the thumb and forefinger. The gills lie under each end flap of the topshell.

2—If you want to eliminate the flour, just brown the butter a little longer and substitute a couple extra tablespoons of Worcestershire sauce. The flavor of the sauce won't change—you'll just get one that's a little lighter and a little thinner.

3—Whisk in the butter gently over low heat. If the heat is too high, the sauce will break, the butter will separate, and the oils will float to the surface.

Dolly Boudreaux's
Fried Cajun Crabmeat Bundles

Down on Bayou Lafourche, about halfway between Galliano and Golden Meadow, a nice Cajun lady named Dolly Boudreaux cooks one of the best-tasting, deep-fried, wonton-wrapped, seasoned crabmeat and spicy cream cheese concoctions you ever put your lips to, m'frien! And because I know that once you fix 'em you're gonna love 'em every bit as much as I do, here's the whole recipe.

1 cup Philadelphia Cream Cheese
½ cup sweetcream butter
1 tsp. onion salt
2 tsp. onion powder
¼ tsp. liquid crabboil
1 lb. special white crabmeat

1 tsp. Frank Davis Seafood
   Seasoning
1 pack wonton wrappers (3 by 3½
   size)
1 qt. peanut oil

First, take a 2½-quart saucepan, place the cream cheese, butter, onion salt, onion powder, and crabboil into it, and cook gently over medium heat—stirring continuously—until all of the ingredients combine smoothly and evenly (which will take you about 5 minutes).

Next, pick through the crabmeat to remove all the shell fragments; then completely blend the full pound of crabmeat with the cream cheese mixture in the saucepan and cook it for another 5 minutes or so to combine all the flavors.

At this point, remove the saucepan from the fire, stir in the seafood seasoning, and allow the stuffing mixture to cool thoroughly. *Note:* for a richer crabmeat flavor, I suggest you make the crabmeat mixture a day ahead of time so that all the ingredients marry into one taste.

Now take the wonton wrappers and place about ¾ of a teaspoon of the crabmeat-cheese mix into the center of each one. Then fold the four corners of the wrappers upward, creating a little bundle of crabmeat and cheese, and squeeze the ends together. They'll stay together if you pinch them slightly.

When you're ready to eat, drop the bundles into hot deep peanut oil—heated between 350 to 400 degrees—and fry them until they turn a crispy golden brown. This takes only a minute or two, so be careful not to burn them.

All that's left is to remove them from the frypan with a slotted spoon, drain them briefly on paper towels, and serve them piping hot alongside a cold crisp salad!

By the way, this recipe will make about 70 bundles.

Chef's Note:

1—While you can make the crabmeat and cheese mixture ahead of time, I don't recommend that you stuff the mixture into the wonton wrappers ahead of time. Made too early, they tend to get sticky on the bottom and won't fry up crisp.

2—You want to make sure you buy wonton *wrappers and not* egg-roll *wrappers. Wonton wrappers come as small 3-inch squares. Egg-roll wrappers are larger, usually 6-inch squares or better. To do the bundles right, I suggest you buy the smaller size, and I recommend the Freida brand.*

3—Be sure to keep the wrappers covered until you are ready to use them—uncovered they dry out, become difficult to shape, and won't get crisp when you fry them.

4—You can use any *preblended seafood seasoning that you like for this recipe. Of course, I'm happy to know that when Dolly makes her Crabmeat Bundles, she uses mine!*

N'Awlins Crabmeat Medallions

Similar to codfish cakes, this recipe transforms simple crab patties into succulent medallions of crab-claw meat, creamer potatoes, and a mirepoix of fresh vegetables that are easy to make yet gourmet in taste. You got to make this recipe soon!

1 stick butter
1 cup finely chopped onions
1 cup finely chopped green onions
½ cup diced celery
¼ cup diced red bell pepper
½ cup finely chopped parsley
3 cloves garlic, minced
1 lb. crab-claw meat
4 cups finely chopped potatoes

⅓ cup of heavy cream
3 eggs, well beaten
2 cups coarsely grated seasoned
   bread crumbs
Seafood seasoning or salt and pepper to taste
4 tbsp. peanut oil
4 tbsp. salted butter

In a 12-inch skillet, melt the butter over medium heat until it begins to foam. Then sauté down the onions, green onions, celery, bell pepper, parsley, and garlic. You don't have to caramelize and brown them, but be sure to cook them until they're completely wilted.

Then in a large mixing bowl, blend the vegetables and the crab-claw meat together. But do it gently—you don't want to break up the crabmeat any more than you have to. When these ingredients are mixed well, gradually begin adding the potatoes and "fold" them into the crabmeat mix. *Note: do this gently too.* You want to have chunks of crabmeat in the medallions, not just fine shreds.

At this point, fold in the heavy cream and the eggs until the consistency is uniform. Then, wet your hands and begin forming the medallions—ideally, they should be about the size of sugar cookies.

Then when the medallions are shaped, lightly coat them with the seasoned bread crumbs and seafood seasoning and set them aside on waxed paper to "set" for about a half-hour. (Actually, you can make them as far as a day in advance and keep them in the refrigerator, separated by waxed paper.)

When you're ready to eat, add a couple tablespoons of peanut oil and a couple tablespoons of butter to a nonstick skillet, bring it to medium-high heat, and pan-sauté the medallions until they turn a golden brown.

I suggest you serve them piping hot, topped with Creole Brandy Sauce.

Franko Duet's Cajun Seafood-Stuffed Pistolettes

Born as an appetizer on Bayou Lafourche, this mouth-watering taste treat has taken on many forms. But only when Franko Duet got hold of it in Galliano, gave it a crabmeat and shrimp stuffing, and added crunch to the texture by frying the pistolettes did it become an entrée that's sure to tempt Cajuns and everybody else. If you never cook anything else out of this book, you got to do this one!

2 sticks real butter	3 lb. boiled and ground shrimp
2 cups finely chopped onions	1 lb. crabmeat (white or claw)
¾ cup finely chopped celery	1 tsp. salt
½ cup finely chopped bell pepper	1 tsp. black pepper
¼ cup finely sliced green onions	½ tsp. granulated garlic
3 cups evaporated milk	½ tsp. cayenne pepper
1 cup water	24 uncooked Brown-N-Serve pisto-
1 lb. Velveeta cheese, cut in chunks	lettes
½ gal. peanut oil	

First, take a heavy 12-inch skillet and melt down the butter over medium heat until it foams. Then stir in the onions, celery, bell pepper, and green onions and cook them for about 12 to 15 minutes until they soften completely. *But be careful not to let the butter burn!*

When the vegetables are ready, pour in the evaporated milk and the water, mix them together thoroughly, and bring the mixture to a slow boil. Then drop in all the Velveeta chunks and, with the heat still set at medium, stir until the cheese melts and the sauce turns smooth and silky. For the most part, this should take you about 5 minutes.

While the sauce is simmering, take a high-sided frypan and heat the peanut oil to 325 degrees.

At this point, fold the ground shrimp and the crabmeat into the hot sauce in the skillet, stir everything together thoroughly, and cook the mixture for 3 minutes. When the stuffing is uniformly blended, sprinkle on and stir in the salt, pepper, granulated garlic, and cayenne. Then take the pan off the fire and allow the stuffing to cool slightly.

Actually, if you want to develop the maximum flavor in the seafood mix, I recommend that you make the stuffing one day, cover it and place it in the refrigerator overnight, and reheat it and stuff the pistolettes the next day. But to be truthful, these are so good that'll probably never happen—you'll stuff the pistolettes as soon as you make 'em!

So ... when you're ready to eat, drop the pistolettes into the hot peanut oil and fry them for about a minute or two on both sides (kinda like doughnuts) until they turn a golden, crunchy brown. Then, *while they're still hot,* hold them with a towel, make a slit in one end with a paring knife (big enough to insert a teaspoon), push down some of the bread with the knife on the inside of the pistolette to make a pocket, and fill the pocket with the stuffing.

While you can fill them all and keep them warm on a tray in the oven for serving later, Cajun Seafood-Stuffed Pistolettes are at their peak best when you serve them as you make them. They are great as appetizers or hors d'oeuvres for parties ... but I prefer to serve 2 per person, accompanied by a cold tossed salad and a good glass of wine, as a dinner entrée.

Maybe 3 per person! Maybe 4!

Chef's Note:

1—If you want to make the stuffing spicy, instead of using regular Velveeta cheese you can substitute the Mexican-style jalapeño Velveeta.

2—If you want to enhance the overall seafood flavor in the stuffing, 2 teaspoons of "Frank Davis Seafood Seasoning" can be substituted for the salt, black pepper, granulated garlic, and cayenne pepper. If the seasoning is not available where you shop, you can order it by direct mail by calling 1-800-742-4231.

3—To serve the pistolettes at a party, go ahead and stuff them all, place them uncovered on a sheet pan, and slide them into the oven at 200 degrees for up to 45 minutes or so. This way, everyone at your party eats at once.

4—If you're thinking an injector or a pastry bag might be an easy way to fill the breads, forget it! You can't get enough stuffing into the center of the bread with an injector or a pastry bag, and what you do get in ends up oozing back out because of the pressure you create inside the bread.

5—Finally, experiment with different stuffings. In addition to just shrimp and crabmeat, make the basic sauce but substitute sautéed crawfish, broiled oysters, Italian sausage and mozzarella, smoked turkey, chopped chicken or ham and bacon. The variations you can come up with are endless—but I guarantee you they'll all be delicious!

Crawfish Jambalaya

Like the taste of crawfish? Like the texture of jambalaya? Well, combine your crawfish and rice in this spicy concoction and you'll come up with one of the tastiest jambalayas you'll ever make. And like all my recipes … this one too is easy!

½ cup Crisco oil
3 cups coarsely chopped onions
1½ cups coarsely chopped celery
¾ cup coarsely chopped bell pepper
½ cup minced shallots
4 cloves garlic, minced
3 cups chicken stock

1 cup water
2 tsp. salt
2 tsp. black pepper
1 tsp. cayenne pepper
2 tsp. paprika
2 lb. peeled crawfish tails with fat
3 cups long-grain rice

To make a really good jambalaya, you need to use a well-seasoned black cast-iron Dutch oven. But if you don't have cast iron, a heavy *aluminum* Dutch oven can be substituted in its place. For this recipe, you want one that measures about 5 quarts.

Place the pot on the stove, pour in the oil, and heat it just until it begins to smoke slightly. Then toss in the onions, celery, bell peppers, and shallots and fry them over high heat until they wilt (which should take you about 6 to 8 minutes). Then when the vegetables are soft, drop in the garlic; you want to cook it for a minute or two, but you don't want it to burn.

Now pour in the chicken stock and the water, stir everything together well, and bring the mixture to a boil. At this point, season the liquid with your salt, black and cayenne pepper, and paprika to taste. *Note:* the seasonings listed in this recipe will give you a mildly spicy pot of jambalaya; if you want it more peppery, add your extra black and cayenne pepper at this point in the recipe.

Next—and this is important!—drop in only *1 pound* of the 2 pounds of crawfish tails you have and cook them into the liquid for 2 minutes. Then pour in the rice, stir the grains into the mixture well, cover the pot, and reduce the heat to *extremely low.* Many jambalaya recipes tell you not to lift the lid or stir the pot during cooking. I'm telling you just the opposite— *every 10 minutes or so, take the lid off the pot and stir the mixture thoroughly.* This keeps the rice cooking evenly and allows it to fluff.

All in all, you want to cook the jambalaya for about an hour. So halfway during the cooking process, right at the 30-minute mark, stir in the *second* pound of crawfish tails. The first pound will release a rich crawfish flavor, but they'll also shrink tremendously because you're overcooking them. The second pound, on the other hand, will stay more plump and provide the whole-crawfish-tail texture you want in the dish.

When all the liquid has been absorbed and the rice is fluffing up, the jambalaya is ready to serve. If you plan to eat it right away (which is the best way), serve it directly from the black pot. If, however, you plan to eat it later in the day—or the next day—spoon it out of the black pot into a large shallow baking pan so that it can cool. If you allow it to remain in the Dutch oven, the residual heat will overcook it to a mush!

Crawfish Jambalaya is best served alongside a cold crisp tossed green salad topped with croutons, bacon bits, and a creamy French-style dressing. Oh—and while wine is excellent for elegant dishes, I kinda prefer a frosty beer with a plate of jambalaya!

Chef's Note:

1—I suggest you add extra salt to this recipe only after you've tasted the chicken broth you intend to use. Some canned broths contain a lot of salt in themselves—you don't want to overseason.

2—If you prefer to use a blended seafood seasoning in this recipe, eliminate the salt, black pepper, and cayenne altogether.

3—The "secret" to a good, fluffy jambalaya is adding just the right amount of rice in relation to the liquid. You have to keep in mind that any ingredient that releases liquids must be counted as "extra liquid." So you either have to reduce the amount of water or stock in the recipe ... or increase the quantity of rice. Fortunately, I've calculated a chart that will give you the perfect texture for a chicken/sausage jambalaya. If you make other kinds of jambalaya, simply make a few compensations on the chart based on liquid-releasing ingredients. Here's your chart:

CHICKEN-SAUSAGE JAMBALAYA RATIO CHART

1 CUP WATER = ¾ CUPS OF RICE
2 CUPS WATER = 1½ CUPS OF RICE
3 CUPS WATER = 2¼ CUPS OF RICE
4 CUPS WATER = 3 CUPS OF RICE
5 CUPS WATER = 3¾ CUPS OF RICE
6 CUPS WATER = 4½ CUPS OF RICE
7 CUPS WATER = 5¼ CUPS OF RICE
8 CUPS WATER = 6 CUPS OF RICE
9 CUPS WATER = 6¾ CUPS OF RICE
10 CUPS WATER = 7½ CUPS OF RICE
11 CUPS WATER = 8¼ CUPS OF RICE
12 CUPS WATER = 9 CUPS OF RICE
13 CUPS WATER = 9¾ CUPS OF RICE
14 CUPS WATER = 10½ CUPS OF RICE

WHATEVER QUANTITY OF WATER = 75 PERCENT VOLUME OF RICE

Crawfish Corn Creole

You've had corn stew, shrimp stew, and corn and shrimp stew. But I want you to taste what happens when you combine fresh, fat crawfish tails with the crunchy texture of white shoepeg corn in a Creole-based red gravy. *Mes amis … this is fine!*

3 tbsp. vegetable oil
2 tbsp. all-purpose flour
2 cups finely diced onions
1 cup finely diced celery
½ cup finely diced bell peppers
4 cloves garlic, finely minced
3 small cans tomato paste
1 can tomato sauce (28-oz. size)
3 cups concentrated chicken stock
2 cups bottled water
4 cups white shoepeg corn, drained
3 bay leaves
½ tsp. sweet basil
⅛ tsp. lemon zest
1 tsp. Frank Davis Seafood Seasoning
½ tsp. cayenne pepper or Louisiana hot sauce
¼ cup minced Italian flatleaf parsley
4 lb. peeled crawfish tails with fat
Salt to taste
6 cups steamed and buttered rice

In a 6-quart heavy aluminum or Visions glassware Dutch oven, heat the oil to medium high, stir in the flour, toss in the onions, celery, bell peppers, and garlic, and sauté the vegetables until they begin to wilt (which should take about 5 minutes or so). *Be sure you stir the pot every once in a while, though, or the flour will stick!*

Then add the tomato paste and combine it thoroughly with the seasoning vegetables, stirring continuously until the mixture is uniformly blended. Oh—be sure to do this over a medium-high heat as well, because you want to fry the tomato paste for a few minutes to ripen it.

Now pour in the tomato sauce, the chicken stock, and the bottled water and stir them into the mixture too. What you eventually want to end up with is a smooth and silky, flavored tomato gravy, which means you're going to have to continue to cook this mixture for another 5 minutes or so.

At this point, stir in the corn and drop in the bay leaves, sweet basil, lemon zest, seafood seasoning, and cayenne pepper and mix everything together well *(still over medium-high heat)*. Then cover the pot, reduce the heat to *low,* and simmer the gravy for about 25-30 minutes until all the flavors have married.

Now, about 5 minutes before you're ready to eat, stir in the minced parsley and the crawfish tails (along with all the fat that comes in the bag), stir everything together one more time, and simmer *covered* over a low fire for 5 to 10 minutes until piping hot and bubbly. Oh—salt to taste at this point.

All that's left is to fill a soupbowl with hot buttered rice and ladle heaping scoops of the Crawfish Corn Creole generously over the top. Serve it with hot baked French bread and a chilled mixed salad that's been tossed with remoulade dressing and you can't find a meal that's more "Naturally N'Awlins."

Chef's Note:

1—When you mix the flour and oil in the Dutch oven, cook it only a few minutes. You don't want to make a roux—all you want to do is use the flour to help thicken the gravy slightly.

2—If you can't find shoepeg corn, you can substitute Green Giant White Corn in its place. Do not, however, use an inexpensive generic whole-kernel corn—it turns too soft and mushy when it cooks. Oh—and cream-style corn is a no-no!

3—Just for the record, lemon "zest" is the ultrathin, deep-yellow peel on the outside of the lemon. It is best removed with a "zester," a small little scraper-type gadget sold in most kitchen shops. But if you're real careful, you can cut it off the lemon with a paring knife. Just don't get any of the white part of the peel—it's bitter tasting!

4—Be careful not to overcook the crawfish tails. You want them to come out plump and tender, not like shriveled rubber bands. About 15 minutes is the maximum amount of time you should allow them to simmer in the hot gravy.

5—This recipe makes about 6 quarts of Crawfish Corn Creole. Yes, you can cut it in half ... but I suggest you make the entire recipe and freeze in portions what you don't eat at the initial sitting. It freezes really well and makes a great Lenten dish.

6—If you can't find a good seafood seasoning where you shop, you can order my seafood seasoning by calling toll-free 1-800-742-4231.

Crawfish Maque Choux

Half-Indian, half-Cajun, and every bit New Orleans ... this classic recipe is quick and simple to prepare, tastes magnificent over rice, and is exceptionally easy on the pocketbook. Try it soon and celebrate!

10 ears fresh corn on the cob	**½ cup rich chicken stock**
2 sticks real butter	**¼ cup light cream**
1 large white onion, coarsely chopped	**1 lb. crawfish tails and fat**
½ cup sliced green onions	**1 tsp. salt (or Frank Davis Vegetable Seasoning)**
1 bell pepper, coarsely chopped	**Black and cayenne pepper to taste**
2 large ripe fresh tomatoes, peeled and diced	

Start off by cutting the corn off the cobs with a sharp knife ... but you're going to have to follow a couple of steps to do it right. First, cut about halfway through the kernels (you don't want whole kernels in the maque choux). Then go back and cut again—this time to the cob. Finally, with a spoon, scrape the cob hard—this releases the "milk" from the cob and makes the maque choux creamy when it cooks. Now, set the cut corn aside for the time being.

Meanwhile, melt the butter over medium heat in a 6-quart Dutch oven and sauté your onions, green onions, and bell pepper until they turn tender and transparent.

Now add the tomatoes and cook them until they soften completely (which should take you about 5 minutes). Then put in the corn, the chicken stock, and the light cream and stir everything together well. At this point, cook the mixture *covered* over medium-low heat for about 20 minutes, stirring occasionally to keep the corn from sticking to the bottom of the pot.

At this point, add your crawfish tails, the vegetable seasoning, the salt, and the peppers and stir everything really well. Then cover the pot again and simmer for about 10 to 15 minutes more so that the flavor of the crawfish and the corn blend uniformly.

When you're ready to eat, serve the maque choux piping hot over steamed rice.

Chef's Note: *Maque choux should be spicy, so I suggest you add an extra touch of cayenne to liven it up! Oh—if corn on the cob is not available, you can substitute 2 cans of whole-kernel niblets and 1 can of creamed corn for the 10 fresh ears. But in all honesty, it's not the same!*

Crawfish Etouffée

There are as many recipes for crawfish étouffée as there are Cajun communities in South Louisiana. But this is mine ... you'll find it rich in flavor, robust in consistency, tantalizing to the taste buds, and—most of all!—very easy to make. So when crawfish season arrives ... try it!

1 stick butter
1 cup finely chopped onions
½ cup finely chopped celery
½ cup finely chopped bell pepper
2 cups crawfish stock (or chicken stock)
4 tbsp. tomato sauce
3 cloves garlic, minced

2 lb. peeled crawfish tails with fat
1 cup finely chopped green onion tops
¼ cup finely chopped parsley
½ tsp. cayenne pepper
1 tsp. Frank Davis Seafood Seasoning
3 tbsp. gravy flour in ½ cup water

First, take a 12-inch skillet and melt the butter until it begins to foam. Then toss in the onions, celery, and bell pepper and sauté them *over medium heat* until they turn clear (about 4 to 5 minutes).

Now at this point, if you were successful in extracting the fat from the crawfish, stir it into the butter-vegetable mixture and cook everything *on low* for about 20 minutes. If you didn't get enough fat, don't worry about it. Go ahead and add your crawfish (or chicken) stock, your tomato sauce, and your garlic and let it simmer for about 20 minutes.

About 15 minutes before you're ready to eat, stir in the crawfish tails, half the onion tops, half the parsley, the cayenne pepper, and the seafood seasoning and let the étouffée *simmer* so that all the flavors come together. This is an important part of the étouffée process—you shouldn't skip it!

After 15 minutes, turn the fire up to medium high and stir in the gravy flour mixture to the consistency you desire *(which should be nothing more than a light sauce—only thick enough to coat a spoon)*. At this point, you should also readjust your seasonings: a little salt, more cayenne, maybe a touch of black pepper. Remember, a true étouffée is "yellow-rose colored," not red!

Finally, reheat the mixture, liberally ladle it over steamed rice, garnish it with fresh parsley and onion tops, and serve it piping hot with butter-toasted French bread!

This is one of the most time-consuming recipes you will ever make … but, believe me, every second you spend on the preparation is worth it! The rich tomato-flavored gravy, the succulence of the crawfish stuffing, the perfect blend of real New Orleans herbs and spices … there's nothing like it!

The Stuffing:

2 sticks margarine	1 cup reduced crawfish stock*
4 tbsp. all-purpose flour	Fresh bread crumbs from 6 slices
2 cups finely chopped onions	bread
1 cup finely chopped celery	2 tbsp. paprika
1 cup finely chopped bell pepper	Salt and cayenne pepper to taste
¼ cup thinly sliced green onions	4 eggs, well beaten
2 lb. crawfish tails and fat	60 crawfish heads, cleaned
6 cloves garlic, minced	2 cups toasted bread crumbs

Start off by taking a 12-inch heavy aluminum skillet, melting the margarine over medium-high heat, stirring in the flour, and making a peanut-butter-colored roux. Then drop in the onions, celery, bell pepper, and green onions and sauté them in the hot roux until all the vegetables soften. Now set the mixture aside and allow it to cool slightly.

Meanwhile, with a chef's knife, finely chop the crawfish tails *(do not use a food processor or they will turn to paste)*.

Then, stir into the roux base the garlic, the chopped tails, and the crawfish stock and blend everything well. At this point, put the skillet back on the fire and simmer the mixture for about 5 minutes or until thoroughly blended.

Next, remove the pan from the fire once more and begin folding in the fresh bread crumbs. You want to use enough to make the mix *semistiff*—not wet and not pasty. Then stir in the paprika, sprinkle on the salt and cayenne to taste, and whip in the eggs to bind the stuffing mixture together.

Finally, using a teaspoon (or your fingers), heap the mixture into the cleaned crawfish heads, almost to the point of overstuffing them. Then gently roll the heads in toasted bread crumbs, place them on a baking sheet, slide the sheet into a 350-degree oven, and bake them for 30 minutes.

When they've cooked for the allotted time, set them aside and begin making your bisque (gravy).

The Bisque (Gravy):

2 sticks margarine
¼ cup all-purpose flour
1 cup finely chopped onions
½ cup finely chopped celery
½ cup finely chopped bell pepper
4 cloves garlic, finely minced
2 cups tomato sauce
1 16-oz. can whole tomatoes, chopped
4 cups reduced crawfish stock*
2 tbsp. paprika

1 tbsp. granulated sugar
1 lemon, thinly sliced
2 bay leaves
2 tbsp. Worcestershire sauce
2 lb. coarsely chopped crawfish tails and fat
Salt, black, and cayenne pepper to taste
6 cups cooked rice
¼ cup thinly sliced green onions
¼ cup finely chopped parsley

Take a 5-quart heavy aluminum Dutch oven, drop in *one stick* of the margarine, melt it over medium-high heat, stir in the flour, and make a rich peanut-butter-colored roux. Then when the roux is ready, remove it from the pot and set it aside in a bowl to cool.

Now, in the same Dutch oven, melt the second stick of margarine over high heat and sauté the onions, celery, bell pepper, and garlic *(watch that the garlic doesn't burn or it will taste bitter!)*. When the vegetables soften, pour in the tomato sauce, the whole tomatoes, and the crawfish stock.

At this point, bring the mixture to a *slow bubble,* blend everything together thoroughly, cover the pot, and cook for about 20 minutes, stirring occasionally.

Next, add the paprika, sugar, lemon slices, bay leaves, and Worcestershire sauce, mix in the roux you made earlier—*along with the crawfish heads you stuffed*—cover the pot again, and simmer everything gently for about 2 hours or so, stirring occasionally but watching that you don't knock the stuffing out of the heads.

Then when the bisque has cooked for the allotted time, drop in the remaining chopped crawfish tails and fat, stir them into the mixture completely, season to taste with salt, black and cayenne pepper, and simmer once more for about 15 minutes.

When you're ready to eat, ladle the bisque over steamed, hot-buttered rice, garnish it with sliced green onions and chopped parsley, and serve it alongside a crisp tossed salad topped with vinaigrette dressing.

Chef's Note: *To make fresh bread crumbs, just drop sliced bread into your food processor and* whip at high speed *until the slices crumble. Fresh bread crumbs keep* the stuffing light; toasted bread crumbs tend to produce a pasty stuffing.

To intensify the flavor of the bisque and the stuffed heads, liberally substitute Frank Davis Seafood Seasoning *to taste instead of using salt, black pepper, and cayenne.*

*If you don't have crawfish fat to put in the dish, just substitute ½ stick of butter in its place. If you don't have reduced crawfish stock on hand, just substitute an equal amount of chicken stock instead. You gotta be versatile!

Caution: *Be extra careful when adding hot roux to liquids and vice versa! It could splatter and cause severe burns. Best advice is to always let the roux cool down first.*

Crawfish on the Rocks

It's a soup! It's a stew! It's a sauce! It's a bisque! Makes no difference what you think it is—when you take a rich Cajun roux base, thicken it up with milk, cheese, and seafood seasonings, simmer it down with a couple pounds of plump crawfish tails, and serve it in a bowl over puff pastry, you got yo'sef a tasty helping of Crawfish on the Rocks!

¼ cup peanut oil
1 stick real butter
2 cups finely chopped onions
¾ cup finely chopped celery
½ cup finely chopped bell pepper
½ cup fresh chopped parsley
4 cloves garlic, finely minced
¼ cup finely sliced green onions
3 cups evaporated milk
½ cup Madeira wine

1 cup Campbell's Chicken Broth
1 lb. Philadelphia Cream Cheese,
   chunked
3 lb. crawfish tails and fat
1 tsp. salt
1 tsp. black pepper
½ tsp. granulated garlic
½ tsp. cayenne pepper
2 cans frozen Crescent Dinner Rolls

First, put the peanut oil and the butter in a heavy 12-inch skillet and melt it down over medium heat until it just begins to foam. Then stir in the onions, celery, bell pepper, parsley, garlic, and green onions and cook them for about 12 to 15 minutes until they soften completely. While the chopped vegetables are simmering, preheat your oven to 350 degrees.

When the vegetables are ready, pour in the evaporated milk, Madeira wine, and chicken broth, mix them together thoroughly, and bring the mixture to a slow boil. Then drop in the cream cheese chunks and, with the heat still set at medium, stir until the cheese melts and the sauce turns smooth and silky. For the most part, this should take you about 5 minutes.

At this point, fold the crawfish tails into the hot sauce in the skillet, stir everything together thoroughly, and cook the mixture for 3 minutes. When uniformly blended, sprinkle on and stir in the salt, black pepper, granulated garlic, and cayenne. Then take the pan off the fire and allow the mixture to cool slightly.

Actually, if you want to develop the maximum flavor in the seafood mix, I recommend that you make the dish one day, cover it and place it in the refrigerator overnight, and reheat it the next day just before you serve it. Just be careful not to recook it—you don't want the crawfish tails to turn into rubber bands! Truthfully, though, this is so good that'll probably never happen.

Then 14 minutes before you're ready to eat, unroll the dinner rolls into triangles. And with a chef's knife, cut out ½-inch squares. Then bake the squares for about 12 to 14 minutes in the oven. These are your "rocks" and you want them to puff and turn a rich, toasty-brown color.

When you're ready to eat, drop the "rocks" into a soupbowl, generously ladle the crawfish over the top, and serve piping hot alongside a cold salad made with sliced tomatoes, avocado chunks, chopped onions, artichoke hearts, hearts of palm, and a dressing made from the artichoke marinade.

This dish can be served family style as an everyday meal or as the entrée for the most elegant, sophisticated dinner party.

Chef's Note:

1—If you want to make the mixture kinda spicy, instead of using just the Philadelphia Cream Cheese and the cayenne, you can drop in a couple of tablespoons of jalapeño peppers.

2—If you want to enhance the overall seafood flavor in the crawfish, instead of using salt, black pepper, cayenne, and granulated garlic, substitute 2 teaspoons of my Frank Davis Seafood Seasoning. If it is not available where you shop, you can order it by direct mail by calling 1-800-742-4231.

3—If the end product thickens too much to spoon over the puff pastry, simply add a little more chicken stock and Madeira wine mixed half and half. Ideally, you want it the consistency of a medium stew!

4—Finally, experiment with different mixtures. In addition to crawfish tails, make the basic sauce and substitute shrimp, crabmeat, broiled oysters, Italian sausage and mozzarella, smoked turkey, chopped chicken or ham and bacon. The variations you can come up with are endless.

In Cajun and Creole country, loggerhead and common snapping turtles are referred to as "cowan" (pronounced cow-whan). And cowan has always been a traditional New Orleans Easter dish. So if you want a good-tasting, full-bodied, rich traditional soup this Easter, you got to fix this recipe for cowan.

3 qt. water	2 cups beef broth
1 lb. lean ground pork	1 tbsp. finely chopped parsley
3 lb. snapping-turtle meat (cowan)	1 tbsp. salt
⅓ cup Crisco oil	1 tsp. black pepper
½ cup all-purpose flour	¼ tsp. oregano
3 cups finely chopped onions	3 bay leaves
1 cup finely chopped bell peppers	⅛ tsp. ground thyme
1 cup finely chopped celery	½ oz. golden sherry per serving
3 cloves garlic, minced	6 hard-boiled eggs, finely chopped
1 can diced Rotel tomatoes with chilies	½ cup minced green onions

First, take a heavy aluminum 5-quart Dutch oven, bring the 3 quarts of water to a boil, and cook the pork and the turtle meat for about an hour at a "slow bubble" until it becomes tender. (Be sure you skim the pot as the meat boils—if you don't remove the "scum" that rises to the surface, your turtle will taste strong and gamey.)

When the meat is cooked, remove it from the pot with a slotted spoon and let it cool on a cutting board. *Then save the water you boiled the pork and turtle in—this is the base for your soup.*

At this point, take the same Dutch oven, heat the Crisco oil, stir in the flour, and make a dark-brown roux. Then take the pot off the fire, stir in the onions, bell peppers, celery, and garlic, and cook them into the roux until the temperature of the roux cools down considerably. (Never add liquid to a piping-hot roux—it practically explodes!)

Now pour in the Rotel tomatoes, the beef broth, and exactly half of the water you cooked the pork and turtle in. Then stir in the chopped parsley, salt, black pepper, oregano, bay leaves, and thyme, put the lid on the pot, put the pot on a low fire, and "simmer" the mixture for about an hour or so. *Don't skimp on this step—it's what develops the full flavor of your turtle soup.*

I suggest you check the cooking process from time to time and stir the pot occasionally. If the soupbase thickens too much, say, it gets thicker than whipping cream, stir in more of the turtle water.

Meanwhile, take a sharp chef's knife and dice the turtle meat into small pieces—half-inch cubes are ideal. Then drop the turtle meat into the pot, pour in the remaining turtle stock, and continue to cook—*covered*—over a low flame for another 30 to 40 minutes, stirring occasionally.

When you're ready to eat, ladle the soup into individual bowls, add about a half-ounce of sherry to each serving, and garnish with the chopped eggs and minced green onions. A big stack of buttered saltine crackers on the side, along with a glass of the chilled sherry, tops off the meal nicely.

Chef's Note:

1—Just as a small amount of pork added to beef in a rich Italian gravy brings out the best flavor, a small amount of pork added to turtle soups and stews also piques their flavor.

2—Of course, if you're Catholic and you plan to serve your cowan on Good Friday, leave out the ground pork and the beef broth to make it a meatless meal. Turtle is technically classified as a "seafood," which makes it a good Lenten substitute.

Crispy Fried N'Awlins Oyster Po' Boys

Piled high on a piping-hot, French-bread pistolette and dressed with shredded lettuce, sliced tomatoes, melted butter, creamy mayonnaise, dill-pickle chips, a splash of ketchup, and a sprinkle of fresh lemon juice … these oysters are some of the best you'll ever eat! All you gotta do is just follow the recipe and they'll come out perfect.

2 cups cornmeal	1 tsp. cayenne pepper
1 cup corn flour (fish fry)	6 doz. fresh-shucked unwashed
½ cup cornstarch or all-purpose	oysters
flour	1 qt. cultured buttermilk
1 tsp. granulated onion	Few dashes Tabasco sauce
½ tsp. granulated garlic	Peanut oil for deep frying
2 tsp. salt	6 French-bread pistolettes
1 tsp. black pepper	

First, take a large bowl and mix together all the dry ingredients—*but mix them together thoroughly.* This is your batter coating mix, so it has to be perfectly blended if your oysters are going to come out crispy and seasoned right.

Next, strain the water from the oysters and pick through them to remove any shell fragments that might have dropped in during shucking. Then place the oysters into a stainless-steel pan, pour the quart of buttermilk over them, and splash on a few dashes of Tabasco. At this point, cover the pan with a sheet of heavy-duty aluminum foil and refrigerate the oysters for at least 3 hours (if you want them the ultimate best that they can be … *refrigerate them overnight!*).

Next, take a heavy aluminum or cast-iron deep fryer, place it on the burner over medium-high heat, and get it hot. Then pour in enough peanut oil to completely cover the oysters when they're frying—remember, you're *deep frying,* so go ahead and add the extra oil.

Keep in mind that to get crispy crunchy oysters, the frying temperature must be *exactly 350 degrees*. But because the temperature is going to drop when you add cold oysters to the hot oil, I suggest you don't begin deep frying until the temperature climbs to almost *375* degrees. That way, it will stabilize at about 350 when the oysters have been added.

One other point: unless you fry all the time on the same stove, in the same pot, and you're familiar with the frying temperature you get at that one particular setting, a deep-fry thermometer is the only way to ensure that you're at the proper temperature.

When you're ready to cook, drain off the buttermilk in a colander, take about two dozen oysters, and toss them around thoroughly in the cornmeal mixture, taking care to completely coat each oyster. Now remove them from the dry mix and let them set in a plate on the countertop *for exactly 1 minute*—this is very important if (1) you want the coating to bind to the oyster and not fall off in the oil, and (2) if you want the oysters to come out crispy and crunchy.

Now drop them into the hot oil ... *one at a time!* Under no circumstances should you attempt to fry more than a dozen oysters at a time! If you put too many into the oil at once, the temperature will drop below 350, the frying action will stop, the cornmeal will soak up the oil like a sponge, and you'll end up with soggy oysters.

Incidentally, while they're frying, gently move the oysters around with a slotted spoon, and fry them for only about 2 to 3 minutes or until they turn a rich golden brown.

When they're cooked remove them from the deep fryer with the slotted spoon and drain them on several layers of paper towels. Then proceed with the next dozen until they're all done!

All that's left is to slice open a hot French-bread pistolette, dress it with butter, mayonnaise, ketchup, pickle chips, lettuce and tomato, and pile on the oysters—*piping hot right out of the fryer!* An extra dash or two of Crystal Hot Sauce and a squeeze from a fresh lemon wedge ... and you got one of the best oyster po' boys you ever had!

Oh—deep-fried tater tots make a great complementary finger snack to chomp on during bites!

Chef's Note: *Do not cover the oysters after they're fried! Don't use a dish, pot lid, aluminum foil, paper towels, or anything else in an attempt to keep the oysters hot. You should eat fried oysters as soon as they are cooked. Trying to keep them hot by covering them only traps internal steam and results in soggy oysters. Leave 'em uncovered—and keep 'em crisp!*

The cornmeal frying mixture that I use in this recipe is available prepackaged as Frank Davis Gourmet Fish Fry. *To order it direct, simply call 1-800-742-4231.*

Old-Tyme Oyster Pudding

More light and fluffy than an oyster dressing, this "puddin" accentuates and completes any holiday meal you prepare and goes with almost anything you decide to cook. And this year it's a perfect match for your Cajun Deep-Fried Breast of Turkey!

½ stick sweetcream butter
2 cups finely chopped onions
1 cup finely chopped celery
2 tbsp. finely chopped parsley
½ cup finely chopped bell pepper
4 cloves garlic, finely minced
1 cup sliced mushrooms
¼ cup thinly sliced green onion tops
6 doz. chopped oysters plus liquor

8 oz. pasteurized clam juice
½ cup whole milk
1 tsp. poultry seasoning
2 tsp. salt
1 tsp. black pepper
6-8 cups unseasoned French-bread stuffing
2 whole eggs, slightly beaten

In a large, black, iron Dutch oven, melt the butter over medium heat and sauté the onions, celery, parsley, bell pepper, garlic, mushrooms, and green onion tops until all of them are tender. The one thing to remember is to keep the butter hot but don't let it burn. Keep stirring the mixture to cook it uniformly.

Next, gradually stir in the chopped oysters (but keep the oyster liquor on the side). Notice I said *gradually stir in the oysters.* The reason for this is that you do not want to reduce the heat, since lowering the heat will cause excessive water to be released from the oysters and you'll have to add too much bread stuffing to the finished dish.

Cook the oysters gently for about 4 minutes, stirring all the while. Then when the ingredients are well mixed, stir in the clam juice, whole milk, poultry seasoning, salt, and pepper. About the salt—check your oysters to see if they are naturally salty before adding the prescribed amount. You may have to reduce the salt if nature has provided her own. At this point you should begin tasting the mixture and making whatever seasoning adjustments are necessary.

Now cover the pot, lower the heat, and simmer for about 5 minutes to allow time for the flavors to blend thoroughly.

After the simmering process is done, remove the pot from the fire and begin stirring in the bread stuffing a little at a time. Note that you do not have to add all of it. If you want your pudding moist, stop adding stuffing crumbs when you get to the texture you desire. If you want a drier pudding, add all 6 cups—even more if your taste and needs dictate.

When the pudding is ready (it should be the consistency of soggy bread floating in milk), rapidly stir in the eggs to tie everything together. Then cover it for a few minutes to let it *"set up."* This is where the body comes in—it's how the final blending brings out full flavor. Oh—and you can make final seasoning adjustments at this point by moistening the dish with the oyster liquor you saved (or a little more bottled clam juice).

All that's left now is to pour out the pudding into a large buttered Pyrex baking pan, lightly sprinkle the top with a handful of coarsely grated bread crumbs, drizzle with a little extra melted butter, and bake it—*uncovered*—about 45 to 50 minutes in a 350-degree oven until browned and set, yet light and fluffy.

Happy Thanksgiving!

Chef's Note:

1—I suggest that when you buy your clam juice you pick up an extra bottle or two. If for some reason your pudding begins to dry out during baking, you can moisten it again by simply pouring on a little more clam juice and fluffing it up with a fork.

2—Ideally, you got the consistency of the finished dish "just right" when you can spoon it out onto a dinner plate and have it look just like an oyster-flavored bread custard.

Spicy Cajun Boiled Lobsters

Order a lobster in a restaurant and it usually comes to your table steamed, split, broiled, then topped with lemon-butter sauce. But when it comes to doing this critter at home, there's nothing any better than a big ol' lobster boiled in a spicy stock. Here's everything you'll ever need to know about cooking them up "family style."

2 large onions, coarsely chopped	3 heads garlic, halved
2 cups coarsely chopped celery	4-6 whole Maine lobsters
6 oz. liquid crabboil	1 lb. butter, melted
6 lemons, quartered	Juice of 2 lemons
⅔ box salt	1 tsp. garlic powder
6 bay leaves	2 tbsp. seafood seasoning

First, fill a stockpot with enough water to completely cover the lobsters you're going to cook. Then bring it to a rapid boil.

Now add the onions, celery, liquid crabboil, lemons, salt, bay leaves, and garlic. The water will stop boiling; but when it comes back to a rapid roll, cook the vegetable seasonings for at least 20 minutes to develop a rich flavored stock. If you want to add a little "lagniappe" (like corn on the cob or small red potatoes), drop those in right at the moment the water begins to boil, time them for about 14 to 16 minutes, then remove them from the pot.

When your lagniappe is ready, very gently drop in the lobsters—I recommend you submerge them claws and head first. Immediately, the water will stop boiling. When it comes back to a boil, that's when you begin timing the lobsters at ... *8 minutes to the pound.*

While they're boiling, make your lemon-butter-garlic sauce by heating the melted butter and thoroughly stirring into it the lemon juice, garlic powder, and seafood seasoning. Then when your lobsters are done, serve them right away and start dipping!

It's all just that simple!

Chef's Note:

1—The best-tasting lobsters average 1¼ to 1½ pounds. These are the younger ones and are usually succulent and tender. These are also the ones you usually find when you shop for lobsters at the store. By the way, it takes 7 years for a lobster to reach a pound in weight!

2—If you prefer to have your lobsters "extra spicy," boil them only 5 minutes *to the pound. Then remove the pot from the burner and allow the lobsters to "soak" in the hot stock for another 20 minutes.*

3—If you'd like to serve your lobsters broiled or grilled, first parboil *them for about 5 minutes. Then take them from the pot, drain them for a few minutes, split them lengthwise (you'll need a meat saw for this!), and finish cooking them on the grill or under the broiler for another 8 to 10 minutes. If you're going to broil or grill, the lemon-butter-garlic sauce should be put on the lobsters at the very beginning of the grilling/broiling process. To grill, put the lobster shell heat-side down with the meat away from the flame; to broil, put the lobster* meat *directly under the broiler element with the shell away from the heat source.*

4—If you'd rather steam your lobsters, place them in a steamer pot containing plain water and the juice of 3 to 4 lemons. Then cook them 10 minutes *to the pound. When they're done, serve them the same way you serve Spicy Cajun Boiled Lobsters.*

5—No ... you can't *microwave a lobster! It explodes!*

6—You cannot *freeze whole lobsters! But you can freeze lobster meat! Simply cook them the way I've described in this recipe and pick out all the meat. Then place the meat in a Ziploc bag, cover it with water, and freeze it for up to 6 months.*

7—All lobsters should be cooked "live." Like their cousins the crawfish, dead ones should be returned to the store or discarded.

8—Live *lobsters can be kept in the refrigerator for 2 days. The best method of storage is to wrap them in a wet dish towel and place them in the hydrator pan (the vegetable pan of your fridge). Never place them in water—they'll die! And don't pack them in ice—they get tough and lose their delicate flavor.*

9—Cooked *lobster—whole or picked meat—will keep in your refrigerator for 3 to 4 days. Here's a hint: if you want to plan a lobster dinner party but don't want to spend "party time" in the kitchen cooking them from scratch, boil them ahead of time and store them in the refrigerator. Then when you're ready to serve them, drop them into plain boiling water for a minute or two just to heat them up. No one will ever know the difference!*

HOW TO EAT SPICY CAJUN BOILED LOBSTERS

A lobster should always be eaten right away while it's still piping hot! First, remove the head from the tail (just like crawfish). Then separate the head shell from the gill and leg portion (you know how you do when you get ready to scoop the fat out of a crawfish head?).

The lobster fat is called "tamale." But unlike crawfish fat it has a greenish rather than yellowish tint. Forget about the color—it's delicious!

Now with a sharp paring knife, split open the cartilage underside of the lobster tail from the top to the bottom. Then grab hold of the tail meat with your hand and pull it out of the shell. It should all come out in one piece! Now take the knife and slice the tail meat crosswise into bite-size pieces—these are your "medallions."

Next, remove the pinchers, crack them open, and take out all the meat—there's a lot in there! And remember, there are three sections in a lobster claw—each one is loaded with meat.

And that's all there is to it! The only thing left is to dip the meat in lemon-butter sauce and pig out!

Okay, okay! I'll tell ya! One more thing! If you like to pick through the shells, there are small pieces of highly flavorful meat located just above the legs in the head. And in a large lobster, some of the sweetest, best-tasting meat is in the leg shells.

But you probably won't want to mess with that, right?

Seafood Muffalettas

So, okay! It's not traditionally *Italian!* But it's as traditionally *Southern* as you're gonna get—fish, shrimp, oysters, and crawfish, all prepared a different way, yet combined with a hint of Italy on a muffaletta bun! Try it!

4 catfish fillets	1 cup Frank Davis Fish Fry
2 lb. fresh shrimp	2 muffaletta breads
1 lb. peeled crawfish tails	¼ cup extra-virgin olive oil
1 pt. fresh oysters	½ lb. provolone cheese
2 cups vegetable oil	1 cup Italian olive salad mix
2 tbsp. bronzing mix	2 tomatoes, thinly sliced
2 tbsp. margarine	2 cups shredded lettuce
1 cup seasoned flour	

First, cut the catfish fillets lengthwise into about half-inch-thick slices. Then sprinkle them liberally with 1 tablespoon bronzing mix, drop them into a hot Teflon-coated skillet dotted with a little margarine, and bronze them on both sides until toasty brown.

Next, peel and devein the shrimp and cut them lengthwise into right and left halves. Then lay them out side by side on a pizza pan, sprinkle them generously with the rest of the bronzing mix, and place them under the broiler until done (they should take about 3-5 minutes to cook). When they're done, set them (and the fish fillets) on a platter and hold them in a warm oven.

Now take a deep fryer or a heavy aluminum Dutch oven and heat the vegetable oil to 375 degrees. While the oil is coming up to temperature, coat the crawfish tails with the seasoned flour and coat the oysters with the fish fry. Then deep fry the crawfish and the oysters—separately—until they are golden brown and crunchy.

At this point, you're ready to make your muffalettas!

First, with a sharp knife split the breads crosswise, liberally brush the olive oil on the top pieces, and place a single layer of the provolone cheese on each piece. Then slide the bread into the oven under the broiler and melt the cheese thoroughly (but do not let it burn!).

While the cheese is melting, take the bottom pieces of the breads, lightly (but evenly!) spread on some of the olive mix, and begin layering on the seafood … fish first, then shrimp, then oysters, then crawfish. Oh, just make a couple of good sandwiches—it's not necessary to overstuff them.

Now drop on a few of the tomato slices and sprinkle on some of the lettuce (it's best if you shred it thinly). Then remove from the oven the bread tops with the melted cheese on them and put the muffalettas together.

All that's left is to slice the "muffs" into quarters and serve them piping hot. I prefer to put both sandwiches back into the oven for about 3 minutes to crisp them up.

Chef's Note: *If you don't have any bronzing mix available, just sprinkle the fish and shrimp lightly with salt, black pepper, cayenne pepper, onion powder, garlic powder, crushed sweet basil, thyme, and paprika. Or you can order it already prepared and blended by calling 1-800-742-4231.*

CHAPTER 7

Beans and Vegetables

Lentils and Italian Sausage

This dish is not only traditionally served in Italy on New Year's Day and is said to bring good luck … in the New Orleans Sicilian community it is usually one of the most popular ways to serve lentils because it's easy to fix and unbelievably rich and tasty! You're gonna like this!

2 lb. Italian sausages
2 cups dried lentils (about 1 lb.)
6 cups water
½ lb. pickled pork, diced
2 large tomatoes, peeled and finely diced

1 large onion, minced
3 cloves garlic, minced
2 whole bay leaves
2 tsp. salt
Freshly ground black pepper to taste

First, place the Italian sausages in a baking pan and add water to a half-inch deep in the bottom. Then, pierce each sausage link several times and place the links in a 350-degree preheated oven.

You want to bake the sausages until they lightly brown and the casings become tender (which should take about an hour to an hour and a half; and be sure you turn the links over once). When the sausages are done, drain off—*but save!*—the drippings, remove the links from the oven, let them cool, and slice them in 1-inch chunks. Then set them aside.

Next, wash your lentils well and pick through them to make sure you remove all the blackened peas and other foreign matter. Then place the lentils in a large saucepan or Dutch oven and add the water, pickled meat, tomatoes, onions, garlic, bay leaves, salt, and pepper.

At this point, bring the mixture to a boil and skim off the foam from the lentils as it surfaces. Then reduce the heat and simmer the mixture— *uncovered!*—for about 45 minutes to an hour, or until the lentils are soft. About halfway through the cooking time add the sliced Italian sausage to the lentils and gently stir in the pieces. This is where the flavor peaks!

Here's a hint: stir the lentils occasionally as they cook so that the bulk of the water evaporates. Remember, you want them creamy, not watery. *But* if the water evaporates too quickly, simply add a little of the sausage drippings you saved instead of extra water (you get a richer flavor that way).

When you're ready to eat, spoon the lentils liberally over thin egg noodles or fettucini (no! not rice!) and top it all generously with a sprinkling of grated Romano cheese! That's Italian!

Southern Butter Beans
with Hamhocks and Pickled Meat

Redfish topped with a creamed shrimp sauce, crawfish in a wine reduction over linguine, roasted wild ducks with an Amaretto glaze ... those are all great dishes. But you just can't eat them all the time—they're too rich! You can eat a big pot of creamy butter beans with braised spinach and a chunk of homemade corn bread all the time, though. 'Cuz that's everyday kinda eatin'! And here is that down-home recipe.

3 qt. water	1 lb. dried butter beans
1 lb. hickory-flavored smoked sausage	3 bay leaves
	⅛ tsp. ground thyme
1 lb. fresh raw hamhocks	½ cup extra-virgin olive oil
½ lb. pickled meat, cut in chunks	2 cans Campbell's Chicken Broth
1½ cups finely diced yellow onions	2 soup cans filled with water
⅔ cup finely diced celery	6 cups cooked buttered rice
2 medium ripe tomatoes, finely diced	

First, take a 5-quart Dutch oven or oval roaster and bring the 3 quarts of water to a rolling boil. Then drop in the smoked sausage, hamhocks, pickled meat, onions, celery, and tomatoes and boil them gently—*uncovered*—for about an hour (replacing the water a little at a time as it steams off and evaporates).

When the meats are done, remove the smoked sausage (and only the smoked sausage) and set it aside. Then drop in the butter beans, along with the bay leaves, the thyme, and half of the olive oil and stir everything together well.

At this point, cover the pot tightly, reduce the heat to medium low, and simmer the limas for about an hour (but be sure to stir the pot occasionally to make certain the beans aren't absorbing the water too quickly). If they are, simply replace the water with a can of chicken broth as necessary.

While the limas are simmering, preheat your oven to 350 degrees. Then when they are just about tender, yet still not fully cooked, remove them from the stovetop, pour in the second can of chicken broth if you need it, slide them into the oven (covered), and bake them for another 30 minutes or until they turn tender and creamy. *Yes,* you will have to check them every 10 minutes or so as they bake, and you may have to add a can or two of the water to the pot. *Hint:* the consistency should be *creamy* but not pasty thick—and don't thin them out with too much water.

About 10 minutes before you're ready to eat, when you stir the pot for the last time, stir in the rest of the olive oil and blend it into the beans thoroughly. All that's left is to spoon out the limas over hot buttered rice and serve them with a link or two of the smoked sausage.

This is home cookin' like yo' grandma usta make!

Chef's Note: *Like all good bean dishes, this one, too, is better the next day. Just put it in the refrigerator overnight and let it mellow; then reheat it and serve it as I've suggested* ... if you can wait that long!

For a complete N'Awlins meal, serve up these butter beans with some of my Pot-Braised Spinach and a big slab of my homemade Black Skillet Corn Bread!

Oh—I suggest you serve the hamhocks and pickled meat on separate saucers to anyone in your family who likes to "pick the bones." I mean, this could be the best part of the meal!

N'Awlins Baked Butter Beans with Ham and Stuff

Slightly sweet with barbecue flavor and lightly spicy with a true New Orleans touch, these butter beans will tempt the taste buds of the most discriminating connoisseur ... yet they're simple enough to be called real down-home cooking!

2 tbsp. bacon drippings	2 qt. chicken stock
1 lb. cooked ham, cut in chunks	2 tbsp. brown sugar
1 cup finely diced yellow onions	2 tbsp. Worcestershire sauce
½ cup finely diced celery	½ cup ketchup
1 small bell pepper, cut in rings	2 tsp. Louisiana hot sauce
1 lb. dried butter beans	2 tsp. sweet basil
½ lb. cooked pork sausage	½ cup thinly sliced green onions
½ cup cooked crumbled bacon	Salt and pepper to taste
4 bay leaves	2 tbsp. minced parsley
1 tbsp. finely minced garlic	

First, take a 5-quart Dutch oven or oval roaster and heat the bacon drippings to *high*. Then toss in the ham, the onions, the celery, and the bell pepper and sauté until the vegetables "wilt" and the ham begins to brown slightly.

Next, drop in the butter beans and—with the heat still on high—stir them into the seasoning mixture and cook them for about 3 minutes (or until the hulls begin to puff).

At this point, remove the pot from the fire and stir in the pork sausage, the crumbled bacon, the bay leaves, and the garlic, along with the 2 quarts of chicken stock (you can use stock you make yourself or substitute canned clear chicken broth). Take time to make sure all the ingredients are fully blended ... then cover the pot, place it into a 425-degree oven, and bake the beans for an hour and a half, stirring occasionally. *Important: if you notice the liquids reducing as the beans bake, gradually add more chicken stock or water to keep the liquids the same level as the beans.*

After the butter beans have cooked for the allotted time, take a mixing bowl and thoroughly blend together the brown sugar, Worcestershire sauce, ketchup, hot sauce, sweet basil, and green onions. Then remove the pot from the oven, slowly stir this mixture into the baking beans *(and stir it in thoroughly!)*, put the pot back into the oven, cover, and continue to bake for another 2 hours or until the liquids turn rich and creamy and the beans become soft and tender.

Five minutes before you're ready to eat, season the beans with salt and pepper to taste and stir in the parsley. Serve over buttered steamed rice, along with a big bowl of turnip greens, corn bread, and iced tea.

Chef's Note: *Yep! Like all good bean dishes, this one is better the next day. Just put it in the refrigerator overnight and let it mellow; then reheat it and serve it as I've suggested ...* if you can wait that long!

N'Awlins Red Beans and Rice

This is one of New Orleans' most controversial recipes! 'Cuz everybody cooks beans! In fact, there are probably as many recipes for red beans and rice as there are Mardi Gras krewes. And don't you know that, strangely enough, most of those recipes produce a fine-tasting pot of beans. So don't throw away your recipe. Just add mine to your collection.

1 lb. red beans	¼ cup finely chopped celery
10 cups water	2 cloves fresh garlic, minced
Pinch baking soda	3 tbsp. finely chopped fresh parsley
2 tbsp. olive oil	2 bay leaves
1 cup julienned tasso	1 tsp. thyme
1 lb. country smoked sausage, sliced	1 tsp. basil
1 hamhock	2 tsp. Louisiana hot sauce
1 large onion, diced	8 cups water + 2 cups water
	Salt to taste

First, rinse the beans well, sort through them, and toss out any broken or blackened beans. Then soak them overnight in 10 cups of water to which you add a pinch of baking soda. Soaking will expand the beans, tenderize the hulls, and make them cook up exceptionally creamy!

Then, when you're ready to cook, take a heavy cast-iron or aluminum Dutch oven, heat up the olive oil, and begin sautéing the seasoning meats. When the meats begin to brown slightly, toss in the onion, celery, garlic, and parsley and cook them until tender (about 2 or 3 minutes).

At this point, drain the beans from the soaking water and add them to the sautéed ingredients. *Stir them around … but do it gently so you don't bruise the beans!* Now cook for about 3 minutes, allowing the steam to expand the beans further.

Next add the bay leaves, thyme, basil, and Louisiana hot sauce *plus* the water and salt to taste and stir everything together well. Go ahead and turn the fire to high and bring the water to a boil … but as soon as it boils, place a heat diffuser under the pot, reduce the flame to "simmer," and cook slowly for about 2 hours—stirring occasionally—or until the beans are soft and creamy.

Most New Orleanians cook and eat their red beans on Monday. But in all honesty, they're much better after they have been in the refrigerator overnight!

Chef's Note:

1—To make your beans even creamier, mash up about a quarter-cup of the beans after they're cooked and stir them back into the pot. Or … add 2 tablespoons of extra-virgin olive oil to the beans and blend it in well until smooth.

2—A heat diffuser prevents the beans from scorching, and nothing is as bad as a pot of scorched beans! So if you don't have one, it may be a good investment if you cook a lot of beans.

3—The only traditional way to serve New Orleans red beans is over fluffy steamed rice with buttered French bread and a tossed green salad with French dressing.

FRANK'S TIPS FOR COOKING N'AWLINS RED BEANS

1—Soak your beans overnight in 10 cups of water to which you've added a pinch of baking soda. This will tenderize the hulls.

2—Pan-sauté your seasoning meats with the onions, celery, garlic, and parsley. Use either olive oil or a good grade of vegetable oil. Never add uncooked seasonings to the beans.

3—Always cook beans in a *heavy* Dutch oven (cast iron or heavy club aluminum is best). Thin metal will form hot spots and cause the beans to burn.

4—To each pound of beans, use 8 cups of water and have 2 additional cups you can add to compensate for evaporation while the beans are cooking. Never use more than 10 cups of water per pound of beans!

5—Cook beans slowly—at a simmer—so they turn creamy and don't burn.

6—Always use a heat diffuser under your pot of beans.

7—All beans freeze well. Store frozen beans in an airtight container. When reheating, always heat up slowly to keep them from burning on the bottom of the pot.

8—Remember ... beans are always better the next day!

Note: Use these cooking instructions not only for red beans, but for all kinds of dried beans—pintos, limas, black beans, great northerns, navy peas, blackeyes, field peas, lentils.

FRANK'S RICE TIPS

In an 8-quart stockpot, bring a gallon of salted water to a rapid boil. Then gradually stir in up to 4 cups of long-grain Louisiana rice and boil gently for 14 minutes. Next, rinse well in a colander and place over a steaming pot of water for 5 minutes. It will serve up grain for grain!

1—Never cook just 1 cup of rice. Cook at least 4 cups and keep it on hand all the time.

2—Rice freezes exceptionally well. Just rinse, drain, and store in Ziploc bags.

3—To use frozen rice, either place in a colander and run hot water over it, or dip in rapidly boiling water for a minute or two. Tastes like just cooked!

How to Make Frank's
Italian Creamed Green Beans

Take 2 cans of Del Monte or Allen brand Italian Cut Green Beans and drain them. Then place them in a buttered Pyrex baking dish.

Then, in a food processor, drop in an 8-ounce package of Philadelphia Cream Cheese and just enough whole milk to give it the consistency of melted ice cream. Blend the mix together thoroughly; then add ½ cup of grated Parmesan cheese and ¼ cup of extra-virgin olive oil and blend it again.

Next, pour the mixture into a bowl and stir in about ½ cup of julienned prosciutto ham. When everything is well mixed, season with either salt and black pepper to taste or sprinkle on a little premixed vegetable seasoning.

At this point, take about a cup of Italian bread crumbs and toss them with about 2 tablespoons of extra-virgin olive oil.

Now pour the cream cheese sauce over the green beans and toss everything together. Then sprinkle the bread crumbs evenly on top of the beans, place the Pyrex casserole dish in a preheated 400-degree oven, and bake *uncovered* for about 20 minutes or until the crumbs toast and brown.

All that's left is to serve 'em piping hot.

Vegetable Bundles with Lemon-Butter Sauce

If you love vegetables, these are some of the tastiest vegetables you'll ever eat … and they're good not only for special occasions, they're good every day of the week, all year long. Fix up a batch with your next meal!

1 cup fresh julienned carrots	**1 stick real butter**
1 cup fresh julienned zucchini	**1 tbsp. all-purpose flour**
1 cup fresh split green beans	**¼ cup evaporated milk**
1 cup fresh julienned broccoli stems	**1 lemon, zested, juiced, and seeded**
1 bunch green onions	**Salt and white pepper to taste**

Preparing this dish may be slightly tedious, but it's really very simple. All you do is take a few of each of the julienned vegetables and lay them out in a little "bundle." Then, strip a green onion with a knife lengthwise, wrap it around the vegetable bundle, and tie it together with an overhand knot—just as if it were a piece of string.

Then place the individual bundles in a vegetable steamer and cook them until they begin to soften. *But don't overcook* 'em—they should be *tender-crisp* (cooked but crunchy).

While the bundles are steaming, take a 9-inch skillet or shallow saucepan and melt the butter. Then stir in the flour and cook it over medium-low heat for about 3 minutes. When the roux is smooth and silky (it doesn't have to brown), stir in the evaporated milk, the lemon zest, and the lemon juice and bring it to a "roll"—*but watch that it doesn't burn!*

Then season the sauce with salt and pepper and cook it (stirring constantly) for another 3 minutes so that the flavors come together and the sauce thickens slightly.

When your vegetables are ready, take them from the steamer and lay them side by side (or stand them up) in a buttered baking pan. Then pour the lemon-butter sauce over each one and slip them into a 350-degree preheated oven for 10 to 12 minutes or until they're piping hot.

Chef's Note: *Feel free to change the basic sauce any way you want to. You can accentuate it with white wine, brandy, shrimp butter, bacon drippings, Grey Poupon mustard, etc. Go ahead—dare to be daring!*

You can substitute Frank Davis Vegetable Seasoning for the salt and white pepper for a more enhanced vegetable flavor. If you can't find it in the stores where you shop, you can order it direct by calling 1-800-742-4231.

Julienned Carrots in a Brown Butter Sauce

The only thing I can say about this recipe is … you can't really say anything about it! It's one of those dishes you just gotta taste! What an innovative way to eat carrots!

¾ stick salted butter
6 fresh carrots, julienned
2 tbsp. dry white wine
Salt and pepper to taste

2 tsp. sweet basil or vegetable
  seasoning
Pinch garlic powder

In a 12-inch skillet, melt the butter over high heat until it just begins to brown. But watch this carefully! Butter has a way of browning rapidly once it starts, and if you don't watch it closely it'll burn before you know it. Remember, you want to make *browned* butter … not *burned* butter.

When the butter starts browning, add the carrots and stir them until each julienne strip is fully coated with the butter. Then reduce the heat to medium and cover the pan. At this point, you want to "sweat" the strips until the beta carotene begins to come out. This is the basis for the sauce. At this point, you can forget about burning! They'll caramelize (turn toasty) maybe, but no longer will the milk solids in the butter burn.

When the carrots begin to "limp," add the wine, the salt and pepper, the sweet basil or vegetable seasoning, and the garlic powder. Then cover the pan once again and simmer the carrots gently until they turn tender-crispy (which should take about 5 minutes more).

While they can be reheated for serving later, they are at their absolute best when eaten right from the skillet!

Tempting Turnip Greens

This, y'all, is gourmet turnip greens. Even if you hate turnip greens … you're gonna love this recipe! Try it!

2 lb. chopped frozen turnip greens
½ cup chicken stock
¾ cup crumbled cooked bacon
1 cup diced ham
1 cup finely diced onions

1 tsp. Frank Davis Vegetable
 Seasoning
½ cup N'Awlins Bacon Butter (see
 index)

First, thoroughly defrost the turnip greens and set the leaves in a colander to drain.

Then, in a 5-quart Dutch oven, bring the chicken stock, the crumbled bacon, the ham, and the diced onions to a boil and cook for about 5 minutes—stirring constantly.

When the onions in the Dutch oven have wilted and turned clear, drop in the turnip greens, stir them into the onion and ham mixture, put the lid on the pot, and cook them over high heat *for 3 minutes,* stirring occasionally. Then reduce the heat to *low* and simmer them for about 15 minutes until they turn tender.

When the leaves are cooked, immediately place them into a colander and squeeze out as much of the steaming liquids as possible—*this will get rid of the bitter, tart taste that most people dislike about turnip greens.*

Finally, transfer the greens, the diced onions, and all the seasoning meats to a casserole dish, sprinkle on the vegetable seasoning, fold in the Bacon Butter, and "toss" everything together until uniformly mixed.

I suggest you serve the greens piping hot immediately! You won't believe how delicious they are with fried chicken, meat loaf, panéed veal, and barbecued pork chops.

Hunting Camp Baked Turnips

Even if you hate turnips, even if you think they're yukky, even if you can't stand to smell 'em cooking … I promise you're gonna love 'em when you fix 'em this way!

8 boiled turnips
Drippings from the cooked bacon
1 large onion, finely chopped
2 ribs celery, finely chopped
½ bell pepper, finely chopped
2 tbsp. finely minced parsley
1 clove garlic, finely minced
½ lb. chopped bacon, cooked crisp

1 tsp. Louisiana hot sauce
2 tsp. Worcestershire sauce
2 tsp. Frank Davis Vegetable
  Seasoning
3 tbsp. butter
½ cup seasoned bread crumbs
1 cup shredded cheddar cheese

First, take the turnips and mash them in a large bowl.

Then, in the bacon drippings, sauté all the vegetables—onion, celery, bell pepper, parsley, and garlic—until they are soft (it should take about 5 minutes).

Next, add the crumbled bacon, Louisiana hot sauce, and Worcestershire to the skillet and blend it into the seasoning vegetables well—I mean mix it in good.

Now stir everything into the mashed turnips, sprinkle on the vegetable seasoning, and fold the mixture well.

At this point, take a Pyrex casserole dish, butter the bottom and sides, and place the turnip mixture into the dish in layers. The way you want to do that is as follows:

Put in a layer of turnips … then lightly sprinkle on some bread crumbs … then sprinkle on a little cheddar. Then more turnips, and more bread crumbs, and more cheddar.

Finally, save a little of the cheddar so that you can top off the casserole with extra cheese and bake the whole dish at 350 degrees until it's golden brown.

Dat's turnips, Doc!

Chef's Note: *To prepare your turnips for this dish, peel them and boil them just as you would boil potatoes for mashing—do them whole or cut into chunks. When they are tender—when a fork pierces them easily—they're done.*

Pot-Braised Spinach

If you enjoyed those gourmet turnip greens I taught you how to make, wait till you taste this spinach recipe! It's a shame Popeye never chomped on these! But forget about Popeye—fix 'em for *your* family!

2 cans Campbell's Chicken Broth	1 cup finely diced onions
2 lb. chopped frozen leaf spinach	2 medium ripe tomatoes, diced
¼ cup extra-virgin olive oil	3 tsp. all-purpose seasoning

First, in a 5-quart Dutch oven, bring the chicken broth to a rolling boil. Then drop in the frozen spinach and cook it over high heat—stirring constantly—just until the broth comes back to a boil.

At this point, remove the pot from the fire, cover it tightly, and let the spinach soak in the broth for 10 minutes.

When it's tender, immediately place it into a colander and squeeze out as much of the chicken broth as possible.

Finally, in the same pot you used to poach the spinach, heat the olive oil to high and sauté the onions and the diced tomatoes until they wilt. Then drop in the squeezed spinach and the all-purpose seasoning and stir-fry the mixture until everything is uniformly blended—which should take only about 5 or 6 minutes.

The dish is great served piping hot right from the pot. But if you plan to serve it at a later meal, simply transfer it to a Pyrex baking dish, cover it tightly with aluminum foil, and refrigerate it until you're ready for it. It can be reheated in the microwave or in your oven (set at 350 degrees) for about 20 minutes.

Chef's Note: *If you can't find all-purpose seasoning where you shop, you can substitute Frank Davis Sprinkling Spice in its place. Sprinkling Spice can be ordered by calling 1-800-742-4231.*

French Market Spinach

If Popeye had a *favorite* spinach dish ... this would be it!

1 lb. fresh spinach	**½ cup diced onions**
½ cup chicken stock	**⅓ cup Shallot Butter (see index)**
¾ cup crumbled cooked bacon	

First, thoroughly wash the fresh spinach, remove the thick stems, and set the leaves in a colander to drain.

Then, in a 5-quart Dutch oven, bring the chicken stock, ¼ cup of the crumbled bacon, and the diced onions to a boil and cook for 3 minutes—stirring constantly.

When the onions have wilted and turned clear, drop in the spinach leaves (just keep adding them to the pot—they'll reduce in volume as they cook), put the lid on the pot, and steam them over high heat *for 3-4 minutes,* stirring them occasionally.

When the leaves turn a rich green and become tender, immediately place them into a colander and squeeze out as much of the steaming liquids as possible. Then transfer the spinach, onions, and bacon to a bowl, add the rest of the bacon bits, fold in the Shallot Butter, and "toss" everything together until uniformly mixed.

Serve immediately!

Oriental Fried Cabbage

If you like cabbage rich, crunchy, and full of flavor, this recipe will be one of your all-time favorites. And it goes exceptionally well with almost any entrée. Try it and see!

1 medium head cabbage	**3 tbsp. Frank Davis Vegetable**
2 tbsp. vegetable oil	**Seasoning**
½ lb. lean shredded pork	**⅛ tsp. garlic powder**
3 green onions, coarsely sliced	**1 tsp. white pepper**
4 tbsp. teriyaki sauce	**1 tbsp. sesame oil**
½ cup concentrated beef stock	**Salt to taste**
½ cup applesauce	

Start off by cutting the cabbage into quarters and removing the "knots" at the base of the head. Then shred each section to the consistency of coleslaw and set it aside for a moment.

Now take the vegetable oil and the shredded pork (pork chops cut into thin strips are excellent for this) and add it either to a 6-quart heavy aluminum Dutch oven or a Chinese wok. Then quickly fry down the meat over high heat until it browns thoroughly. *Remember to stir continually during the cooking process.*

Next, add the shredded cabbage and the green onions to the wok and mix everything together uniformly, making sure that all the cabbage is coated with the oil. At this point, put the cover on the pot and let the cabbage cook for about 3 minutes—*stirring occasionally.* Don't worry about the little bit of cabbage that slightly burns on the bottom of the pot. This is *caramelization* (natural acids turning to sugar) and it's supposed to happen.

Now take the cover off the pot again, add the next 6 ingredients (one at a time, stirring between the additions), and *stir, stir, stir!* The seasonings have to coat all the cabbage shreds well; otherwise the dish will lack uniformity. And when you are satisfied that you've blended everything together as best you can, put the lid back on the pot, reduce the heat to low, stir in the sesame oil, and let the cabbage continue to "smother" for about 15-20 minutes or until it turns al dente (tender, but crispy).

Finally, just before you plan to serve the dish, adjust your salt content. Remember, there's going to be salt in the vegetable seasoning and the teriyaki sauce and it has to cook into the dish before you can determine its potency. So add the salt last!

I suggest you serve this alongside a bowl of buttered rice with pepper steak, grilled or baked pork ribs or pork chops, fried chicken fillets, or bronzed shrimp.

Eggplant-Italian Sausage Parmigiana

You should know that the classic "Eggplant Parmigiana" is made with olive-oil-sautéed eggplant dipped in eggs and bread crumbs (along with ricotta cheese). But this lighter, "fully baked" version gives you a second recipe to try on your Italian (and not-so-Italian) guests!

2 large smooth-skin eggplants, peeled
1 gal. water + 3 tbsp. salt
4 cups Tomato Gravy (Sugo) (see index)

Drippings from the Italian sausage
2 lb. Italian sausage, baked and finely chopped
2 cups shredded mozzarella cheese
1 cup grated Parmesan cheese

Start off by cutting your eggplants in thin slices and soaking them in the cold salted water (this removes the so-called bitter taste that comes from the broken seeds).

Next, on the bottom of an 11-by-16-by-2-inch Pyrex baking pan, place a couple tablespoons of Tomato Gravy (with the sausage drippings stirred in) and spread it around evenly. Then begin covering the bottom of the pan with single slices of the eggplant.

At this point, sprinkle on some of the finely chopped Italian sausage (but do it evenly). Then sprinkle on some of the mozzarella cheese. Then sprinkle on a little Parmesan. And finally, ladle on some more gravy—but don't ladle it on too heavily! You want just enough to go into the eggplant as it cooks!

Repeat the procedure over and over until you have used all the sliced eggplant (or filled the baking pan). But be sure you end up with the top layer being gravy and a final sprinkling of mozzarella.

All that's left is to place the dish—uncovered—in a preheated 350-degree oven and bake the Parmigiana for about an hour or so.

Similar to "Veal Parmesan," this rich Sicilian dish will make you honestly believe that your grandparents came from downtown Palermo!

Chef's Note: *When you're ready to eat, I suggest you serve it piping hot alongside an Italian Salad with Caesar Dressing and a big chunk of fresh-baked Italian bread. And for a little added pleasure, I also recommend a chilled glass of Gallo Hearty Burgundy! Mama mia!*

Broccoli Tchoupitoulas

There's plain, steamed broccoli, lightly buttered broccoli, and broccoli with cheese. And then there's Broccoli Tchoupitoulas. Wait till you taste this!

¼ stick margarine
4 cups fresh broccoli florets
2 tsp. salt
1 tsp. white pepper
½ tsp. cayenne pepper

2 cups chicken stock (reduced)
2 tbsp. fresh-squeezed lemon juice
3 tbsp. cornstarch + 1 cup cold
   water
1 stick sweetcream butter

Basically, all you're doing with this dish is lightly stir-frying then steaming, which means you can cook this dish in a 12-inch skillet. But I prefer to fix it in a 5-quart Dutch oven with a lid.

So take your pot, toss in the margarine, heat it over *high heat* until bubbles form, and drop in the trimmed and washed broccoli florets. Then, with a slotted spoon, stir the florets gently until they are thoroughly coated with the margarine and begin to soften slightly.

Next, sprinkle on the salt, white pepper, and cayenne, mix thoroughly, and continue stir-frying for 3 minutes.

At this point, remove the broccoli from the pan, pour in the chicken stock and the lemon juice, bring it to a boil, and reduce to two-thirds its original volume. Then mix together the cornstarch and water and gradually stir it into the chicken stock (reduce the heat to a simmer once the sauce begins to boil).

When the sauce smooths and reaches the consistency you desire, begin stirring in small amounts of butter until the mixture "creams."

Then, finally, drop the broccoli back into the sauce and put the lid on the pot. For a crunchy, barely cooked texture, you can serve the broccoli about a minute or two after dropping it back into the sauce. But for a more softened vegetable, I suggest you wait for about 5 minutes or so before serving. Either way … this is great stuff!

Baked Broccoli-Cauliflower-Carrot Casserole

Combine gently steamed broccoli, cauliflower, and carrots, cover with a rich chicken stock and butter sauce, top with toasted bread crumbs, and bake till brown and bubbly, and you got one of the best vegetable medleys ever concocted!

4 cups chicken stock
1 medium cauliflower, cut into florets
1 large broccoli, cut into florets
½ lb. carrots, julienned
¼ cup sliced green onions
1 stick butter
1 can Campbell's Cream of Chicken Soup

2 tbsp. cornstarch + ½ cup water
1 tsp. Frank Davis Vegetable Seasoning
½ cup bread crumbs
¼ cup grated Parmesan cheese
¼ cup margarine

First, pour the chicken stock into a vegetable steamer and bring it to a rolling boil. Then, one ingredient at a time, begin steaming the cauliflower, broccoli, and carrots in the chicken stock until they are tender-crisp (not raw, but not soft either). When each vegetable is cooked, dip it quickly in ice-cold water to stop the cooking, drain it in a colander, and set it aside in a buttered 11-by-17 baking pan.

Now, bring the chicken stock back to a boil and reduce it to one-half of its volume. Remember that all the essence from the vegetables will have dripped into the stock during steaming and will have flavored it. So the sauce you make from the stock will be intensely rich.

Next—*still over high heat*—drop the green onions into the stock, stir in the butter, and blend in the cream of chicken soup. Then when the mixture is smooth (use a wire whip to get a creamy consistency), mix the water and the cornstarch together and stir it into the sauce to thicken it. At this point, remove the pan from the heat, lightly season the sauce with vegetable seasoning (or salt and black pepper to taste), and liberally spoon it over the vegetables in the baking pan.

Meanwhile, in a food processor, blend together the bread crumbs, Parmesan cheese, and the margarine until the crumbs are the consistency of moist sand. Then generously sprinkle them over the saucy vegetable medley, place the pan into a preheated 450-degree oven, and bake for 15-20 minutes until the top is brown and bubbly.

All that's left is to serve the veggies—sauce and all—piping hot with your favorite entrée. Even folks who *hate* vegetables will love this!

Chef's Note: *If you don't have a vegetable steamer, you can* microwave *the broccoli, cauliflower, and carrots in chicken stock. But they still have to be done separately ... and be careful you don't overcook them!* They have to be tender-crisp or they will turn out mushy after they're baked.

CHAPTER 8

Pasta, Rice, and Potatoes

Pasta Peppina

This is one of the best pasta dishes I ever tasted. Peppina Loreto, the mother of my Italian exchange student, taught me how to cook this San Genesio creation in my kitchen the night after her daughter and mine graduated from high school. We've made it at least once a week ever since then!

½ cup water
2 tbsp. extra-virgin olive oil
1 small onion, thinly sliced
½ lb. rendered bacon, crumbled
½ lb. Canadian bacon, chopped
2 cans peeled tomatoes (28-oz. size)
4 cloves garlic, minced

1 cup Cabernet Sauvignon wine
5 strips anchovies, minced
3 pickled chili peppers, thinly sliced
Salt and black pepper to taste
1 lb. Luxury perciatelli pasta
1 heaping cup grated Parmesan
    cheese

First, take a 4-quart Dutch oven and place it on a low fire. Then pour in the water and the olive oil and drop in the sliced onions. Now, with the lid off, simmer the onions over low heat until they completely soften—but do not let the water come to a boil! This should take about 20 minutes.

Next, stir in the rendered bacon and the Canadian bacon. Then, still with the pot uncovered, cook the meats in the stock over low heat until they are fully wilted (another 15 minutes or so). You'll begin to detect a full-bodied aroma developing.

Now, drop in the peeled tomatoes (along with the liquid they came packed in) and add the minced garlic. And with a wooden spoon, break everything in the pot into small pieces. Once again, with the lid off, cook the sauce for about 20 minutes—but this time over medium heat so that the tomatoes begin to soften.

Then pour in the red wine, the anchovies, and the chili peppers and stir everything together for about 3 minutes. Now reduce the fire to medium low, put the lid on the pot, and let the sauce slow-cook for about 30 minutes.

At this point, taste the sauce and add salt and black pepper if you so desire. By the way, the sauce should be slightly peppery—it's supposed to be! Remember, it's going to be mixed with pasta later and for the flavor to hold it needs to be a tad on the hot side.

Now cover the pot again, bring the fire back to low, and simmer the sauce for another 15 minutes.

Meanwhile, boil your perciatelli pasta in salted water, but boil it only until it is *al dente*. Take special care not to overcook it even slightly; otherwise it will soften too much when you stir it into the sauce.

Now here's the secret to Pasta Peppina. ...

When it's ready, pour the pasta into a colander and drain it thoroughly—*but do not wash it!* Instead, transfer it directly to the pot with the sauce and toss everything together well, making sure you coat every strand of pasta. Then immediately fold in the Parmesan cheese, bring the pot to the table, and serve it right away … piping hot!

I promise that very few things you will eat in your life will ever taste this good!

Chef's Note: *Perciatelli pasta is the thin macaroni with the hole in the center.*

The bacon should not be rendered until crisp. There should still be a slight amount of visible fat present to give the sauce added flavor. Oh—if you can find prosciutto ham, use it instead of Canadian bacon. It's more authentic.

Warning! Do not leave out the anchovies. *You will never taste them, so it doesn't matter whether or not you like anchovies. What they do is combine with the tomatoes and the red wine to give the dish a superrich Italian flavor that can't be duplicated any other way. Trust me!*

Cucuzza Pasta Pomadora

Cucuzza is a long Italian squash with a delicate sweet taste that's rich in vitamin C and high in natural fiber. But you forget how good it is for you when you combine it with stewed tomatoes, toss it with acini pepe pasta, and top it with Romano cheese. All that matters at this point is … seconds!

½ lb. acini pepe pasta	1 cup chicken stock
¼ cup extra-virgin olive oil	Pinch Italian seasoning
1 medium onion, finely chopped	½ tsp. black pepper
2 cloves garlic, freshly minced	2 fresh cucuzza
1 can Big R stewed tomatoes (303	Romano cheese for topping
size)	Parsley for garnish

Before you begin preparing the cucuzza (pronounced ku-koot-za), take a 3-quart stockpot and boil the acini pepe pasta until it is *al dente* (acini pepe pasta is a very tiny pasta usually found in soups). Then drain it in a colander, wash off the excess starch, and set it aside to cool.

Then, in a 5-quart Dutch oven with a tight-fitting lid, heat the olive oil to medium high, drop in the chopped onions and garlic, and sauté them only until the onions turn clear—*do not let them caramelize.*

Next, chop up the tomatoes and toss them into the pot along with the chicken stock, Italian seasoning, and black pepper. Then stir everything together well and *simmer* the mixture over low heat for about 10 minutes.

While the tomato stock is cooking, take a potato peeler or paring knife and strip the green skin from the cucuzza. Then cut the cucuzza into half-inch diced pieces. And when the tomato stock is ready, drop the pieces into the stock, stir everything together well, cover the pot, and cook the cucuzza over medium-high heat until soft (which should take you only about 20-30 minutes).

Then when the cucuzza is tender, stir in your pasta, cover the pot again, let the dish simmer once more for about 2 minutes, and serve it up in big bowls … piping hot and generously topped with Romano cheese and parsley.

Delizioso!

Chef's Note: *Whether you like squash or not, I guarantee you're going to like cucuzza! It's delicate and sweet, light in flavor, rich in vitamin C, and goes well with almost everything. Prepared according to the recipe above, it's a versatile vegetable. But you can embellish the dish and change its taste by adding about 2 pounds of raw peeled shrimp during the last 5 minutes of the cooking process.*

Oh—you should also know that this dish freezes well!

Pasta d'Roma

Light and healthy and truly authentic, this pasta dish goes great with almost any entrée … but it is especially good with my Italian Shrimp Scampi. In fact, it's good all by itself!

¼ cup extra-virgin olive oil
2 tsp. red wine vinegar
1 cup marinated Italian olive mix, chopped
⅔ cup Greek olives, pitted and chopped
2 oz. diced pimientos

¼ cup marinated artichoke hearts, chopped
3 cloves fresh garlic, finely chopped
1 lb. No. 4 spaghetti, cooked al dente
½ cup grated Parmesan cheese for topping

In a large glass or ceramic container, combine all the ingredients except the cheese and the pasta, cover them with plastic wrap, and allow them to marinate at room temperature overnight.

Then when you're ready to eat, pour the mixture into a saucepan and sauté it until it's hot (but don't let the oil come to a boil).

All that's left is to pour it over the pasta, toss it into the strands well, top with grated Parmesan cheese, and serve piping hot with fresh crusty French or Italian bread.

Oh—that's Italian!

Chef's Note: *This olive mixture also makes a great dressing for Italian salad. I suggest you pour it over tossed shredded lettuce, diced tomatoes, and sliced cucumbers. It also goes great as a sandwich spread on sliced cold cuts (Genoa salami, prosciutto ham, mortadella, and provolone cheese). In other words … it's just what you need to make a muffaletta!*

Sicilian Spaghetti Aglio e Olio

One of the tastiest—*and healthiest*—ways to serve spaghetti, this dish dates back to the early days of Rome and Pompeii. Initially it was served without cheese, but my Sicilian roots won't allow that! So go ahead and top it with Romano! You'll be surprised just how good pasta "as pasta" can be.

1 lb. imported No. 4 spaghetti	½ cup grated Romano cheese
½ cup + 4 tbsp. extra-virgin olive oil	2 tbsp. finely chopped parsley
6 garlic cloves, finely minced	2 tsp. coarse-ground black pepper
2 red chili peppers, finely chopped	

First, bring a large pot of salted water to a rapid boil and cook the spaghetti until it is *al dente* (which means it's cooked, but it's still slightly firm). This should take you about 11 minutes or so. I recommend you add 2 tablespoons of olive oil to the water to keep the pasta from sticking together.

When the spaghetti is done, drain it in a colander, pour the remaining 2 tablespoons of olive oil over it, and stir it gently into the strands to keep them separated.

Meanwhile, take a heavy 12-inch skillet and fry half of the garlic in half of the olive oil over medium-low heat *(do not let the garlic burn!)*. As soon as the garlic begins to take on a light beige color, drop in half of the pasta and thoroughly toss it with the garlic and olive oil over medium heat for 2 to 3 minutes.

At this point, transfer the spaghetti to a warm platter and do the second half of the pasta, garlic, and olive oil. When the entire batch is ready, liberally sprinkle it with the chili peppers and the Romano cheese, top it with parsley and freshly ground black pepper, and serve it piping hot.

Chef's Note:

1—Pasta doesn't always have to be served with marinara, red Italian gravy, or heavy cream sauce. This dish gives you an excellent—to say nothing of delicious—way to provide your family with a high-energy complex carbohydrate that is low in salt, low in cholesterol, and superhealthy because it contains garlic and the monounsaturated fat of the olive oil.

2—If you can't find fresh chili peppers at your grocery store, you can substitute about a half-teaspoon of dried red pepper flakes instead.

Eggplant Crabmeat Pasta

Excellent served piping hot over pasta or ice cold over snack crackers, this eggplant creation makes a great hors d'oeuvre as well as an entrée. And no matter which way you serve it the flavor will make it one of your family favorites.

¼ cup extra-virgin olive oil
1 cup finely diced yellow onions
4 garlic cloves, baked and mashed
2 medium eggplants, peeled and sliced in strips
10 ripe plum tomatoes, diced
½ lb. prosciutto ham
1 cup chicken stock

2 tbsp. Frank Davis Sicilian Seasoning
Salt and pepper to taste
1 lb. white crabmeat
1 lb. No. 3 thin spaghetti, cooked al dente
Romano cheese for topping

First, take a 5½-quart Dutch oven and heat the olive oil to just below the smoking point. Then drop in the diced onions and cook them for about 5 minutes or until they wilt. When they have softened and turned clear, toss in the garlic and the eggplant and cook the mixture over *very high* heat—*stirring constantly*—until the eggplant begins to brown slightly.

Next, add the diced tomatoes and the prosciutto ham, and *(again stirring constantly)* cook everything together until most of the juices have been rendered from the tomatoes and they turn soft. Now pour in the chicken stock and mix everything thoroughly once more. At this point, reduce the heat to low, cover the pot, and *simmer* the dish for about 20 minutes.

After the allotted cooking time, remove the cover from the pot, toss in the Sicilian seasoning, along with your salt and pepper to taste, and gently mix everything again. You'll notice that the eggplant is becoming very soft, so be gentle when you stir. You don't want it to turn to mush! Now cover the pot once more and continue to simmer the dish for another 45 minutes to an hour.

Then about 5 minutes before you're ready to eat, *very gently* fold in half of the crabmeat—be careful not to break it up into shreds. While the flavors are marrying, put your pasta on a warm serving tray. Then ladle all the smothered eggplant over the top, and sprinkle on the remaining crabmeat and the Romano cheese.

I suggest you serve this dish with thinly sliced raw zucchini, topped with Italian olive salad and complemented with Pompeii-style garlic bread (see below). *Mama mia!*

Chef's Note: *You can bake garlic by slicing the top off the entire head, placing it in a pie pan, pouring a couple of tablespoons of olive oil over it, and baking it covered with aluminum foil for 45 minutes at 400 degrees. When it's done, just squeeze the softened garlic right out of the pod. It's great for garlic bread, garlic spread, garlic chicken, etc.*

Be sure to soak the eggplants for about 20 minutes in salted water prior to cooking them. The salt removes the "bite" peculiar to eggplants and prevents them from soaking up the olive oil.

If you can't find plum tomatoes, 4 large regular tomatoes—peeled and finely diced—can be substituted. And if you want to cut the cholesterol from your diet, you can also substitute imitation crabmeat (which you simmer in crabboil seasoning for a few minutes) for the real thing.

Frank Davis "Strictly N'Awlins" Sicilian Seasoning is a high-quality subtle blend of authentic Italian herbs and spices. It is not available in grocery stores or gourmet shops, but it can be ordered by direct mail by calling 1-800-742-4231.

Pompeii-style garlic bread is regular garlic bread thickly topped with either shredded mozzarella or provolone cheese and placed under the broiler until it bubbles and browns.

To use the dish as a cold appetizer, eliminate the pasta and chill the eggplant in the refrigerator overnight. Then when you're ready to eat, simply spoon it out on thin slices of Italian bread, melba toast, garlic rounds, or table wafers.

Cajun Dirty Rice Dressing

Very few side dishes can complement the rich flavor of fried chicken, pork chops, or any other meat entrée as well as real Cajun dirty rice. And if you use this recipe, you can whip up one of the best batches you ever had, even though nobody in your family remotely resembles a Cajun. Here's how it's done!

1 stick butter	½ lb. lean ground pork
1 cup finely chopped onions	½ lb. chopped chicken livers
¾ cup finely chopped green onions	¾ cup concentrated chicken stock
½ cup finely chopped celery	3 tsp. Louisiana hot sauce
¼ cup finely chopped bell pepper	2 tsp. Kitchen Bouquet
4 tbsp. finely chopped parsley	Salt and black pepper to taste
½ lb. lean ground beef	6 cups cooked rice

First, take a heavy Dutch oven or 12-inch skillet (with a tight-fitting lid) and heat the butter just until it starts to brown. Then quickly toss in and stir-fry all of the seasoning vegetables. Remember—you just want them to wilt! Don't let them get too soft!

Now turn up the heat to high, add the beef, the pork, and the chicken livers, and cook until the meats brown. At this point, stir in the chicken stock, the Louisiana hot sauce, and the Kitchen Bouquet, and season with your salt and pepper. You might want to overseason slightly—I said *slightly!*—because this is the only seasoning the rice will get.

Next, put the cover on the pot, turn the heat down to low, and simmer the meat and vegetable mixture for about 20 minutes or until tender.

Finally, using a strainer spoon, remove the meat and the vegetables from the liquid base and fold them gently into the cooked rice until everything is thoroughly blended. Then gradually add just enough of the liquid to moisten the rice to the consistency you desire.

By the way, you can serve this piping hot right from the pot … but for the richest flavor, it is best if you allow the mixture to rest for an hour or two in a warm oven.

Chef's Note: *Dirty rice comes out best if you stir the meat and the vegetable mixture into hot rice rather than cold rice. And, just like jambalaya, it always seems to be best the next day!*

Love Dem Pommes Petites!

When you talk about staples on the table—the rice, the pasta, the grits, all the things that help fill you up and provide the carbohydrates necessary to your diet—it seems that none of them beats *potatoes*.

Like most New Orleanians, I love 'em—fried, baked, boiled, smashed, mashed, creamed, brabant, scalloped, and stuffed. But you want a recipe the way I like them best? Here it is. It's called "Pommes Petites"—little potatoes!

What you do is take some little "B"-size creamers—that's those baby red potatoes about the size of Ping-Pong balls. You want to try to get the smallest ones you can find. Then drop them into rapidly boiling salted water. Leave the skins on—don't peel them. Then boil them until an ice pick pierces them easily (about 17 minutes).

Now pour them out into a colander and let them drain until they are just cool enough to handle. Remember—a good rule of thumb is to peel a boiled potato while it's still hot so that the heat activates the starch and makes the potato sweet.

When they're all peeled, take a skillet (a nonstick kind works best), get it hot, and pour in just enough olive oil to lightly coat the potatoes as you swirl them. When the oil begins to smoke, drop in the creamers and continuously agitate them in the skillet. Don't overcrowd them, though! You want them to be free to roll around on the hot surface of the pan. And incidentally, you're cooking on *high!*

What you want is the outside of the potatoes to turn a crispy, crunchy brown (and believe me, they'll brown!). What you end up with is a crusty potato on the outside and a soft, tender, moist, creamy potato on the inside.

Ummmmmmmm ... I'd love about a dozen of them right now!

N'Awlins Cheese-Baked Potatoes

Baked potatoes never tasted better! The combination of creamery sweet butter, Velveeta cheese, heavy cream, and crumbled bacon bits tempts the taste buds of the most discriminating palate. This dish goes great with anything!

½ stick real butter, unsalted	2 tsp. sweet basil
¾ cup heavy cream	½ cup finely chopped parsley
4 oz. Velveeta cheese	Salt and pepper to taste
10 "B"-size creamer potatoes, sliced	Paprika
6 strips bacon, cooked and crumbled	

Start off by melting the butter over medium heat in a heavy 12-inch skillet. Then add the heavy cream, bring it to a gentle boil, and begin the "reduction" process. When the cream and butter blend evenly and start to thicken, slowly add the Velveeta and melt it into the sauce. *Remember ... you have to continually stir this sauce and scrape the sides of the skillet.* Consistency should smooth out in about 5 minutes.

Next, lightly butter an 11-by-14 Pyrex baking dish and lay out the potato slices evenly in layers. But between each layer, liberally spread on enough of the cheese sauce to coat the potato slices. Between each layer, you should also lightly sprinkle on a little of the bacon bits, a little basil, a little parsley, and a little salt and pepper. Repeat the process again and again until all the potatoes, all the cheese sauce, and all the seasoning ingredients are in the baking dish.

Finally, top the casserole with paprika and the last of the bacon bits, and bake in a preheated 350-degree oven until the cheese sauce bubbles (which should take about 30 minutes or so). *But do not overcook or the potatoes will be mushy.*

Chef's Note: *This potato casserole goes well with fried, baked, grilled, broiled, and barbecued chicken, fish, beef, pork, lamb, shrimp, crab, crawfish, and whatever else you can think of! And if you add cooked julienned strips of meat, poultry, or seafood to the layers as you put the casserole together, it becomes a complete one-dish meal!*

N'Awlins Fluted Potatoes

This potato casserole combines butter, Velveeta cheese, whole milk, and crumbled bacon for a tempting taste treat. It enhances any meal!

1 stick real butter, unsalted
4 heaping tbsp. all-purpose flour
1½ cups whole milk
4 oz. Velveeta cheese
6 large Idaho potatoes,
    waffle sliced

Salt and pepper to taste
2 cups finely diced onions
6 strips bacon, cooked and
    crumbled

Start off by melting the butter over medium heat in a 12-inch skillet. Then mix the flour and the whole milk together until smooth and slowly stir it into the butter. When the mixture is creamy, bring it to a gentle boil, and begin the "reduction-thickening" process. You might want to add a little extra milk if the sauce thickens too much for your taste.

When the consistency is right (similar to melted ice cream) slowly add the Velveeta and melt it into the sauce. *Remember ... you have to continually stir this sauce and scrape the sides of the skillet.* The texture should be silky and creamy in about 5 minutes.

Next, lightly butter an 11-by-14 Pyrex baking dish and set out the potato slices evenly in layers. But between each layer, liberally spread on enough of the cheese sauce to coat the potato slices. Between each layer, you should also lightly sprinkle on a little salt and pepper, a handful of chopped onions, and a little bit of the bacon bits. Repeat the process again and again until all the potatoes and all the other ingredients are in the baking dish.

Finally, cover the casserole with aluminum foil and bake in a preheated 350-degree oven for about an hour or so, or until the potatoes are tender and bubbling in the cheese sauce.

Chef's Note: *This potato casserole goes well with fried, baked, grilled, broiled, and barbecued chicken, fish, beef, pork, lamb, shrimp, crab, crawfish, and whatever else you can think of! And if you add your cooked meat to the layers as you put the casserole together, it becomes a complete one-dish meal!*

Duchesse Potatoes

You know those stuffed potatoes you like so much? Well, this is the stuffing without the hulls. And they go good with anything from fried shrimp to breaded pork chops! Try this!

6 large Idaho potatoes, peeled and
  quartered
4 tbsp. butter + ½ stick butter
½ cup finely diced onions
¼ cup finely diced celery
¼ cup finely diced bell peppers
¼ cup bacon bits
3 egg yolks, well beaten

2 tbsp. chopped green onions
1 cup shredded colby cheese
½ tsp. white pepper
½ cup heavy cream
Salt to taste
3 egg whites, slightly beaten
1 tsp. paprika

First, cook the potatoes in rapidly boiling salted water until they are tender (which should take about 25 minutes). When they're done, drain them in a colander—*but immediately put them back into the hot pot they were boiled in to allow all the excess moisture to evaporate.*

While the potatoes are drying, take a 12-inch skillet, melt the 4 tablespoons of butter, and gently sauté the onions, celery, and bell peppers until they soften.

Meanwhile, using an electric mixer, cream the potatoes to a semismooth texture (do not overmash at this point). Then—using a spoon—blend in the seasoning vegetables, along with the remaining butter, the bacon bits, the egg yolks, the green onions, the cheese, and the white pepper.

Now, when everything is uniform, take the electric mixer again, slowly whip in the heavy cream, and beat the potatoes until they turn stiff. Then add your salt to taste and make whatever other seasoning adjustments you desire.

Finally, lightly butter a baking sheet. Then put the whipped potatoes into a pastry bag with a fluted star-shaped tip, pipe them out in little mounds on the sheet, brush the tops with the egg whites, lightly sprinkle with paprika, and brown them in a preheated 475-degree oven until toasty.

I recommend you serve them piping hot!

Succulent Bronzed Potatoes

This dish was created as an accompaniment to almost any entrée. You can do it at home on your stove or in your commercial kitchen … it's relatively low in calories … and best of all, it gives you succulence, taste, tenderness, and crispness without a lot of fuss! Try it! I promise you it'll soon be among your favorites!

1 Teflon- or Silverstone-coated skillet (12-inch size)
3 lb. "A"- or "B"-size creamer potatoes, boiled and peeled
2 tsp. Frank Davis Sicilian Seasoning
Salt, white, black, and red pepper to taste

2 tbsp. sweet paprika
2 tbsp. extra-virgin olive oil
3 tbsp. chopped shallots
4 tbsp. white wine
¼ cup minced parsley for garnish

Start off by turning your stovetop or range to *high* and placing the skillet on the burner. It is essential that this recipe be done in a Teflon- or Silverstone-coated skillet to compensate for the small amounts of oils used. Note, too, that the skillet must be heated to "hot" prior to adding the olive oil (it's hot enough when a drop of water sizzles off quickly).

Meanwhile, season the peeled potatoes with the Sicilian seasoning, salt and peppers, and paprika, tossing them to make sure each potato is coated evenly.

At this point, add a little of the olive oil to the skillet (enough to handle the portion of potatoes you're cooking), swish it around in the pan to coat the bottom, and drop in the shallots (stirring them in quickly and cooking them for about a minute or so).

Now drop in the potatoes and let them cook over high, rolling them around and around, until the olive oil begins to turn them a *toasty bronze* color.

When they're done, remove them from the skillet and set them on a warming platter. Then add the white wine to the skillet, deglaze the bottom, and reduce the wine to about half of its original volume. Now put the potatoes back into the pan, roll them around so that each one picks up the sauce, garnish with a sprinkling of parsley, and serve piping hot.

Chef's Note: *You can also use bourbon, cognac, or fine brandy instead of wine to vary the flavor. Experiment with them and treat your taste buds.*

This recipe can also be used to bronze *shrimp, soft-shell crabs, crawfish tails, and even thinly sliced cuts of beef, pork, veal, and chicken.*

How to Make Instant Potatoes Taste Homemade

One of the best commercial products we have on the American market today is instant potato flakes. *But* ... you just can't fix them according to the directions you read on the side of the box and expect them to taste homemade.

You can, however, doctor 'em up with a few additional ingredients and turn them into gourmet! In fact, fix your next batch like this and I defy you to tell me that they didn't come right out of the garden! Here's what you do:

1—Fix them according to box directions so that you get basic mashed potatoes. Oh—make 'em a little stiff 'cuz you gotta add some stuff!

2—Then, while they're still piping hot, thoroughly stir in a little shredded cheddar or colby cheese. Mix until it's all melted. How cheesy you want it is up to you.

3—Then whip in some melted margarine. How much? Well, when you think you have enough ... add a little more!

4—Then stir in some *whipping cream*—not milk as the box directions tell you. You want these potatoes silky—whipping cream gives you that taste. Again, how much? I never add less than a half-pint! But you should add enough to thin out the potatoes to the consistency you want. Remember how you made 'em stiff to begin with? This is how you loosen 'em up!

5—Finally, crumble up a handful of Durkee Canned Fried Onions and fold them in (this gives you a nice crunchy taste), then season the potatoes with salt and black pepper.

And that's it, y'all! Fix these guys and I promise you you'll never boil and peel spuds for mashin' again!

CHAPTER 9

Wild Game

Stuffed Venison Pinwheels

It's a combination of venison backstrap, a layer of thinly sliced bacon, and a mixture of melted cheese and Rotel tomatoes, all tightly rolled into a pinwheel and cut into inch-thick, serving-size pieces. Baked to juicy perfection, they're hard to beat for a family-style, everyday dinner or for an elegant dinner party. You gotta try 'em!

2 whole venison backstraps, rolled out ¼ inch thick	1 can Rotel tomatoes with diced chilies
1 qt. whole milk	2 lb. thinly sliced lean bacon
2 tsp. wild game seasoning	½ cup thinly sliced green onions
1 lb. Velveeta cheese	8 cloves garlic, finely minced

First, prepare the backstrap fillet. It's an extremely tender tubelike piece of meat about 12 inches long and 2 to 3 inches in diameter. And because of its shape, it can be cut around the perimeter, ¼ inch thick, and rolled out flat. To do this, you need a very sharp knife.

Start by laying out the fillet perpendicular to your body and making a shallow slice about ¼ inch deep in the meat. Then, as if slicing through and unrolling paper towels from a roll, begin working around the outside perimeter of the fillet until the backstrap comes out looking like a round steak. It takes a little practice to do … but you can do it!

When the meat is ready, place both pieces into a glass or plastic container and cover them with whole milk. You want to marinate the venison for at least 6 hours, but preferably overnight. The milk tenderizes the deer and helps to remove any unwanted gamey flavor.

After the marination process, remove the meat from the milk (you can discard the milk), and pat the venison dry with several paper towels. Then liberally sprinkle both sides with wild game seasoning and rub it briskly into the meat.

At this point, preheat your oven to 400 degrees. Then, in your food processor, mix together the Velveeta cheese and the Rotel tomatoes until smooth and creamy.

When you're ready to make the pinwheels, spread a thin layer of the cheese mixture evenly over one side of the deer. Then place a layer of bacon strips—side by side—on top of the cheese. Finish up the preparation by lightly sprinkling on a little sliced green onions and a little minced garlic.

Now tightly roll up the flattened fillets and set them aside momentarily. Then on the same work surface, lay out another 8 to 10 strips of bacon side by side and put one of the rolled backstraps on top of the them. Now wrap the bacon strips around the venison and pin them in place with toothpicks. When you are finished, the backstrap should be completely encased in bacon strips. Repeat with the other backstrap.

All that's left is to take a sharp knife, slice the rolled venison into 2-inch-thick pinwheels, position them on a shallow cookie sheet, and bake them—*uncovered*—in the oven for about 40 to 45 minutes. You'll notice that a light sauce will form in the bottom of the cookie sheet: you can use this to baste the pinwheels as they cook. The one thing you don't want to do is overcook the venison—it will come out dry and chewy instead of juicy and tender if you do!

When you're ready to eat, serve up the pinwheels piping hot from the oven, alongside a big helping of Tempting Turnip Greens (see index) and a couple of Oven Crusted Potatoes (see *Frank Davis Cooks Naturally N'Awlins*).

Even if you *hate* venison with a passion, you're gonna *love* this meal! And if you happen to *love* venison, well … !

Chef's Note: *If you don't have wild game seasoning on hand, you can lightly sprinkle the venison with salt, black pepper, onion powder, garlic powder, and sweet basil as a substitute. Unfortunately, most spice manufacturers don't make a pre-mixed wild game seasoning, but my company does. If you'd like me to send you some, simply call 1-800-742-4231.*

Venison Chaurice

In Creole patois, the word for "hot sausage" is chaurice. And since I wanted this recipe for venison to take on a Creole flavor, I took a couple pounds of hot sausage, rolled it out, plugged a trimmed venison backstrap fillet with fresh garlic, and wrapped the sausage around the venison. Sounds good, huh? But the way it sounds comes nowhere close to how good it tastes! If you love venison … you're gonna love this!

2-3 lb. venison backstrap fillet	1 large onion, finely diced
½ gal. whole milk	½ large bell pepper, finely diced
3 large cloves garlic, thinly sliced	Drippings from the venison roast
2 tbsp. wild game seasoning	2 cups beef stock
1 roll extra heavy duty aluminum foil	2 cups hearty Burgundy
	4 tbsp. all-purpose flour
2 lb. bulk hot sausage	Salt and black pepper to taste
2 sheets waxed or parchment paper	

First, with a sharp knife carefully trim away all the excess fat from the venison fillet—*it's the fat that makes wild meat gamey-tasting.* Then place the fillet into a glass or plastic container, completely cover it with the milk, and marinate it for at least 4 hours (but overnight is better). You'll find that the milk will totally remove any of the harsh unwanted flavors from the venison.

After the marination time, pat the fillet dry with paper towels and lay it out on a cutting board. Then, with a small paring knife, cut deep slits into the fillet about an inch or so apart and stuff each slit with a slice or two of garlic. Now liberally sprinkle the wild game seasoning all over the meat and rub it in briskly. When it's seasoned, set the fillet aside momentarily.

At this point, preheat your oven to 400 degrees. While it's heating, place on the countertop a sheet of aluminum foil large enough to completely wrap the fillet. Then place the hot sausage in the center of the foil. Next, lay 2 sheets of waxed paper—*side by side and overlapping*—on top of the hot sausage and begin pushing down on the sausage to flatten it out. When you've reduced the bulk somewhat, take a rolling pin or a wine bottle and continue to flatten out the sausage until it's uniformly about ¼ to ½ inch thick.

Now remove the waxed paper and place the seasoned fillet in the center of the hot sausage. Sprinkle on top of the fillet a handful of diced onions and diced bell pepper. Then lift both ends of the aluminum foil upward, forcing the sausage up against the sides of the venison fillet.

Then, working with one side of the foil at a time, use your fingers or a plastic spatula to loosen the flattened-out sausage from the foil and drape it over the fillet. (You might want to trim away a little of the sausage from the edges before you make the final wrap so that it only slightly overlaps the fillet.) Now moisten your hands and pat down the edges of the sausage to completely seal in the venison (be sure you seal the ends too!).

Now gently roll the wrapped fillet over so that the roast rests on the sealed sausage edge. When this is done, *tightly* wrap the foil around the roast—*this will allow the roast to keep its shape and will seal in the juices as the fillet cooks.*

All that's left to do now is to place the roast on a shallow baking sheet (just in case some of the juices leak out!), slide it into the oven, and bake it for about 2 hours.

When you're ready to eat, unwrap one end of the roast and drain off the drippings into a skillet. Then stir the beef stock into the drippings and bring the mixture to a slow boil on top of the stove. At this point, thoroughly mix the flour into the wine, stir it into the drippings, and bring it back to a slow boil—*you want the wine mixture to cook for at least 5 minutes to burn off the alcohol and begin to thicken.* When it turns silky smooth, adjust your seasonings by adding salt and black pepper to your taste.

When everything is ready, thinly slice the venison roast and cover it with a big helping of the sauce. I recommend you serve this venison dish alongside a creamy baked potato and a generous scoop of buttery turnip greens.

Chef's Note: *While it might surprise you, the hot sausage is not going to make the roast hot nor greasy! Because wild game is very lean, it will absorb whatever fat is extruded from the hot sausage.*

Be sure to use extra heavy duty aluminum foil when cooking this venison recipe. Thinner foil breaks too easily.

If you can't find wild game seasoning where you shop, you can order the one I use in this dish by calling 1-800-742-4231.

Black Pot Venison and Vino
(With Tossed Noodles)

I dearly love to cook wild game dishes! I think there's nothing more tasty than a big pot of squirrel stew, or rabbit sauce piquante, or roasted duck, or smothered quail. Well ... yes there is! It's this recipe for Black Pot Venison and Vino, smothered in chopped onions and served with extra-wide egg noodles. One taste and you can't stop eating!

4 lb. trimmed venison roast, quartered
½ qt. whole milk
1 lb. lean bacon plus drippings
3 extralarge onions, coarsely diced
6 cloves fresh garlic, finely minced
2 tbsp. wild game seasoning

1 cup unseasoned all-purpose flour
¼ cup vegetable oil
1 cup Johannisberg Reisling white wine
Salt and pepper to taste (if needed)
1 lb. extrawide egg noodles, cooked al dente

The first thing you want to remember is that in order to remove the pungent "wild and gamey" taste from venison (and all other wild game, for that matter) you must take time to strip off all the sinew, fat, and muscle covering from the meat. Most of the unwanted flavor is concentrated in those parts.

Next, wash the meat well in cold running water to remove any traces of blood pigment.

And finally, you need to marinate the meat for at least 3 hours ... but preferably overnight. And don't marinate in vinegar! *Marinate in whole milk.* One, it sweetens the meat; and two, the lactic acid helps to break down tough muscle fiber and produce a tenderness similar to prime fillet.

So now that you've taken care of the preparation, let's cook!

Start off by rendering the bacon and cooking it in a 5-quart cast-iron Dutch oven until it turns crisp—*but save the drippings.* Then remove the bacon from the pot, set it on a paper towel, let it drain, and chop it rather coarsely.

Meanwhile, reheat the drippings over high heat, toss in the diced onions, and cook them over high heat until they *caramelize* (turn a dark brown color). But note something: when the onions just start to brown, it's time to drop in the garlic and the bacon (the slight amount of onion juices will keep the garlic from burning). Now finish browning the onions, remove them from the pot, and set them aside.

At this point, take the venison out of the milk marinade and liberally sprinkle each piece with the wild game seasoning (it is not necessary to wash off the excess milk). Then dredge the meat in plain, unseasoned all-purpose flour and set it aside on a platter. While the meat is "resting," pour the vegetable oil into the Dutch oven and get it hot. Then put the venison into the oil and brown it on both sides. When the meat is ready, remove it from the pot.

Then place half of the onions back in the pot, lay the venison over them, and spread the remaining onions over the venison. *You'll notice there is no liquid whatsoever in the Dutch oven.* The onions and the venison will create their own liquid as they cook. Now cover the Dutch oven, place it into a preheated 350-degree oven, and bake for about 2-3 hours or until the meat is tender and a fork pierces the thickest part of the roast easily.

When you're ready to eat, gently remove the meat from the pot (I say *gently* because it's almost gonna fall apart!) and place it on a serving platter. Then place the Dutch oven and the drippings back on the stove over medium-high heat, stir in the wine, and reduce the pot liquor to at least half of its original volume. The resultant sauce it makes should be ready in about 10 minutes. All you do at this point is take the pot off the fire and thoroughly toss in the noodles.

I suggest you slice and serve the roast as the entrée, and serve the noodles right from the black pot (the cast iron will keep them hot during the entire meal).

Of course, a bottle of red wine and a cold crisp salad complements the offering. But do me a favor: don't say you don't like venison until you taste this! It's absolutely delicious!

Chef's Note:

1—You can order my "Strictly N'Awlins" Wild Game Seasoning by calling 1-800-742-4231. But if you don't have any on hand when you cook your venison, you can lightly sprinkle on a little salt, black pepper, red pepper, thyme, basil, onion powder, garlic powder, and nonfat dry milk.

2—Because wild game cooking is sometimes considered difficult, if you have any questions concerning the cooking of venison, rabbit, squirrel, duck, goose, dove, quail, or any other kind of wild game, just drop me a note at Frank Davis Productions, P.O. Box 722, Slidell, Louisiana 70459. I'll help you learn to cook it all!

Succulent Double-Baked Christmas Goose
(With Old-Fashioned Sugarplum Sauce)

This year, why not do an old-fashioned traditional Christmas? It simply means that instead of cooking a turkey, you fix a goose—but not just any goose! A double-baked, slow-roasted version that even Charles Dickens and Ebeneezer Scrooge would come back to have seconds on! And be sure to top it off with some of my Sugarplum Sauce!

1 goose (8 to 10 lb. average)	2 Florida oranges, quartered (peel
Salt and black pepper to taste	on)
4 tbsp. poultry seasoning	2 large red onions, quartered
1 tbsp. rosemary	8 bay leaves
2 Granny Smith apples, quartered	
(peel on)	

The first thing you do is wash and clean the goose well, both inside and out, with cold running water. Then remove the giblets—but save them if you decide to make an oyster or corn-bread dressing later.

Do not, however, remove any of the goose fat! It's not going to make the bird greasy using this cooking method and it's what makes the goose self-basting! Incidentally, while you're doing all this prepping, go ahead and preheat your oven to 450 degrees.

When the goose is washed, pat him dry with paper towels and fold the neck skin under the body to get it out of the way. Now liberally sprinkle on the salt, pepper, and poultry seasoning (inside and out) … *and rub it in well.*

Next, sprinkle the rosemary inside the cavity and make sure it's evenly distributed. Then pack the cavity full with the apples, oranges, onions, and bay leaves. At this point, you should take a piece of butcher's twine and tie down the wings and legs to hold the goose in an appetizing position as he bakes. I also suggest you take small pieces of aluminum foil and wrap the ends of the drumsticks and the tips of the wings to keep them from drying out during baking.

Okay—now you're ready to put the critter into the oven. But remember, you want him greaseless. So here's how you do that.

Take a baking pan large enough to hold the goose, add enough water to the pan to cover the bottom about an inch deep, and place a baking rack on top of the pan. Now put the goose on the rack, breast side up, and bake him until he turns a rich honey brown all over. Then when he reaches the right color, reduce the oven temperature to 225 degrees and slow-cook him (uncovered!) for about 30 minutes to the pound or until a meat thermometer indicates a 180-degree internal temperature. If you bake him right, the goose should turn out golden brown, moist, tender, and grease free.

At this point remove the bird from the oven and set him on the countertop to cool for approximately 1 hour. While he's resting, make your Sugarplum Sauce.

Sugarplum Sauce:

Goose drippings with fat removed   **1 jar plum jelly (10-oz. size)**
¼ cup strained applesauce   **1 tsp. soy sauce**
½ cup peach brandy   **¼ cup Grenadine syrup**
¼ cup white raisins

In a 2-quart saucepan, bring the pan drippings, the applesauce, and half of the peach brandy to a rolling boil. Then reduce the heat to low and simmer until the mixture is shiny and smooth.

In the meantime, while the glaze is cooking, soak the white raisins in the remaining peach brandy until they swell (which should take about 15 minutes). Then run them through the food processor just long enough to cream them slightly.

Next, gradually add the jelly to the saucepan, stirring it constantly until it melts thoroughly.

Then whip in the raisin puree, the soy sauce, and the Grenadine syrup and continue to cook over low heat (you'll have to stir occasionally) until a sheen forms on the sauce. This should take no more than 5 minutes.

Then, 20 to 30 minutes before you're ready to eat, again preheat your oven to 450 degrees and slide the goose back in (still on the rack). This will reheat the inside of the goose and finish "crisping" the outer skin.

When you're ready to eat, carve and serve up several slices of the goose and top them generously with the Sugarplum Sauce. I promise, y'all … it'll be the highlight of your holidays!

Chef's Note: *To remove the goose fat from the drippings, put all the pan juices from the baked goose in a Pyrex measuring cup and place it in the refrigerator until the fat congeals. Then lift the fat off the natural juices and discard it. It's that easy!*

The sauce is good not only on goose, but on practically every kind of poultry, especially turkey, duck, and game hens.

CHAPTER 10

Lagniappe

Frank and Tommy's
Egg Rolls and Spring Rolls

Whenever I want to learn new Oriental recipes and cooking techniques, I ask my old friend Tommy Wong of Trey Yuen Restaurant in Mandeville to teach me. So when I wanted to learn how to do authentic Chinese egg rolls and spring rolls, guess who got together with me in the kitchen?

Egg Rolls:

1 gal. water
1 gal. peanut oil for deep frying
1 cup finely shredded green cabbage
1 cup finely chopped celery
1 cup fresh bean sprouts
6 cups cracked ice
2 cups finely chopped cooked meat
    or seafood

1½ tsp. salt
½ tsp. black pepper
1 tsp. five-spice powder
1 tbsp. sesame-seed oil
2 pkg. egg-roll wrappers
1 egg, well beaten

First, bring the gallon of water to a rapid boil in a large pot and preheat the peanut oil to 325 degrees.

Now *separately* blanch the green cabbage, celery, and bean sprouts in the boiling water for about a minute or so—you should start timing the blanching process after the water comes back to a boil. This works best if you use a boiling pot that has a strainer that fits inside of it.

Then as you remove each vegetable from the water, dunk it immediately in an ice-cold water bath to stop the cooking and to keep the vegetables crisp. When they are thoroughly cold, place the vegetables in a colander and forcefully press out all the excess water.

At this point, put all the vegetables together in a large bowl, drop in the cooked meat or seafood, and drop in the salt, pepper, five-spice powder, and sesame-seed oil. Now, with your hands, toss everything together thoroughly until the mixture is uniformly blended.

When you're ready to fry, position an egg-roll wrapper in a baseball-diamond configuration in front of you on the countertop. Then place 2 to 3 heaping tablespoons of the vegetable-meat mixture where the pitcher's mound would be and spread the filling across the wrapper, stopping about an inch from the left and right corners.

To roll, begin with the corner nearest you, fold it over the stuffing firmly, and tighten it into a rounded cylindrical shape. Then fold in the left and right corners and continue to roll toward the corner farthest from you (while you still apply firm pressure on the stuffing). To finish up, just before the roll is complete, brush on a little bit of beaten egg to seal the wrapper together.

All that's left is to drop the egg rolls in peanut oil and deep fry them until they are a rich golden brown (which takes about 3 to 4 minutes). I suggest you serve them piping hot with hot mustard and Chinese plum sauce.

Spring Rolls:

6 oz. lean pork, finely shredded	1 tsp. salt
1½ tsp. soy sauce	3 tbsp. light soy sauce
1 tsp. cornstarch	1 tsp. sesame-seed oil
2 tbsp. peanut oil	2 tsp. sugar
½ tsp. minced garlic	½ tsp. white pepper
4 oz. bamboo shoots, finely shredded	½ cup canned chicken broth
6-8 medium dried black mushrooms, rehydrated	2 green onions, thinly cut on a bias
	2 tsp. cornstarch (dissolved in 2 tbsp. water)
1 lb. green cabbage, finely shredded	20 spring-roll wrappers
2 tbsp. dry sherry	1 egg, well beaten
	1 gal. peanut oil for deep frying

First, mix the shredded pork with the half-teaspoon of soy sauce and the teaspoon of cornstarch for about 5 minutes. Then preheat your wok or a heavy aluminum skillet over high heat for about 2 minutes with nothing in it. Then add the peanut oil and the marinated shredded pork and quickly stir-fry it for about 30 seconds. When it's cooked, remove it from the wok with a slotted spoon and allow the excess oil to drain off.

Now immediately reheat the wok to high and drop in the garlic, bamboo shoots, black mushrooms, and cabbage and stir-fry the mixture for about 2 minutes. Then put the shredded pork back into the wok, shower in the sherry, sprinkle in all the seasonings, along with the chicken broth, and stir-fry for another 2 minutes. Then add the green onions and the cornstarch and stir the mixture again until the liquids in the wok thicken (which should take only a few seconds).

At this point, remove the stuffing from the wok, place it in a colander to cool, and let it drain for a minimum of 2 hours.

When you're ready to wrap your spring rolls, place a wrapper *squarely* in front of you (not in the diamond shape you used for egg rolls). Then put about 2 heaping tablespoons of the stuffing just below the center line of the wrapper and spread it evenly crosswise. Now fold the edge nearest to you over the mixture and roll the wrapper up tightly. After the wrapper is rolled about ¾ of the way, fold over both edges and continue to roll away from you. To finish off the roll and seal the wrap, brush the edge with a little bit of beaten egg.

All that's left is to deep fry the spring rolls to a crispy golden brown in hot peanut oil set at 350 degrees. I suggest you drain the rolls for a minute or two on absorbent paper towels before you serve them. And like egg rolls, they should be served with hot mustard and Chinese plum sauces.

Chef's Note:

1—You can find five-spice powder at all Oriental markets and at most supermarkets in the international foods section. These same markets also have hot mustard and plum sauces.

2—It's up to you as to which kind of seafood or meat you want to use in your egg rolls and spring rolls. Shrimp, crawfish tails, lobster meat, calamari, scallops, pork, beef, and chicken all make great additions.

3—If you want to prepare egg rolls and spring rolls for a party, go ahead and assemble them and partially deep fry them. Then let them cool completely, wrap them in plastic film, and place them in the refrigerator. Then when you're ready to serve, take them from the fridge, allow them to warm up slightly, and "refry" them at 325 degrees until they are crisp and crunchy. This considerably reduces your cooking time.

4—Spring-roll wrappers, unlike egg-roll wrappers, are extremely thin and flaky, almost pastry-like. For that reason they tend to dry out quickly and become difficult to roll once the package is opened. To prevent this from happening I suggest you keep them covered with a damp towel as you're rolling them.

N'Awlins Pickled Onions

To maintain your identity as a real New Orleanian, you gotta have a jar of these on the pantry shelf at all times. Why? Because Monday red beans and rice just wouldn't be the same without them! Make some ... they're easy to do!

2-3 lb. tiny yellow onions
1 gal. cool water
¼ cup salt
2 tbsp. crushed red pepper
2 tsp. sweet basil

6 small bay leaves
1 qt. distilled white vinegar
½ pt. water
2 tbsp. liquid crabboil

First, peel the onions and place them in a glass, crock, or plastic container *(no metal!)*. Then mix the water and the salt together well, pour it over the onions, and allow them to soak overnight to "cure."

The next day, when you're ready to "put up" the onions, take a clean jar and sprinkle some of the crushed red pepper, sweet basil, and bay leaves on the bottom. Then pack about a third of the onions on top of the seasonings. Just continue layering the ingredients—onions, pepper, basil, bay leaves—until they're all used.

When the jar is packed, mix the distilled vinegar, the half-pint of water, and the crabboil together well and pour the mixture over the onions. Then cap the jar and allow the onions to "set" in the bottom of your refrigerator for at least a week before slicing them into red beans and rice, fried liver, jambalaya, and whatever else you want them to accompany.

Y'all ... it's just that simple!

Chef's Note: *Yellow onions are traditionally used for pickling, but you can also use small white pearl onions too. Note that this recipe will give you* spicy *onions, but if you want them hotter go ahead and add more crushed red pepper, birdseyes, jalapeños, or whatever. You can also add extra crabboil to taste. Note: I recommend you dilute the vinegar with water 3:1 (three parts vinegar to one part water). If you use undiluted vinegar, the onions will turn out extremely tart!*

They should keep well in the refrigerator for about 6 months. Of course, they never last that long at my house! And don't worry if they discolor and turn dark—they always do!

Old New Orleans Gourmet Stuffed Bell Peppers

If you think bell peppers are stuffed only with chopped shrimp and bread or ground meat and rice, wait till you fix these stuffed peppers! Lots of onion, celery, parsley, and garlic are mixed with seasoned bread stuffing and combined with lean ground beef and pork, then blended with Monterey Jack and colby cheese, topped with buttered bread crumbs, and baked to succulence! I promise—you're gonna love these!

6 medium-size bell peppers	1 small can V-8 juice
1 stick margarine	3 cloves garlic, minced
1 cup finely chopped onions	¼ cup Madeira wine
⅔ cup sliced green onions	1 tsp. Worcestershire sauce
½ cup finely chopped celery	2 whole eggs, well beaten
1 cup finely chopped bell pepper	4 cups French bread stuffing mix
1 medium tomato, diced	½ cup mixed Monterey Jack and
¼ cup finely minced parsley	colby cheese
1 lb. extralean ground beef	1 tsp. salt
1 lb. extralean ground pork	½ tsp. black pepper
½ cup whole milk	¼ cup buttered bread crumbs

First, cut the tops off the bell peppers, remove the seeds, and wash them well inside and out. Then place them into lightly salted boiling water and cook them until they just begin to wilt slightly. *Do not overcook!*

Next, remove them from the pot, shock them with cold water to stop the cooking, and place them cut-side down on paper towels to drain.

At this point, take a 12-inch skillet, melt the stick of margarine over medium heat, and gently sauté the onions, green onions, celery, bell pepper, diced tomato, and parsley until tender (which takes about 5 minutes).

In the meantime, mix together the ground beef and pork with the whole milk and the V-8 juice (get in there with your hands to ensure that everything is evenly blended). Then drop the seasoned meat, *along with the garlic, the wine, and the Worcestershire sauce,* into the sautéed vegetable mixture and cook it over medium heat—stirring constantly—until it lightly browns and renders out the bulk of its juices.

When the mixture is done, transfer it to a large mixing bowl (do not drain off the juices!) and allow it to cool to room temperature. Then fold in the beaten eggs, French bread stuffing mix, cheese, salt, and pepper. Remember ... you don't want the mixture stiff and dry, but you also don't want it runny and wet, either. Blend it just to the point of it being *moist.* Depending upon your cooking temperature and the grade of meat you used, the stuffing mixture could require either a little more bread or a little extra liquid than what is called for in the recipe.

If that's the case, I suggest that if you need a little more bread, add it; and if you need a little more liquid, use either chicken broth, milk, or more V-8 juice. Use something with flavor—don't use water!

All that's left now is to stuff the mixture into the cooled bell peppers and set them into a shallow baking pan. Then liberally sprinkle the tops with the buttered bread crumbs and bake them—*uncovered*—at 350 degrees for about 30 minutes (or until the crumbs turn a toasty golden brown).

I've said it before and I'll say it again ... that's *Naturally N'Awlins.*

Chef's Note: *First, don't buy a lesser grade of ground beef and pork when you make these stuffed peppers. Lesser grades give you a great deal of fat in the meat, and you want the ground meat* lean *so that your stuffing doesn't come out greasy.*

Second, I recommend you serve these peppers with a side dish of scalloped potatoes, maybe some buttered carrots, a cold lettuce-spinach-tomato salad (with all the trimmings), and a glass of chilled Madeira wine.

Nora's "Don't Tell Me You Can't Make These!" Hot Tamales

On page 239 of my *Naturally N'Awlins* cookbook, I've got an old, time-tested recipe for hot tamales that I think is one of the best anywhere. But it takes a little effort and a lot of cooking to put them together. This one, on the other hand, concocted by my kitchen assistant Nora DeJoie, is probably the easiest tamale recipe you'll ever fix. Everything gets mixed and rolled "raw"! Only after you've put the tamales together do you cook them! You gotta try these bad boys!

The Tamale Meat Mixture:

120 tamale papers	½ tsp. black pepper
3 lb. extralean ground beef	5 tsp. salt
3 medium onions	½ tsp. Italian Chili Pepper Sauce
5 cloves fresh garlic	½ cup yellow cornmeal
10 oz. Rotel tomatoes with green chilies	2 oz. hot chili powder
	8 oz. tomato sauce
2 tsp. red pepper	

The Seasoned Cornmeal Coating:

3 cups yellow cornmeal	2 tsp. red pepper
2 tbsp. salt	1 oz. chill powder

The Tamale Sauce:

10 oz. tomato sauce	4 small aluminum loaf pans
1 oz. chili powder	Boiling water
1 tsp. Italian Chili Pepper Sauce	

First, place the tamale papers in a shallow baking pan and soak them in just enough water to keep them wet—they're easier to work with if they're wet.

Next, put the ground meat into a large mixing bowl. Then with your food processor, puree the onions, garlic, and Rotel tomatoes. (Yep! You're also gonna pour in the liquid that the tomatoes came packed in.) Then pour the pureed mixture over the ground meat, along with the red pepper, black pepper, salt, Italian pepper sauce, cornmeal, chili powder, and tomato sauce and work everything together by hand until the meat mix is uniformly and thoroughly blended. *(You might want to wear rubber gloves to do the mixing—the chili powder tends to stain your hands red if you don't.)*

Now set the tamale mix aside at room temperature for about 30 minutes so that the seasonings can marry. And while the meat is resting, mix up your cornmeal coating and your tamale sauce. Here's how easy they are to do.

In a shallow baking pan, blend together the cornmeal, salt, red pepper, and chili powder until thoroughly mixed. Set it aside. Then take an 8-cup Pyrex measuring cup and whip together the tomato sauce, chili powder, and Italian Chili Pepper Sauce until completely blended. Set it aside, too.

Now you're ready to roll hot tamales! Notice—nothing's been cooked yet!

First, place a large sheet of aluminum foil on the table in front of you—this is your workspace; this is what you're gonna roll the tamales on.

Next, situate the tamale papers, the bowl of meat mix, the cornmeal coating, and the loaf pans where you can easily reach each one. Then using about 1 tablespoon of the meat mix, take your hands (again, you might want to wear rubber gloves) and roll out an oblong tamale about the size of a Vienna sausage and toss it around in the cornmeal mixture. You don't have to pack the cornmeal on! Just a light outer coating is all you need.

Now remove it from the cornmeal and wrap it in one of the wet tamale papers (and it works best if you wrap them from point to point diagonally, tucking in the edges of the paper as you wrap).

As you finish each one, place it in an aluminum loaf pan. You'll know you're doing it right if you'll get three layers of tamales, with 10 tamales on each layer. And they should fit into the pans perfectly. I do suggest you crisscross the layers, however, so that the tamales cook evenly.

When all the pans are loaded, pour the sauce evenly over the tamales and fill each loaf pan with boiling water. Then tightly cover each pan with aluminum foil and place them into an oval roaster. Finally, fill the roaster with just enough water to come about three-quarters of the way up the sides of the pans. *Don't overfill!*

All that's left is to place the roaster on the stovetop, cover it tightly, and simmer the tamales for about 2 hours.

You should end up with 120 tamales ready to eat!

Chef's Note:

1—You can buy both the Italian Chili Pepper Sauce and the tamale papers at Central Grocery, 923 Decatur Street, New Orleans 70130.

2—It's a lot easier to make these hot tamales if you got help. It works best if one person rolls the meat and another person wraps the coated tamale. Of course, the more help you get the faster you'll go!

3—If you want to double the recipe and make tamales for the freezer, do it! They freeze well. You can roll and wrap them, place them into the loaf pans, ladle on the sauce, cover them with heavy-duty aluminum foil, and freeze them uncooked. Or you can make them, fully cook them, freeze them, and just reheat them whenever you want a quick and easy meal.

Cliff's Southern Fried Hush Puppies

I've eaten a lot of hush puppies in my lifetime. But none were ever as good as those concocted by the late Cliff Hagewood one evening at Johnny Glover's fishing camp just below Houma! You talk about pig out! One taste and you keep on eatin'! This is one recipe you want to follow to the letter!

2 cups self-rising white cornmeal	**½ cup shoepeg corn, well drained**
1 cup self-rising flour	**Buttermilk to form mixture**
½ bunch green onions, thinly sliced	**Salt and pepper to taste**
1 whole egg, slightly beaten	**64 oz. peanut oil for frying**
¼ cup granulated sugar	

First, take a large mixing bowl and combine the cornmeal and the flour until they are thoroughly blended. Then stir in the green onions, beaten egg, sugar, and shoepeg corn and thoroughly blend all of the ingredients together again.

Now begin stirring in the buttermilk a little at a time until the mixture is just thick enough to hold its shape on a teaspoon. *You don't want it runny— but you don't want a dough either!* If you can "heap" a teaspoon of the mixture ... it's the right consistency!

At this point, season the mix with salt and pepper to your taste, cover it with plastic wrap, and let it "set" on the countertop for 15 minutes (this will give all the flavors a chance to marry). While the hush-puppy mix is marrying, go ahead and preheat the peanut oil to 350 degrees in a heavy aluminum frypan.

Then, when you're ready to eat, take 1 teaspoon of the mixture at a time and gently push it off the spoon into the hot oil with your finger. You want to fry them just like doughnuts—to a golden-brown color. And if you've made the mix properly, you won't even have to turn them over … they'll turn over by themselves!

When they're done, remove them from the oil, drain them on several layers of paper towels, and serve them piping hot alongside some of my Crispy Fried Sheepshead fillets. Ooooooweeee!

THE INSIDE STORY ON EGGPLANTS

Eggplants are just like mirlitons. They're extremely versatile, but a lot of folks have trouble handling them.

Take frying eggplants, for example. There's only two ways to fry eggplants—the right way and the wrong way, and any way that leaves the eggplant soggy and greasy is the wrong way. Let me teach you how to cook eggplants so that they turn out grease free, tender, tasty, and crispy.

First, pick a young eggplant. Those gigantic long eggplants are the worst ones you can buy. You know the "bite" you often get in eggplants? That's because you bought old, oversize eggplants full of seeds—and it's the seeds that bite.

Next, pick an eggplant with smooth purple skin. Avoid the wrinkly kind. Then, unless you're planning to make *caponata,* peel the eggplants and either slice them crosswise or dice them into sticks and soak them in the sink in a gallon of water and a tablespoon of salt. The brine solution seals the eggplant so that it can't absorb oil.

Then, while the eggplant slices are still wet, dip them first into seasoned all-purpose flour, then into an eggwash, then into a pan full of coarsely ground seasoned bread crumbs (make sure the crumbs contain a generous portion of Romano cheese). But before you fry the slices, set them on a piece of waxed paper for a few minutes so that the gluten (the sticky stuff in flour) can do its job and stick to the eggplant.

All that's left is to drop the slices into a pan of deep peanut oil that's set to 350 degrees. What you end up with is a greaseless platter of Sicilian-style eggplant that's supercrispy on the outside and creamy tender on the inside. I promise you, it will be the best fried eggplant you ever had!

TIPS FOR BOILING PASTA

There must be over a hundred different kinds of pasta—spaghetti, macaroni, rigatoni, cavatuni, ziti, and so on. But regardless of the kind, good pasta should never be overcooked (or put another way, *Italian* pasta is never soft and soggy!). So to keep it firm, tender, and *al dente,* here are some cooking tips:

1—Always have enough water in the pot to give the pasta lots of room to boil and roll over. It may be okay to steam rice in just a little water, but if you do that with pasta it is going to turn into a sticky mess. A good rule of thumb is *4 quarts of water to 1 pound of pasta.*

2—Always add about a teaspoonful of salt and about 2 tablespoons of olive oil to the boiling water. This will season and flavor the pasta and keep the strands from sticking together.

3—Do not put the pasta into the water until the water is *rapidly boiling.* Even then, make sure you stir it as it goes into the water.

4—You should always cook pasta *uncovered* ... and *stir it* every 3 or 4 minutes. Uncovered, it won't boil over and the stirring will give you consistency in each strand.

5—Cook it only long enough to completely soften the semolina flour. It should offer a "slight resistance" to the tooth—which is what "al dente" means. It should never ever be soft. For perfect pasta, ideal cooking time is 10 to 15 minutes depending upon the kind of pasta you're cooking.

6—When it's cooked, take it off the fire immediately and drain it in a colander. If you're planning to use the pasta in salads, rinse it in *cold water* ... if you're going to serve it hot with a sauce, either rinse it in *hot water* or don't rinse it at all. Just make sure all the water has drained off before you serve it. Otherwise it will thin out your sauce and make it watery.

7—Just for the record, 1 pound of spaghetti will serve 6 normal people (or 4 really hungry Italians).

8—A 2-ounce serving of spaghetti contains 210 calories, 6 grams of protein, 43 grams of carbohydrates, 1 gram of fat, and 3 milligrams of sodium. Of course, that's plain pasta—once you splash it down with gravy, cover it with Romano, and dish it up with two meatballs, a half-loaf of French bread, and a bottle of Bordellino ... hey, you're on your own!

Chef's Note: *You can cook pasta in advance for your guests and your family. All you do is boil it as I've suggested, drain it, wash it in cold water, mix in about 4 to 6 tablespoons of olive oil, put it into a Ziploc bag, and store it in the bottom of the refrigerator.*

Then when you're ready to eat, either add it to the piping hot sauce and stir it around, or put the pasta back in the colander and dip it quickly into boiling hot water. It will taste like you just cooked it.

Incidentally, pasta will keep in your refrigerator this way for about 5 days.

HOW TO COOK FRESH HOMEMADE SAUSAGES

There are two recommended methods for preparing fresh homemade sausages—*grilling* or *water-baking*.

Grilling: Pork, hot, or Italian sausages can be cooked on the barbecue pit. Simply take the links or patties and place them on a charbroil grill about 4 inches over the coals or lava rocks. As they heat you should continually turn them over with a pair of tongs to ensure that they cook evenly (do this gently if you're cooking patties or they'll break apart). Incidentally, cooking time over the open grill usually runs about 15-20 minutes, and your sausages are done when they come out a toasty brown.

If you're cooking sausage links in natural casings, I also recommend that before you fire them up on the grill you prick each link in about 3 places with an ice pick to allow the fatty juices to leak out. You will have to watch for the occasional "flare up," however. Escaping fat tends to catch fire when it reaches the flames.

This is the method I suggest you use if you intend to serve your sausages as sandwiches on buns or French bread. I think they taste best when they're dressed with tomatoes, lettuce, mustard, mayonnaise, grilled onions, and melted mozzarella or provolone cheese.

Water-Baking: This is the method I suggest you use if you plan to put your fresh homemade sausages in sauces and gravies, because the water bath significantly reduces the amount of excess fat that eventually goes into the sauce or gravy.

What you do is take a high-sided baking pan and place the sausage links in a single layer on the bottom (you don't do this with patties!). Then pour just enough water into the pan so that it comes about halfway up the links.

At this point, prick each link about 3 times with an ice pick, tightly cover the pan with heavy-duty aluminum foil, and place it in a 400-degree oven for approximately 30 minutes. Then uncover the pan, pour off the water (along with the excess fat), turn the sausages over, and continue to bake them—*uncovered*—for another 10 minutes or until the links turn a toasty brown.

All that's left is to drop them into your Italian gravy, stew, gumbo, sauce piquante, red beans, or whatever else you want to cook.

How to Make Homemade Sicilian Ricotta Cheese

It goes into stuffed manicotti, it's the main ingredient in cannoli, and most Sicilians love it so much they eat it right from the spoon. But to buy the commercial variety, you're talking expensive. Why not make your own homemade ricotta? It's not as difficult to do as it sounds.

1 gal. whole milk (not skim or low fat)	**1 qt. cultured buttermilk**
½ tsp. rennet	**Pinch salt**

Start off by taking a large pot and pouring the gallon of milk into it. Then bring the milk to a near boil (actually, the cheese comes out best if you use a thermometer and bring the temperature of the milk up to exactly 180 degrees). In fact, you should never let the milk go over 180 degrees, never let it drop below 170 degrees, and keep it stabilized at 180 until you have added the rennet and stirred it in well.

Once you have the temperature constant, remove the pot from the fire and begin adding the buttermilk 8 ounces at a time. What you want to do is add 8 ounces, stir it in vigorously, wait for about 5 minutes, then add another 8 ounces. Continue to add buttermilk and agitate vigorously until you see what looks similar to cornmeal starting to float up to the surface. This is the ricotta taking shape. And once it starts forming, *never stop stirring it.*

Once you've noticed the floating cheese, wait about 15 minutes for it to set. If it sets well, you can remove it from the pot and put it into molds to drain. If it doesn't set well, add more buttermilk until it does.

Unlike Creole cream cheese, ricotta should be refrigerated immediately upon it setting. Allow the excess water to drain out in a pan in the refrigerator. Before forming the molds, you can add salt to taste. Also unlike Creole cream cheese, ricotta will keep only for about 8 to 10 days in your refrigerator.

Chef's Note: *Rennet (or rennin) can be purchased at most large drugstores or at most cheese shops.*

How to Make Homemade Creole Cream Cheese

Remember that wonderful Creole cream cheese you used to get from Gold Seal Creamery? Well, the creamery has long since shut down, but before he retired Mr. Centenni gave me his prized recipe. So with a whole lot of pride and gratitude to my friend, I share it with you!

1 gal. skim milk	**½ tsp. rennet**
4 oz. cultured buttermilk	**6 cream cheese molds**

Start off by putting a gallon of skim milk into a large container, preferably stainless steel. Be sure the temperature of the milk is no cooler than 70 degrees and no warmer than 80 degrees.

Then, to the milk add the buttermilk and stir the mixture together well. Then pour in the rennet and agitate everything vigorously for exactly 1 minute. After stirring, do not stir again or you'll break the cheese formation.

At this point, cover the container and let it stand at room temperature for 12 to 15 hours. All the while, the rennet will be converting the milk solids into a "caked" cheese. Remember, the longer it stands, the firmer the cheese will be.

After the cheese has set, ladle it out into the molds (which can be steel cheese molds you get from a kitchen supply store or simply plastic containers similar to those crabmeat comes packed in). If you use the homemade variety, just poke a bunch of holes in the containers (sides and bottom) so that the water drains off the cheese.

Once the cheese has molded, set the containers into a baking pan to catch any excess moisture leaking from the cheese and place the pan in the refrigerator for at least 4 to 6 hours to allow the cheese to form. When it reaches the consistency you want, transfer it to a permanent storage container (preferably glass or plastic cartons). Note that cream cheese will keep in your refrigerator for at least a month. When you're ready to eat, spoon what you want into a bowl, cover it with heavy whipping cream, sprinkle it with granulated sugar, and have yo'self a real N'Awlins breakfast.

Chef's Note: *Rennet (or rennin) can be purchased at most large drugstores or at most cheese shops.*

CHAPTER 11

Sauces, Gravies, and Toppings

Creole Brandy Sauce

Want to make a rich velvety sauce to serve over pork, poultry, and seafood? Learn to do this one! It's so good you'll want to drink it with a straw!

½ stick butter

1 tbsp. all-purpose flour

1 cup evaporated milk

¼ cup brandy

2 tbsp. Creole mustard

Salt and white pepper to taste

2 tbsp. chopped green onions

Pinch lemon zest

In a saucepan, melt the butter, stir in the flour, and cook it over medium heat until it takes on an ever so slight shade of beige. Then pour in the evaporated milk, blend it thoroughly into the butter roux until smooth, and continue to cook it until the sauce base starts to thicken.

At this point, stir in the brandy and the Creole mustard and work it into the sauce. In fact, continue stirring until only a slight essence of the alcohol remains and the sauce resumes its thickness (which should take you about 4 minutes or so).

When it's ready to serve, whisk in your salt and pepper, sprinkle in the green onions and lemon zest, and liberally ladle it over fried, baked, or sautéed pork, braised beef or veal, or bronzed, pan-fried, or grilled seafood. It's a delicate accompaniment to almost any entrée.

Spicy Shrimp Cocktail Sauce

Follow my Perfect N'Awlins Boiled Shrimp recipe to the letter and you won't need a dipping sauce. But if you'd like one anyway, whip up a batch of this one! It's some good, cher!

2 cups ketchup

½ cup mayonnaise

¼ cup Creole mustard

¼ cup chopped onions

3 tbsp. fresh lemon juice

3 tbsp. Worcestershire sauce

1 tsp. prepared horseradish

1 tbsp. minced jalapeño peppers

1 tbsp. Louisiana hot sauce

½ tsp. garlic powder

2 tsp. salt

This couldn't be easier to make! Very simply, take your food processor and with the steel cutting blade whip all the ingredients together until they are uniformly blended.

Then place the mixture into your refrigerator for about an hour to chill. Amen! That's it! All that's left is to serve it with your boiled shrimp.

Chef's Note: *If you prefer, go ahead and double the recipe, because this sauce can be stored for several weeks in your fridge in an airtight container. In fact, the longer it sets ... the better it gets!*

Mary Clare's Sicilian Tomato Gravy (Sugo)

Traditionally, in Southern Italy and Sicily pasta is served with every meal … and over the top of the pasta is a rich Italian gravy made with tomatoes. But unlike the gravies made in America, "real Italian gravy" is rich but not thick! So if you want to make gravy authentically Italian, you got to make it just like my wife does. Here's how it's done!

4 tbsp. extra-virgin olive oil	1 tsp. sweet basil
1 medium onion, finely chopped	½ tsp. oregano
1 large can Contadina tomato paste (18-oz. size)	1 tsp. Italian seasoning
	2 whole bay leaves (medium size)
2 cups crushed peeled tomatoes (303-size can)	3 Contadina cans filled with water (1½ qt.)
2 cloves garlic, finely minced	Salt and black pepper to taste

First, in a 5-quart Dutch oven, heat the olive oil to medium high and fry down the chopped onions until they wilt. Then drop in the tomato paste, stir it well into the softened onions, and cook the mixture for about 2 minutes. The trick is to sauté the tomato paste until the consistency is *velvety smooth*. I recommend you stir the mixture constantly.

Next, drop in the crushed tomatoes and the garlic and blend them well into the tomato-paste mixture. Then stirring constantly, cook everything together for another 2 minutes.

At this point, toss in the basil, oregano, Italian seasoning, and bay leaves. And—yep!—stir them in well too! Remember, everything has to be smooth.

Then slowly stir in the water—simply fill the tomato-paste can three times to get an accurate measurement—and mix all the ingredients once more. I suggest you use a wire whip for the final mixing—it's the best way to get a uniform blending.

Finally, season the gravy with salt and pepper to taste. Then cover the pot, reduce the heat to low, and let the sauce simmer for about an hour to an hour and a half before serving it over hot pasta.

Remember, "real" Sicilian sauce is not pasty-thick; it's just *rich*.

Chef's Note: *Instead of water, I suggest you use a good rich beef or chicken stock for making your gravy. If you want to drop eggs, chicken, sausage, pork chunks, or meatballs into the sauce, you should put them in immediately after the salt and pepper is added so that the flavors can marry together. And always remember, a good Italian gravy must contain some form of pork—it's where the traditional distinctive flavor comes from!*

Any excess oil from the meats that accumulates on top of the gravy can be skimmed off before serving or absorbed by floating several lettuce leaves on the surface of the sauce. Discard the leaves before serving the sauce.

Just for the record, fresh-boiled spaghetti should not be rinsed when you plan to serve it with Sicilian tomato gravy. It should simply be drained then coated with the gravy while still hot (it's the hot starch in the pasta that helps the gravy to adhere to each strand).

Creamed Horseradish Sauce

Nothing goes better with corned beef and cabbage than this condiment dressing. And I guarantee you it'll beat anything you'll buy at the store!

1 bottle pure horseradish
1 small container sour cream

1 tbsp. chopped chives
Pinch salt

All you do is mix all the ingredients together in a bowl until they are thoroughly blended. Then after chilling it for about an hour, spread it with a knife—to taste—over the sliced corned beef.

Meine Freunde, das ist gut!

N'Awlins Bacon Butter

The absolute best way to flavor any dish is to enhance it with a flavored butter. They're all easy to make, but this one could possibly be the easiest. I know it's the tastiest!

1 lb. softened butter (room
    temperature)
⅔ cup diced yellow onions
¼ cup diced celery
½ cup finely crumbled cooked
    bacon

¼ cup bacon drippings
3 tbsp. Louisiana hot sauce
Salt and black pepper to taste

First, take a couple of tablespoons of the butter, place them into a heavy skillet over medium-high heat, toss in the onions and celery, and sauté the vegetables until they wilt.

Then take a large bowl and mix together the remaining butter, the onions, the celery, and the crumbled bacon. And, one at a time, fold in the rest of the ingredients and whip them thoroughly until the mixture is smooth, creamy, and uniformly blended.

Now place the bowl in the refrigerator until the mixture just begins to "set up"—it's easier to work with when it's chilled. When it's ready, spoon out the mix into heavy-duty plastic wrap and roll it tightly into "tube-shaped" blocks. This recipe should give you 4 to 6 tubes of flavored butter, which can be kept either in the refrigerator for 2 weeks or in the freezer for several months.

Use it to sauté seafood, beef, pork, veal, and chicken. Use it as a baste for grilled meats. Brush it on barbecue. And melt it over steamed vegetables, mashed potatoes, pasta, and even grits. It's that versatile ... and it turns a simple recipe into one that's truly gourmet!

N'Awlins Nectar Syrup

Remember all those great nectar snowballs you used to buy when you were a kid? Ever wonder how they made that great-tasting topping? Here's the recipe!

3 cups granulated sugar	2 tbsp. almond extract
3 cups water	4 drops red food coloring
1 tbsp. vanilla	

This is so simple to make! Just mix the 3 cups of sugar and the 3 cups of water together in a saucepan and heat until the sugar dissolves thoroughly and the water comes to a rolling boil.

Then take the mixture off the fire and add the vanilla, the almond extract, and the food coloring and blend it together well.

And presto ... you got old-time N'Awlins nectar syrup!

CHAPTER 12

Desserts

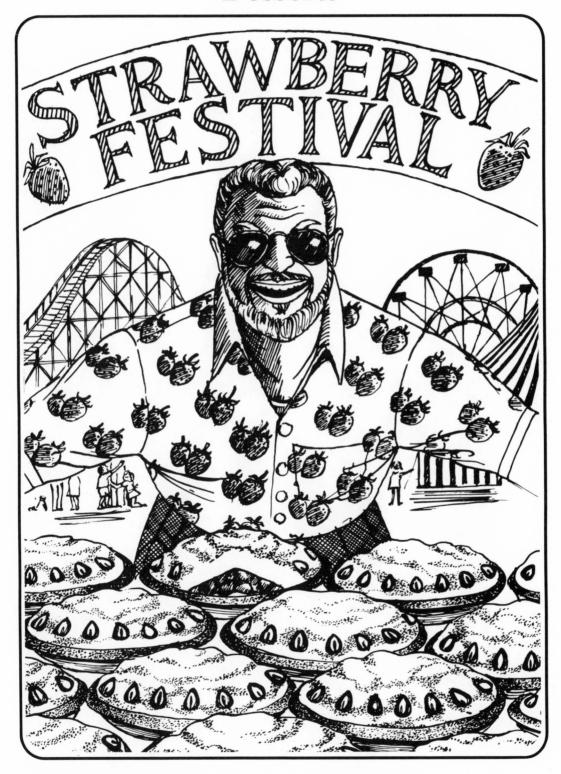

The Original New Orleans Beignet Recipe
(Circa 1813)

I have no idea where I got this recipe! At some time over the past few decades somebody either sent it to me, or I picked it up at a cooking demonstration, or I found it in a neighbor's recipe file box, or ... who knows! All I do know is that this recipe will give you some of the best batches of beignets "from scratch" that you ever tasted in all your born days!

¼ cup whole milk
¼ cup granulated sugar
1 tsp. salt
¼ cup vegetable shortening
¼ cup very warm water (110-15 degrees)

1 pkg. active dry yeast
1 egg, well beaten
3 cups sifted all-purpose flour
Oil for deep frying
Powdered sugar for dusting

The first thing you do is take a pot and scald the milk ... then stir in the sugar, salt, and shortening and allow the mixture to cool to lukewarm. While it's cooling, take a large bowl, pour your very warm water into it, and sprinkle in the yeast. You want to take your time and stir it around until it all dissolves. That's important!

Then add the lukewarm milk mixture, the egg, and half of the flour to the bowl and beat it well with a mixer or a spoon for about *1 minute*. Then add the rest of the flour (and even a little more if needed) to make a soft dough.

When it's mixed, turn the dough out onto a lightly floured surface and knead it until it becomes smooth and elastic. At this point, put the dough down inside a greased bowl, cover it with a towel, and let it rise in a warm place—free from draft—until it doubles in size (which will take about an hour). Then punch the dough down, re-cover with the towel, and let it rise again (this time for a half-hour).

Now you're ready to make beignets!

Roll out the dough to a ½-inch thickness and cut out 2½-inch squares. Then place the squares on a greased baking sheet and let them rise slightly until light ... about an hour. *Under absolutely no circumstances should you handle them during the final rising—if you do, they'll fall and they'll turn out as tough and heavy as hardtack when they're fried.*

When you're ready to cook them, heat the oil in your deep fryer (or Dutch oven) to 375 degrees and fry them for 2 minutes (or until golden brown on both sides). Then drain the beignets on absorbent paper towels, sprinkle them with generous amounts of powdered sugar, and serve them piping hot alongside a steaming cup of café au lait!

They'll taste like N'Awlins in the Quarter after dark!

Chef's Note: *This recipe should give you about 2 dozen beignets.*

Old New Orleans Calas

The original recipe dates back to between 1750 and 1800, and the crunchy, tasty rice cakes were once sold as breakfast items on the streets of the city by Creole women who wrapped them in towels and carried them in a basket on their heads. Today, they're no longer sold on the streets ... but they're still popular among the old-line Creole families of New Orleans—especially at Mardi Gras and Holy Communion time!

3 cups water
1 heaping cup long-grain rice
2 whole eggs
½ cup granulated sugar
1 tsp. vanilla
½ tsp. apple-pie spice
¼ tsp. salt

1 cup whole milk
1½ cups self-rising flour
Vegetable oil for frying
Powdered sugar for dusting
Steen's Pure Cane Syrup for
   topping

First, take a 4-quart Dutch oven or saucepan containing 3 cups of water and bring it to a rolling boil. Then stir in 1 heaping cup of long-grain rice. When the water comes back to a boil, reduce the heat to simmer, cover the pot, and cook the rice for about 15-20 minutes until it is "softened" (slightly overcooked but not extramushy). At this point—*without washing the rice!*—set the pot into the refrigerator to cool.

Next, you're going to need a large bowl and a wire whip. Take the bowl, toss in the eggs, granulated sugar, vanilla, apple-pie spice, and salt and whip everything together into a smooth and frothy custard—*about 3 to 5 minutes.*

Now, pour the cup of milk into the egg/sugar mixture and, again using the whip, blend it thoroughly into the custard. Then, a little at a time, add the flour and whip everything together until you get a smooth batter.

At this point, mix the batter and the cold rice together thoroughly, making sure that every grain is uniformly coated, and let the mixture stand for about 30 minutes so that the flavors "marry."

Meanwhile, pour about an inch of high-quality vegetable oil into a heavy 12-inch skillet (you want to almost cover the calas as they cook) and heat the oil on *high* (between 375-400 degrees). Then, when the oil reaches the right temperature, drop the calas mixture into the skillet by large spoonfuls (you want them to form thin 3-inch fritters), fry them for about a minute on both sides until golden brown and crunchy, and place them on paper towels to drain.

Finally, serve them *immediately*—piping hot—covered with a generous sprinkling of powdered sugar and a large helping of Louisiana pure cane syrup.

Chef's Note: *Apple-pie spice is a mixture of cinnamon, nutmeg, allspice, and ginger. Several spice manufacturers prepackage it.*

For calas to be light, crispy, and crunchy, they need to be eaten as soon as they come out of the skillet. Once they cool and set, they tend to get tough and greasy. I also recommend that you fry them in only the highest quality vegetable oil.

Some recipes call for cooking calas in a lightly greased skillet. I want you to know that this method produces heavy "rice pancakes" rather than light and crispy calas. I suggest you fry them—authentically!—in deep fat.

Naturally N'Awlins Strawberry Festival Pie

Here it is, y'all! Right from the folks who make the 900 pies for the annual Ponchatoula Strawberry Festival. This is some kinda delicious—complete with calories and all!

1 pt. fresh strawberries, sliced and quartered
1 graham-cracker-crumb piecrust
3 tbsp. cornstarch
1½ cups cold water

1 box strawberry Jell-O (3-oz. size)
1 cup granulated sugar
Cool Whip or whipped cream for topping

First thing you do is place the sliced and quartered strawberries (and you should slice half of the pint and quarter the other half) into the graham-cracker-crumb piecrust and set it aside.

Then mix the cornstarch and cold water together and stir it around briskly until all the starch is dissolved. When it's smooth, pour the mixture into a deep pot and bring it to a boil.

Next add the strawberry Jell-O and the granulated sugar to the pot and stir the mixture over a medium-high heat until it turns silky smooth and thoroughly uniform. *In fact, you want to continue to stir the mixture without stopping until it thickens. This is the most important part of the whole recipe!*

So how do you know when it's just right? Easy!

Just put a tablespoon or so of the glaze mix into a teacup and swirl it around to cool it off slightly. When the cooled sauce doesn't run when the cup is inverted, the glaze is ready to put on the pie.

All that's left is to evenly ladle the hot glaze over the fresh strawberries in the pie shell, making sure that every single strawberry is covered. Then set the pie aside to cool. And when it's cool enough, cover it with either whipped cream or Cool Whip, slide it into the refrigerator to chill, and … well, the rest is up to you!

Chef's Note: *For an elegant presentation, you can decorate the top of the pie by placing a few fresh halved strawberries around the edges and a scant shaving of chocolate in the center.*

Sweet-Potato Praline Pie à la Mode

If you can combine the delicate richness of Louisiana yams with the classic taste of Creole pralines and bake them together in a crusty pie shell, you have a wintertime bayou-style dessert anyone would savor. But when you top it off à la mode ... it don't get no better than dat!

2-3 sweet potatoes	1 tsp. vanilla
1 stick butter, melted	¼ cup praline liqueur
½ cup white sugar	½ tsp. ground cinnamon
1 cup lightly packed brown sugar	½ tsp. ground pumpkin-pie spice
4 tbsp. all-purpose flour	Pinch ground nutmeg
½ cup chopped pecan pieces	1 unbaked 9-inch pastry shell
3 whole eggs, well beaten	Vanilla ice cream
½ cup heavy whipping cream	Marshmallow creme
½ tsp. lemon juice	

First, bake your sweet potatoes at 350 degrees until they are tender and set them aside to cool (you'll need 2 or 3 for this pie, depending upon their size—you want to end up with 2 cups mashed). Then remove the peelings and mash the pulp until it turns lump free and creamy smooth.

Next, take a large mixing bowl and blend together the butter, mashed potatoes, white sugar, brown sugar, flour, and pecan pieces. *Note: don't skimp on this step!* Uniformity is very important.

Now add the eggs, whipping cream, lemon juice, vanilla, and praline liqueur. But don't just mix it. *Whip* it into the potato mixture! The batter you get must be uniform for the pie to bake evenly.

At this point, sprinkle on the cinnamon, the pumpkin-pie spice, and the nutmeg and stir it into the batter.

All that's left is to pour the mixture into the pie shell and bake it for about 45 minutes on the center rack of a preheated 325-degree oven. You'll know the pie is ready when the filling firms up and a sheen forms on the surface.

I recommend you allow the pie to cool thoroughly before serving (it's hard to cut a hot sweet potato pie!). I also recommend that when you serve it you top it with a generous scoop of softened vanilla ice cream and a large dollop of warm marshmallow creme.

Chocolate Pecan Truffle Pie

A tasty, crisp, chocolate-crumb crust loaded to the brim with a rich truffle-pecan filling! Ummmmmmmmm! This is so good I guarantee you're gonna have a hard time sharing this with your dinner guests ... or even the members of your family!

⅓ cup cold orange juice
1 envelope Knox unflavored gelatin
1 tbsp. instant coffee
1 tbsp. coffee-flavored liqueur
¾ cup semisweet chocolate chips
1 tsp. pure vanilla
2 whole eggs, slightly beaten

⅓ cup granulated sugar
2 cups Cool Whip
¾ cup finely chopped pecan pieces
9-inch chocolate-crumb crust
1 Hershey bar, refrigerated
¼ cup sweetened shredded coconut

First, take a 3½-quart saucepan, pour in the orange juice, sprinkle the gelatin evenly over the surface, and let it set for 1 minute to soften. Then place the pan on the stove, heat the juice over a medium-low flame, and stir until the gelatin is completely dissolved.

Next, sprinkle in the instant coffee, pour in the coffee liqueur, and drop in the chocolate chips. Then stir—*almost constantly!*—until the chocolate is thoroughly melted, the alcohol evaporates, and the blend is smooth.

Now remove the pot from the fire, stir in the vanilla, and set the mixture aside for about 10 minutes (or until it becomes lukewarm).

While the chocolate base is cooling, take a large bowl and an electric mixer and beat together the eggs and the sugar at high speed. The object is to whip them until they thicken (which should take about 5 minutes or so).

Then, with the mixer running at medium speed, gradually add the lukewarm gelatin mix and beat it only until blended.

At this point, fold in the whipped cream and the chopped pecan pieces, and transfer the mixture from the bowl to the crumb crust. Then, with a hand grater, shred the Hershey bar over the top of the filling, sprinkle on the coconut garnish, and chill the pie in the refrigerator until firm.

If you're a chocoholic ... you're gonna love this!

Chef's Note: *If extra calories don't bother you and you want a superrich truffle filling, instead of Cool Whip use 2 cups of real, freshly prepared, homemade whipped cream. Ummmmmmmmm!*

Chocolate-crumb crusts are available in the frozen-food section of most supermarkets.

Pecan Fudgey Pudding

If you're addicted to chocolate, this is one of those desserts that you have to hide until everyone has finished eating. 'Cuz if you don't, the dessert will all be gone before you get the entrée on the table. And you talk about easy to make! Wait till you try this!

1 cup all-purpose flour	2 tbsp. melted butter
1 tsp. baking powder	1 cup chopped pecans
½ tsp. salt	¾ cup dark brown sugar
¾ cup granulated sugar	½ cup cocoa
2 tbsp. cocoa	1¾ cups hot water
½ cup whole milk	1 cup real whipped cream
1 tsp. vanilla	½ cup Kahlua liqueur

First, in a large bowl, sift together the flour, the baking powder, the salt, the granulated sugar, and the cocoa. In fact, first mix it all together *then* sift it to make sure the blend is totally uniform.

Next, to the blended mix add the milk, the vanilla, and the butter and mix everything well again. At this point, go ahead and drop in the pecans and fold them in so that they are evenly distributed throughout the pudding base. *Note:* take your time and don't hurry this step because this is what forms the texture and consistency of the finished pudding.

Now pour the mix into a buttered 8-by-8 cake pan and let it rest for 3 minutes. In the meantime, take a wire whip and mix together your brown sugar and second measure of cocoa. Then sprinkle it evenly over the batter.

Now here's the trick to getting the pudding to come out just right!

Very gently—*and uniformly!*—pour the hot water over the entire contents of the baking pan. Then immediately slide the pan into the oven and bake the pudding at 350 degrees for 40 to 45 minutes.

When it's ready, take it out of the oven and allow it to cool slightly. Then dish out heaping spoonfuls from the pan into small bowls.

I suggest you serve it warm, topped with whipped cream or Cool Whip and splashed with a dash of Kahlua liqueur.

Old New Orleans Vanilla Ice Cream

Remember the rich vanilla flavor of the ice cream your grandma used to make in the hydrator pan of the 'frigerator when you were a kid? Well ... I've duplicated that recipe for you to use in your ice-cream freezer! Wait till you taste!

½ pt. whipping cream	2 tsp. pure vanilla
1 pt. Half & Half	1 cup granulated sugar
2 cans evaporated milk	Pinch salt
1 can condensed milk	1 packet Salada
4 eggs	

First, take a large bowl and mix together the whipping cream, the Half & Half, and the evaporated milk. Then, using a wire whisk, whip in the condensed milk until the mixture is completely blended and slightly frothy.

Next, separate the eggs, whip the whites into stiff peaks, and set them in the refrigerator to chill. Then whip the egg yolks, the vanilla, and the sugar together until the mixture turns smooth and creamy.

At this point—with an electric mixer on low speed—blend the salt and the yolks into the milk base until fully incorporated. Then whip in the Salada until it, too, is nice and smooth.

Finally, *gently fold in the egg whites* and chill the ice-cream mixture for about a half-hour. You'll notice that the cream will harden in less time (and come out less grainy) if the mixture is cold when you put it into the freezer.

All that's left is to pour the ice-cream mix into your freezer and let it form. It should take an average running time of 20 to 30 minutes to become finished ice cream.

Chef's Note: *When the ice-cream freezer stops running, the ice cream inside the can will be the consistency of mush. So I suggest that when the ice cream thickens and the motor stalls, you remove the dasher from the can, wipe away all the rock salt from the can cover, recap the can, add more ice, and let the ice cream "cure" for about an hour before you serve it. If you wrap a bath towel completely around the freezer—and over the top as well—the cream will ripen quicker.*

Incidentally, this is also the time when you add solid *ingredients—shredded candy bars, chocolate chips, chopped cherries, minced nuts, etc.—to the ice cream. If it is done earlier, the pieces will merely precipitate to the bottom of the can. After you remove the dasher, just fold the solids in slightly.* Liquid *flavorings like chocolate syrup and pureed fruit can be added to the ice cream at the very start of the freezing process. By the way, baby foods (like Gerber strained peaches) make excellent flavoring ingredients!*

Always use crushed ice rather than cubes whenever possible. It causes the mixture to freeze slower, thereby giving you a smooth, less grainy ice cream.

Avoid using table salt to make ice cream. The fine granules cause the mixture to freeze too rapidly and your ice cream turns out grainy. Use ice-cream salt.

Layering is another technique that prevents grainy ice cream. Once the can is in the freezer, add about 3 inches of ice and top it with 5 ounces of rock salt. Then add another 3 inches of ice and another 5 ounces of rock salt. Continue repeating the process until the freezer is filled with ice … but do not place the ice and salt on top of the can!

To start the freezing process, add 1 cup of cold water when the freezer is half-filled with ice and salt. Then add a second cup of cold water when the freezer is completely filled. The water helps the ice settle and melt evenly, reducing the possibility of graininess.

Salada is an ice-cream base that binds all the ingredients together to give the finished product a smooth silky consistency. It is available at most major food stores and at specialty shops where ice-cream supplies are sold.

For a richer taste, make the ice-cream mixture a day ahead of time, store it in an empty gallon milk jug, and let it rest in your refrigerator overnight before you freeze it.

Low-Calorie Vanilla Ice Cream

Want the full flavor of a good rich ice cream without all the calories? Well … I've got the recipe you're looking for!

6 eggs, separated	¼ cup hot water
6 cups skim milk	3 tbsp. Knox gelatin
6 cups prepared nonfat dry milk	4 tbsp. vanilla
14 saccharin tablets (½ grain)	¾ tsp. salt

First, take two bowls and, with an electric mixer, beat the egg yolks creamy smooth and the egg whites into stiff peaks.

Next, mix together the skim milk and the nonfat dry milk in a saucepan over low heat—*don't let it boil!* Then dissolve the saccharin tablets into the mixture and whip in the egg yolks.

At this point, combine the hot water and the gelatin and add to it just enough of the egg custard to fully dissolve the gelatin. Now set the gelatin aside for a moment to cool.

Next, add the softened gelatin, vanilla, and salt to the custard and mix all the ingredients together until they are fully blended.

Finally, *gently fold in the egg whites* and chill the cream mixture for about a half-hour. All that's left is to strain the mixture, pour it into your freezer, and let it form. It should take an average running time of 20 to 30 minutes to become finished low-cal ice cream.

Chef's Note: *When the ice-cream freezer stops running, the ice cream inside the can will be the consistency of mush. So I suggest that when the ice cream thickens and the motor stalls, you remove the dasher from the can, wipe away all the rock salt from the can cover, recap the can, add more ice, and let the ice cream "cure" for about an hour before you serve it. If you wrap a bath towel completely around the freezer—and over the top as well—the cream will ripen quicker.*

Always use crushed ice rather than cubes whenever possible. It causes the mixture to freeze slower, thereby giving you a smooth, less grainy ice cream.

Avoid using table salt to make ice cream. The fine granules cause the mixture to freeze too rapidly and your ice cream turns out grainy. Use ice-cream salt.

Layering is another technique that prevents grainy ice cream. Once the can is in the freezer, add about 3 inches of ice and top it with 5 ounces of rock salt. Then add another 3 inches of ice and another 5 ounces of rock salt. Continue repeating the process until the freezer is filled with ice ... but do not place the ice and salt on top of the can!

To start the freezing process, add 1 cup of cold water when the freezer is half-filled with ice and salt. Then add a second cup of cold water when the freezer is completely filled. The water helps the ice settle and melt evenly, reducing the possibility of graininess.

For a richer taste, make the ice-cream mixture a day ahead of time, store it in an empty gallon milk jug, and let it rest in your refrigerator overnight before you freeze it.

Low-Cholesterol Vanilla Ice Cream

The "Doc" says you can't have the cholesterol, right? And you think that means having to give up ice cream, right? Wrong! I've got a low-cholesterol ice cream recipe for you! Oh—it doesn't taste like Blue Bell or Häagen-Dazs … but it's pretty doggone good for something that's good for you!

2 cups skim milk	**2 cups skim evaporated milk**
1 envelope Knox unflavored gelatin	**2 tsp. pure vanilla**
1¼ cups sugar	

First, take a saucepan and heat the skim milk just to scalding—*but do not let it boil!* Now remove it from the heat and stir in the gelatin and the sugar until the mixture is fully dissolved and smooth.

Next, take a blender and "spin" the mix on the medium setting for about 4 minutes. Then take the evaporated milk, add it to the blender, and "spin" it again on the medium setting for another 2 minutes.

At this point, transfer the mixture to a stainless steel bowl, cover it, and chill it in the refrigerator for 3 hours.

Then when you're ready to make ice cream, remove the mixture from the refrigerator, stir in the vanilla, and pour the mixture into your ice-cream freezer. It should take an average running time of 20 to 30 minutes to become finished ice cream.

Chef's Note: *When the ice-cream freezer stops running, the ice cream inside the can will be the consistency of mush. So I suggest that when the ice cream thickens and the motor stalls, you remove the dasher from the can, wipe away all the rock salt from the can cover, recap the can, add more ice, and let the ice cream "cure" for about an hour before you serve it. If you wrap a bath towel completely around the freezer—and over the top as well—the cream will ripen quicker.*

Always use crushed ice rather than cubes whenever possible. It causes the mixture to freeze slower, thereby giving you a smooth, less grainy ice cream.

Avoid using table salt to make ice cream. The fine granules cause the mixture to freeze too rapidly and your ice cream turns out grainy. Use ice-cream salt.

Layering is another technique that prevents grainy ice cream. Once the can is in the freezer, add about 3 inches of ice and top it with 5 ounces of rock salt. Then add another 3 inches of ice and another 5 ounces of rock salt. Continue repeating the process until the freezer is filled with ice … but do not place the ice and salt on top of the can!

To start the freezing process, add 1 cup of cold water when the freezer is half-filled with ice and salt. Then add a second cup of cold water when the freezer is completely filled. The water helps the ice settle and melt evenly, reducing the possibility of graininess.

Banana Split Crepes
with Southern Comfort Topping

I could write two pages trying to explain just how good this dessert is, but there's no way it really can be explained. It's a banana split ... it's crepes suzette ... it's rich ... it's light ... it tastes like a million calories ... and I'll bet you can't eat just one!

The Crepe Filling:

3 bananas, julienned
1 fresh pineapple, finely chopped
2 cups chopped Maraschino
  cherries

2 cups chopped walnuts
1 large container Cool Whip

First, take a large bowl and fold all the ingredients together gently—try not to break the bananas any more than you have to. Then when you got everything mixed well, cover the bowl with plastic wrap and refrigerate it for at least 3 hours to allow the flavors to "marry."

The Egg Crepe Batter:

4 whole eggs, well beaten
1 tsp. all-purpose flour

4 tbsp. water

At this point, whip together the eggs, flour, and water until uniformly blended. Then using just enough egg batter to completely cover the bottom of a lightly buttered nonstick skillet, roll the batter around to form an extrathin crepe ... *but see to it that the skillet is hot when you put the batter into it.* Then, when the crepe has cooked (usually when the edges curl up), spoon out the banana split filling into the center and fold the crepe edges over it.

The Southern Comfort Topping:

2 cups Häagen-Dazs Vanilla Ice
  Cream

½ tsp. cinnamon
¼ cup Southern Comfort

Meanwhile, drop the Häagen-Dazs into another nonstick skillet (and it should be hot enough to begin melting the ice cream), sprinkle on the cinnamon, and pour the Southern Comfort over the top. Then flame the alcohol immediately! And when the ice cream is about half-melted, ladle it over the crepe.

It'll take you a few tries before you get the ice cream and the Southern Comfort the right texture, but once you get it right ... wow!

Chef's Note: *Just one word of caution—be extra careful whenever you flambé. Don't do it over a kitchen stove vent or near anything that can catch fire! Don't pour the alcohol directly from the bottle—use a spoon or ladle. In other words ... be careful!*

Miraculous Mousse

Whadaya do for a formal dessert when friends drop in unexpectedly for supper? You make *Miraculous Mousse,* which is probably the best name you can give it because it's a *miracle* that you can make it so fast and still have it taste so good! Here's the recipe!

First, take a big bowl—preferably stainless steel—and put it in the refrigerator or freezer to chill it. Then dig out the hand mixer and some whipping cream and pour the cold whipping cream in the cold bowl.

Now, start beating the cream until the peaks *almost* form! But don't beat it too much—you don't want it fully whipped, yet you don't want it liquid either.

Anyway, when you start to see the peaks, open up a box of—you ready for this?—*Jell-O Instant Pudding!* Yep—good ol' J-E-L-L-O! And with the beaters going on high, you start sprinkling in the contents of the box! And, podnuh, when you finally get the whole box in the whipping cream, you got yourself one fantastic chocolate mousse! It's simple, unbelievably quick, and if you don't blab to folks how you did it they'll swear you graduated as a pastry chef from the Culinary Institute of America!

Of course, there are a few variations you can use. For instance, if you want a dark chocolate mousse, just whip in a squirt or two of Hershey's Syrup while the beaters are going. Or let's say chocolate isn't your main flavor. Well, whip up a mousse with strawberry or cherry or lemon or banana or whatever else you like. If they make Jell-O Instant Pudding in that flavor, you can transform that flavor into a quickie mousse! No—a miraculous mousse!

And believe me, it's heavenly!

CHAPTER 13

Frank's Handy Kitchen Tables

MEASUREMENT EQUIVALENTS

3 teaspoons = 1 tablespoon
4 tablespoons = ¼ cup
8 tablespoons = ½ cup
12 tablespoons = ¾ cup
16 tablespoons = 1 cup
½ pint = 1 cup
1 pint = 2 cups
1 quart = 4 cups
1 quart = 2 pints
2 quarts = ½ gallon
4 quarts = 1 gallon
4 ounces = ½ cup
4 ounces = ¼ pound
8 ounces = 1 cup
8 ounces = ½ pound
16 ounces = 2 cups
16 ounces = 1 pint
16 ounces = 1 pound
32 ounces = 1 quart
64 ounces = ½ gallon
128 ounces = 1 gallon
1 ounce (liquid) = 2 tablespoons
2 ounces (liquid) = 4 tablespoons
2 cups of liquid = 1 pound

COMMON INGREDIENT WEIGHTS

1 pound cornmeal = 3 cups
1 pound cornstarch = 3 cups
1 pound all-purpose flour = 4 cups
23 soda crackers = 1 cup
15 graham crackers = 1 cup
1 medium lemon = 2½ tablespoons lemon juice
1 medium lemon = 1 tablespoon grated zest
1 medium orange = 3 tablespoons orange juice
1 stick butter = ½ cup
8 egg whites = 1 cup (approximately)
16 egg yolks = 1 cup (approximately)
1 cup raw pasta = 2 cups cooked pasta
12 ounces uncooked spaghetti = 6½ cups cooked spaghetti
1 cup raw long-grain rice = 4 cups cooked rice

1 cup soft bread crumbs = 2 slices fresh bread
2 sticks butter = 1 cup
1 pound butter = 2 cups
1 cup whipping cream = 2 cups whipped cream
4 ounces block cheese = 1 cup shredded cheese
1 pound block cheese = 4 cups shredded cheese
¼ pound shelled nuts = 1 cup chopped nuts
1 pound shelled nuts = 4 cups chopped nuts
1 pound granulated sugar = 2 cups
1 pound powdered sugar = 3½ cups

RECOMMENDED BAKING CHART

Just in case you get confused and you're not quite sure what oven temperature to use when you're cooking your favorite recipes, here's an easy reference chart I've put together.

Food Item	Degrees F.	Minutes
White Bread	400	45-60
Corn Bread	425	20-25
Drop Cookies	375	10-12
Brownies	400	25-30
Muffins	425	15-20
Pie Shell	450	10-12
Double-Crust Pie	425	30-35
Casseroles (Uncooked)	350	60-90
Casseroles (Precooked)	350	35-40
Baked Fish (Fillets)	400	20-25

OVEN TEMPERATURES

250-300 Degrees ....Slow Oven
300-325 Degrees...Moderately Slow Oven
325-350 Degrees...Moderate Oven
350-375 Degrees ....Moderately Quick Oven
375-400 Degrees...Moderately Hot Oven
425-450 Degrees..Hot Oven
475-500 Degrees ....Very Hot Oven

CHART OF INTERNAL
COOKING TEMPERATURES

People tell me all the time, "Frank, I can never tell when my meat dishes are done! Is there a trick to it?"

Yes, there is! It's called a *food thermometer.*

And it is the only method that is certain to give you correct and consistent results time and time again. What's more, the thermometer guarantees that when the meat you cook reaches the temperature on the chart, the internal heat has killed *all* present and harmful bacteria and the meat is safe to eat.

So let me make a suggestion. Buy yourself a good food thermometer … and use it!

Meat Is Cooked When Food Thermometer Reaches This Temperature

Beef Rib Roast (Rare) ....140 Degrees

Beef Rib Roast (Medium) ....155 Degrees

Beef Rib Roast (Well Done)...170 Degrees

Beef Rump (Boneless—Well Done) ....170 Degrees

Venison Roast (Rare) ....140 Degrees

Venison Roast (Medium) ....155 Degrees

Venison Roast (Well Done)..170 Degrees

Veal Roast..170 Degrees

Lamb Roast ....177 Degrees

Pork Roast ....170 Degrees

Smoked Ham (Whole—Raw) ....160 Degrees

Smoked Picnic Ham..170 Degrees

Baked Ham (Cured) ....140 Degrees

Baked Chicken...180 Degrees

Baked Turkey ....180 Degrees

Baked Goose ....180 Degrees

Baked Duck..180 Degrees

CHAPTER 14

Understanding the Secrets of Kitchen Basics

About every five years or so, a whole new generation of cooks joins the culinary ranks. They could be newlyweds, graduating seniors going off to college for the first time, new working moms, recent divorcées or singles living alone, retired senior citizens, and numerous others who are contented with—and who only have time for—*simplicity*. These are the folks who are satisfied with just the kitchen basics ... as long as what they create in the kitchen tastes great.

Well, that's what this chapter is all about. On the following pages, I'm going to share with you a barrage of kitchen and cooking tricks that will make cooking simple but tasty. Of course, take my instructions, hints, and suggestions and mix in a generous portion of your own creativity and personal taste and you will be amazed at just how much your cooking talents will improve.

Ready? Here we go!

Part 1: Cooking on the Barbecue Grill

It's one of the easiest ways to cook at home. It's just about fuss free, it doesn't heat up or smell up your house, there's very little cleanup involved, and it's as healthful as you can get because all the harmful oils and fats drip off during the cooking process and are converted into a smoke that flavors your food.

And don't think you can grill only during summer. I use the pit all year long. Even on our coldest days you can slip on a sweater or a light jacket, fire up the coals, and you're cooking!

MEATS

Whole chickens, game hens, steaks, roasts, pork chops, ribs, sausages, fish, shrimp, oysters on the half-shell—they can all be done on the grill.

1—Cook steaks, chops, and ribs on high heat—very close to the heat source—for the first half of the cooking process. Then reduce the heat (or move the meat farther from the heat source by raising the grating) and finish them by the slow-cooking method.

You also want to cook one side all the way till done before you turn the meat over. What you cook will come out a lot more juicy that way. Don't be a meat flipper! And use tongs or a spatula! Forks make holes that allow juices leak out.

Keep the lid closed during most of the cooking process. It will prevent updrafts and flare ups. Season or marinate the steaks, chops, or ribs before putting them on the grill.

2—For chickens, roasts, and game hens, you want to slow-cook for the entire time they're on the grill.

Season or marinate them for a few hours, drop them on the grating, and close the lid. You should insert a cooking thermometer in chickens and roasts and cook by internal temperatures to be sure these thicker cuts are done to your liking. Just for the record, chickens and game hens are properly cooked when the internal temperature reaches 185 degrees. A beef roast is cooked to "medium" when the internal temperature reaches 160 degrees; a pork roast is ready to serve when it reaches 170 degrees internally.

Never never overcook! If you do, whatever you cook will come out tasting like shoe leather!

3—Sausages, fish fillets, fish in scales, shrimp in their shells, and oysters on the half-shell should all be cooked over medium heat with the lid down for the first part of the cooking process and with the lid up for the second part of the cooking process.

When you cook sausages, prick the casing several times to allow excess fats to escape. Then simply toss them on the grating and cook them until they turn a toasty brown. Should flare ups occur, simply sprinkle on a little water to control the flames.

When you cook fish and shrimp, they should be marinated first in some type of oil-based coating—*seasoned olive oil or Italian salad dressing*—or basted as they cook with butter or margarine. Just remember, seafood is protein and protein cooks quickly. Don't overcook! When fish fillets flake apart, they' re done. When shrimp sizzle inside their shells, they're done.

Oysters on the half-shell need to be dabbed or drizzled with a couple of teaspoons of Italian salad dressing or a blended mixture of olive oil, garlic, lemon, Romano, and parsley prior to putting them on the grating. And just so you'll know ... oysters on the grill are done when the edges curl.

VEGETABLES

Vegetables and potatoes can also be cooked on the grill—either wrapped in aluminum foil or raw in their own skins.

1—Wash russet or baking potatoes thoroughly, dry the skins, liberally coat them with vegetable oil, wrap tightly in foil (shiny side toward the food), and grill them for about an hour until cooked.

2—Slice red potatoes into medallions, place them on a sheet of aluminum foil, salt and pepper them generously, dab on a little squeeze margarine, wrap the slices tightly in the foil, and cook on the grill for about 45 minutes until done.

3—Shuck fresh corn, remove the silk, butter thoroughly, season with salt and pepper, wrap tightly in aluminum foil, and cook for about 30 minutes till plump and tender.

4—Zucchini, yellow squash, white squash, and mushrooms should be grilled in their own skins. Slice the squash in lengthwise strips (to keep them from falling through the grating), baste them with margarine or seasoned olive oil, salt, and pepper, and place them on the grating for about 15 minutes. Mushrooms should also be basted and seasoned with margarine or olive oil and grilled whole for about 12 minutes on the grating. Just remember to keep vegetables that you cook in their own skins as far from the heat and flames as possible (or reduce the heat as low as it will go).

Note: some vegetables don't grill all that well in their own skins. They include eggplant, cauliflower, broccoli, and green beans. Of course, that doesn't mean you can't cook them *on* the grill. Just cut them into small pieces or florets, place them on a sheet of aluminum foil, season them with butter, salt, and pepper, wrap them tightly, and place them on the grating.

As with meats, however, do not overcook your vegetables. The proper texture is what's called "tender crisp." This means they are tender, but the texture still has a little crunch and crispness.

OTHER CHEF'S SECRETS

• Before cooking on any barbecue grill, first spray the grating with Pam or Vegelene to keep the food from sticking. After spraying, replace the grating on the coals or lava rock and fire up the grill to high. Make temperature adjustments after the grill gets hot.

• To cook chicken breasts evenly (so that the thin side doesn't dry out before the thick side is done), either pound out the meat or fillet and flatten out the thick side with a boning knife.

• Whole chickens, game hens, ducks, and turkeys will cook more evenly on a grill if you cook them on a *stand-up roaster rack* (every newlywed couple should have at least two of these). When using a rack, however, be sure to leave the skin on the poultry; because as it renders out the fats it bastes itself and comes out extremely moist and juicy. If you have a dual-control grill (separate settings for both the left and right sides), fire up only one side. Then place the poultry to be slow-cooked on the "cold" side.

• To get the best flavor in your steaks (rib eyes, filets mignons, T-bones, New York strips, porterhouses, etc.), first marinate or season the meat for at least 3 hours. It is possible, however, to cook good steaks without marinating them first—just season them with salt and pepper and baste them with melted butter as they cook on the grating. And yes—you can cook frozen steaks on the grill!

• If you want your barbecued ribs to come out extremely tender, be sure to remove the silverskin (that white membrane on the backside of pork ribs) before grilling them. It is not necessary to boil ribs before grilling them. Boiling will make ribs a slight bit more tender, *but ... boiling also removes a lot of the flavor of the meat.* Slow-cooking on the grill will achieve the same results. Just buy "baby-back" ribs to barbecue—tell your butcher you want ribs that are "3 and down" (which means that the whole rack weighed 3 pounds or less).

Never put barbecue sauce on your grilled meats until they are just about done. A good rule of thumb is: when you figure you have about 10 minutes' cooking time left, that's when the barbecue sauce goes on. See, all barbecue sauces contain sugar of some kind ... and sugar caramelizes on the grill, which causes your meats to become charred, burned, and bitter. To get your grilled meats to brown evenly, I suggest you use a BBQ brush and baste with liquid margarine as they cook.

• I'll go into it in greater detail later, but soups can be transformed into excellent sauces for grilled meats and vegetables. You got to understand that the one thing you don't get when you grill is *"pan drippings,"* which means you don't have a *base* to use to create a sauce. Well, you'll be surprised just how many gourmet sauces you can create with a collection of Campbell's soups.

Chef's Note: *While everything you've just read may sound complicated I assure you it isn't. It's all quickly done and extremely simple. Even new brides, incoming freshmen, and confirmed bachelors who've never cooked before in their lives can cook like this. With the exception of a large roast, a whole chicken, and a full rack of ribs, all the other techniques I've explained can be accomplished in, say, 15 to 20 minutes. Which means that within a half-hour after arriving home from work ... you're dining in gourmet style.*

And no TV dinner even comes close!

Part 2: Cooking on the Stovetop

You now know all kinds of tricks for using your BBQ pit. So you're ready for "Part 2: Cooking on the Stovetop"! But what kind of cooking can you do on a stovetop?

Well, you can pan-fry, deep fry, stir-fry, sauté, braise, poach, pan-broil, bronze, stew, and boil. And on the next couple of pages I'm going to teach you how to do all of that with the confidence of a master chef. You ready?

PAN-FRYING

That's taking beef round steaks, hamburgers, pork chops, veal cutlets, chicken breasts, turkey slices, filleted fish, shrimp, soft-shell crabs, squash, zucchini, eggplant, and green tomatoes in thicknesses no larger than ½ to

¾ of an inch and frying them—coated or uncoated—in a very small amount of oil no more than ½ to 1 inch deep.

You can pan-fry breaded or nonbreaded foods, but they must be turned over to pan-fry both sides during the cooking process. A good vegetable oil works great for pan-frying; but if you want to accentuate the specific flavor of a food, you should use peanut oil or olive oil instead. Peanut oil gives seafoods a nutty flavor and makes them more robust; olive oil makes foods taste unmistakably Italian.

To remove all excess oil from your fried foods, I suggest you drain whatever you cook on several layers of super-absorbent paper towels after cooking. I prefer Job Squad!

Just don't use solid shortening or lard for pan-frying if you want to cut back on your fat and cholesterol intake. Lard and solid shortening also give your food a heavy greasy taste when you try to eat it cold.

DEEP FRYING

That's taking chicken pieces, quartered game hens, turkey legs, and split ducks, as well as fish fillets, shrimp, oysters, soft-shell crabs, calamari, julienned clams, eggplant sticks, zucchini strips, squash slices, whole button mushrooms, and sliced okra and frying them *totally submerged* in deep vegetable or peanut oil—usually in a high-sided frypan or cast-iron Dutch oven. General frying temperature is between 325 and 375 degrees.

You can deep fry both breaded and nonbreaded foods. But unlike pan-frying, they do not need to be turned during the cooking process. I don't recommend that you deep fry in olive oil—it's cost prohibitive and it burns too quickly at high heat.

Like pan-frying, don't use solid shortening or lard for deep frying if you want to reduce the greasy taste and cut back on your fat and cholesterol intake.

To remove all excess oil from your deep-fried foods, I suggest you drain whatever you cook on several layers of super-absorbent Job Squad paper towels after frying.

STIR-FRYING

This is that wonderful form of Oriental cooking that is usually done in a wok, but which can also be done in a nonstick skillet. Technically, stir-frying uses a very small amount of oil (usually a tablespoon or less), which is dropped in a *very hot* wok or skillet and swooshed around to coat the metal. Then equally cut (all the same size) pieces of meat, poultry, seafood, and vegetables are quickly fried while being continuously stirred to keep them from sticking and burning.

In all cases, the meats are stir-fried first. A good all-purpose seasoning or a specifically blended spice is used to flavor the julienned chicken, pork strips, beef slices, butterflied shrimp, or crawfish tails. Then the meats are temporarily removed and the *bias-cut* vegetables (these are vegetables cut on a sharp angle to expose as much surface as possible) are dropped in.

A good vegetable mixture consists of any combination of about a half-cup each of onions, celery, bell peppers, snow peas, mushrooms, broccoli florets, water chestnuts, bamboo shoots, and miniature corns on the cob. But you can also stir-fry yellow squash, zucchini, carrots, and cabbage. Just make certain that everything is cut to approximately the same size so that it's all cooked at the same time. Generally, it takes about 3 minutes to stir-fry vegetables, and they should come out "tender-crisp" (cooked but still slightly crunchy).

When the veggies are done, drop the meats back into the wok or skillet, toss everything together again, and pour in a small amount of chicken stock (you can use canned Campbell's Chicken Broth). Then cover the wok or skillet with a lid and steam the ingredients for another minute or two.

Just before you serve, stir in a couple of teaspoonfuls of cornstarch mixed with about a quarter-cup of chicken stock and cook it—*still constantly tossing everything!*—for about 30 seconds (or until it thickens).

If you'd prefer, instead of using the cornstarch you can stir in about a half-can of one of the numerous creamed soups I've outlined below to make a sauce. Or you can simply serve the vegetables *au naturel* with just a little butter, yogurt, or margarine and a twist of lemon.

SAUTEING

This is almost like pan-frying ... but you use only enough oil to keep the food from sticking to the skillet. In New Orleans cookery, when the directions say to *sauté*, most cooks and chefs will tell you it usually means to cook your "mirepoix" of vegetables (that's the onions, celery, bell pepper, garlic, and parsley) over medium heat to soften them before continuing with the recipe.

And even across the rest of Louisiana as well, *sautéing* generally is the first step you must complete in the recipe before you can go on to the rest of the recipe. For example, you sauté your mirepoix before you make a stew, a pot roast, a gumbo, an étouffée, a sauce piquante, a jambalaya, a soup, a chowder, a gravy, or a sauce.

Once your mirepoix is sautéed, then the rest of the ingredients go in (chunked chicken, chopped pork, ground meat, julienned turkey breast, sliced sausage, peeled shrimp, beef slices, or crawfish tails), along with whatever you're going to use to provide the liquid in the dish—chicken broth, beef broth, canned soup, Rotel tomatoes, wine, beer, milk, heavy cream, you name it! Just remember—all these liquids must be added in small amounts just to give the dish "moisture" (you don't want a full gravy!). And all sautéing is done over medium heat without a lid on the skillet! Because once a lid is clamped on and significant liquids become present, you're *braising!*

BRAISING

This is the kind of cooking you do on the stovetop to turn tough foods into tender foods. It can be done both in a skillet or a Dutch oven and is usually used for cooking round steak, flank steak, brisket, rump roast, chuck roast, venison, squirrel, rabbit, other wild game, and other foods that have a tendency to turn out dry and stringy when cooked. It always requires cooking for a longer period of time with a tight-fitting lid.

Here's the procedure.

First the food is thoroughly browned all over in a small amount of very hot vegetable or peanut oil. It's then covered tightly and slowly and gently simmered in a small amount of concentrated, highly flavored stock (a court bouillon, diluted soup mix, a light butter-roux gravy, an onion stock, a mixed vegetable stock, a seafood stock, a thin wine sauce, etc.).

Just remember one thing—whenever you're braising, the liquid never comes to a boil. It just simmers and barely bubbles.

POACHING

This can best be explained as a very very slow boil without the liquid ever coming to a bubble. It is a great method of cooking for eggs, fish, oysters, shrimp, and whole chicken (especially when you're making chicken salad). The way you do it is … bring seasoned water (and you can season it with herbs and spices, crabboil, wine, lemon juice, or just salt and pepper) to a full boil. Then drop in the food you want to poach.

When the water looks like it's about to return to the boil, reduce the heat to keep it from doing so. *You must know that poached foods are never to boil or bubble!* You want to keep them right on the edge and allow the heat of the seasoned water (which is called bouillon) to do the cooking.

A good rule of thumb is to allow 10 minutes per 1 inch of thickness to properly poach fish, 3-4 minutes for medium shrimp, and about 1 hour for a 2½-pound whole chicken. And oysters should be poached only until the edges curl. If you poach oysters too long, they turn into rubber bands!

A couple of cautions: (1) Never leave poached foods in the poaching stock after they're cooked—they'll overcook in a hurry and become very tough! And (2), never throw away the poaching stock. It can be thickened with a butter roux or a little cornstarch and converted into a great-tasting gravy or sauce.

PAN-BROILING

This is probably the most difficult form of stovetop cooking because if you don't do it right ... you'll burn the food and the pan. Pan-broiling must be done with a very heavy bottomed skillet with a tight-fitting lid that you keep lifting off and on ('cuz remember, if liquids form ... you're braising!). So as the food pan-broils, you cover it for just a few minutes, then uncover it to release the liquids. In fact, for steaks and fatty chops you'll have to sop up some of the grease with paper towels as it accumulates. Be very cautious doing this, though, so that you don't burn yourself!

Usually, the only thing that's still pan-broiled in New Orleans is a thin-cut rib-eye steak or pork chop because the process creates a nice crusty outside. Aside from that, though, everything else is either grilled or broiled in the oven. Unless you have some old, well-seasoned cast-iron skillets hanging around, you'll probably want to pass up the pan-broiling. Besides ... it smokes up your house!

BRONZING

This is a technique I developed back in the early seventies. My old buddy Chef Paul Prudhomme had just taken the nation by storm with his "blackening" technique (which uses a considerable amount of real butter cooked in a "white-hot" cast-iron skillet to create the blackened taste and effect). So I came up with using a nonstick skillet instead of cast iron, a small amount of margarine instead of a lot of butter, and a light sprinkling of specially blended seasoning (I market a product I call bronzing mix) to cook coarse fish fillets, butterflied shrimp, thinly sliced pork chops, whole button mushrooms, pounded-out chicken breast fillets, and a variety of julienned vegetables. In fact, it has virtually replaced pan-broiling across Louisiana because it's easy to do and yields a healthful method of cooking.

Simply take a nonstick skillet, lightly spray it with Pam or Vegelene or brush it with about a tablespoon of margarine, and heat it to medium high. Then season the food you want to bronze with a *light* sprinkling of salt, black pepper, onion powder, garlic powder, ground thyme, basil, oregano, cayenne, and paprika (or my bronzing mix) and drop it into the hot skillet.

A couple of notes: (1) You want to cook the food on both sides only until a nice toasty-colored bronze hue appears. (2) You want to keep the food moving in the skillet (you can slide it back and forth as it bronzes). (3) The thinner the cut of meat the better it will bronze and the juicier it will come out when it's done (I've found that a 4- to 6-ounce portion works best). And (4) when it's cooked, a little wine or chicken stock can be used to deglaze the skillet and create a rich, delicate, and light sauce that you can use for topping the bronzed meat or vegetables.

Bronzed foods also serve well cold since they contain very little fat. Try julienning a chicken breast or pork chop, or try chopping bronzed shrimp for adding to a cold tossed salad. It's wonderful!

STEWING

This is the form of cooking that is the reverse of braising. While braising uses very little liquid, stewing requires that first you start with a rich gravy, then add the meats, seafoods, or vegetables to it.

What you do is make a roux using equal parts of oil and flour and turn it into a gravy by adding a sautéed mirepoix and either chicken or beef broth, Rotel tomatoes, wine, beer, or whatever else you want to use as a base. Then season the gravy to taste and drop in cubed beef, chunked pork, chopped venison, cut-up chicken or rabbit, sausages, meatballs, or anything else you want to stew (I also suggest you add small peeled "B"-size creamer potatoes, a couple of quartered carrots, and a cup or two of fresh green beans to your stew).

Remember, stewing requires small pieces of meat cooked—no, over-cooked!—in a highly flavored gravy. See, you want the meat to literally "fall apart" and have the flavor spread throughout and totally dominate the gravy. So that means two things: (1) you don't have to be so precise about timing the cooking process, which in turn means that (2) you can put on a pot of stew, cut the fire down to low, and do other things while supper is cooking! If you happen to remember it 30 minutes late ... no big deal!

Just keep the heat low as it cooks, make sure you never run out of gravy in the pot, and you can't mess it up!

BOILING

This is the easiest form of stovetop cooking, even though we've all heard the line ... "I can't boil water without it burning." I'm here to tell you that you can.

Bring a large pot of water to a rapid boil—212 degrees Fahrenheit. And use the boiling technique to cook shrimp, crabs, crawfish, lobsters, eggs in the shell, potatoes, corn on the cob, rice, and pasta.

Flavor the water with onions, celery, lemons, garlic, bay leaves, salt, pepper, and crabboil to cook your shrimp (2 minutes), crawfish (2 minutes), crabs (8 minutes), and live lobsters (6 to 12 minutes). Add a couple of teaspoons of vinegar to the water to boil eggs in the shell (10 minutes for hard boiled). Boil potatoes in plain water for about 17 minutes. Pour a cup of whole milk in the water to boil corn on the cob (it takes no more than 11 minutes). Slightly salt the water to boil your rice (14 minutes). And add not only a little salt but a little olive oil to the water to boil pasta (which takes 10 to 15 minutes, depending on the kind of pasta you are going to boil).

And aside from that ... don't boil any other kind of food in plain water. *Water has no flavor!* Whenever and whatever you cook you want to cook in a flavored stock. You want to put as much rich taste as you can in your stews, sauces, sautés, gravies, and everything else at the very outset. It s probably the No. 1 Commandment for folks learning to cook.

ONE MORE THING ABOUT SAUCES

No one is going to expect a new bride, a college student, a working mom, a senior citizen, a single parent, or anyone else just learning the science of the kitchen to conjure up the classic sauces. But make no mistake about it, a nice topping sauce adds extreme flavor and a certain elegance to any dish. So what do you do about this sauce thing?

As I said earlier, utilize the Campbell's canned soups and make a few conversions. You have 16 canned soups in the supermarket that can be transformed into "instant" gourmet sauces and gravies for topping and cooking steaks, chops, shrimp, fish, vegetables, pasta, rice, and potatoes.

Obviously, some of them won't do the job—like chicken noodle and turkey and rice. But the ones that do work, *and the ones you should have stocked in your pantry,* are:

Cream of Shrimp	Cream of Mushroom
Cream of Celery	Cream of Potato
Cream of Asparagus	Cream of Broccoli
Nacho Cheese	Cheddar Cheese
Broccoli and Cheese	Creamy Onion
Creamy Chicken and Mushroom	Golden Mushroom
Cream of Chicken	Chicken Broth
Beef Broth	Cream Corn

Simply open the can, pour out the soup, thin it to your desired taste with either chicken broth, beef broth, whole milk, consommé, whipping cream, wine, or V-8 juice (notice I never said plain water once!), and bring it up to heat in a skillet or saucepan. To make it even more tasty, first sauté a mirepoix in a little butter and add the soup base to it.

Then stew or braise in the prepared soup sauce, finish off steamed or stir-fried vegetables by tossing them with the soup sauce, or use the concocted mixture to ladle over fried, grilled, broiled, barbecued, bronzed, or roasted entrées.

No ... you won't have created the classic béarnaise, béchamel, bordelaise, or mornay, but what you will have created will be extremely easy to make. And you won't ever have to apologize to anyone for the flavor you'll get.

So start using your stovetop! Now you know how!

At this point, you're halfway to mastering your kitchen. So far you can cook on the grill and you can cook on the stovetop. Now it's time to learn to put the oven to work.

So what kind of cooking do you do in the oven? Easy stuff—stuff you don't have to stand around and watch, like baking, dry roasting, pot roasting, broiling, and making casseroles. Let's tackle them one at a time!

BAKING

You can bake beef, pork, veal, chicken, fish, shrimp, oysters, crabs, crawfish, potatoes, corn on the cob, pies, cookies, cakes, pizza, all kinds of vegetables, and lots of other great foods. And you can bake them covered, uncovered, in bags, in pots, and wrapped in foil. For example:

1—Take a whole chicken, game hen, or turkey; sprinkle it with poultry seasoning; position it on a stand-up roaster (you can buy them at any kitchen shop); and bake the whole fowl uncovered at about 300 degrees until the internal temperature reaches 180 degrees. Simple, huh? And ... it's done!

2—Cut up a chicken into pieces, generously season the pieces with salt and pepper, dip them into an eggwash or spray them with butter-flavored Pam, roll them in Italian seasoned bread crumbs, and bake them uncovered at 350 degrees on a shallow, lightly greased cookie sheet for about an hour or until they turn a crusty golden brown. Couldn't be easier!

3—Take a couple of center-cut pork chops, generously sprinkle them with salt and pepper (or you can use a premixed pork seasoning), dip them into an eggwash, roll them in Italian seasoned bread crumbs, and bake them uncovered at 350 degrees on a shallow, lightly greased cookie sheet for about 30 to 40 minutes or until they turn a crusty golden brown. You can do the same thing with a couple of fish fillets—just brush on a little melted butter and squeeze on a little lemon juice while the fillets are cooking.

4—Place a whole fish that has been scaled and gutted into a lightly greased baking pan (Pyrex, Corning, or metal), sprinkle it inside and out with salt and pepper or a premixed seafood seasoning, top with a little paprika and a few lemon slices, and bake uncovered at 350 degrees until the fish just begins to flake apart. At this point, pour on a can of Rotel tomatoes and a little white wine and continue baking until the fish is tender throughout and falling off the bone.

You know those cans of soups I suggest you use to make sauces? Well ... after you remove the fish (and you're going to have to do that carefully or it will crumble up), take the drippings from the baking pan, stir it into a skillet with a can of cream of shrimp or golden mushroom or creamy onion soup, for example, and pour it over the fish as you serve it. All you need is a few baked potatoes or a little rice on the side and you got yourself a gourmet meal! See how quick?

5—Speaking of baked potatoes … to make great creamy baked potatoes every time, wash them well with a scruffy pad to remove the dirt and the scaly outside skin, dry them thoroughly with paper towels, rub them generously all over with vegetable oil, tightly wrap them in heavy-duty aluminum foil, and bake them in a 500-degree oven for 1 hour.

Now you can serve them as baked potatoes or … you can chop them up into pieces and toast them lightly in a buttered skillet as brabant potatoes; or peel them and slice them, put them in a Corningware dish, and cover them with one of the canned soups for an au gratin-type dish; or peel them and squoosh them up, whip in heavy cream and butter, and serve them as mashed potatoes; or peel them and mix them with a few chopped hard-boiled eggs, a little mayonnaise, some finely diced onions and celery, a dash of yellow mustard, salt, and pepper, and serve them as potato salad. All that … from a couple of baked potatoes!

6—Baked macaroni is another great dish to do in the oven. And it's not that difficult. First, boil your pasta (I like the kind with the hole in the middle for baked mac) until it's just tender (al dente). Then drain it well in a colander and set it aside for awhile.

In the meantime, take a skillet, open and heat a can of cheddar cheese soup, thin it out ever so slightly with a little bit of evaporated milk, pour it over the pasta, and toss everything together well with one raw egg. Then transfer the macaroni mix to a buttered baking pan, sprinkle on some coarsely ground black pepper, and top with a heaping cup of grated cheddar cheese. All you have to do then is bake the dish uncovered at 400 degrees until the cheese melts and begins to brown on top of the pasta. It's a whole lot better than the boxed stuff!

7—Pizzas are another great food to do in the oven; but you've got to have a clay pizza stone to get the bottom crust to come out crispy. Cooking pizza just in a metal pizza pan is going to give you a soggy crust every time. Oh, by the way—until you get to the advanced stages in your culinary science, I suggest you forget about making your own pizzas from scratch and go with the frozen varieties. Just buy the high-quality ones. They're almost as good as homemade!

8—Same story goes for baking pies and cakes. This gets awfully technical. So until you get all the basics mastered, ain't nothing wrong with buying Mrs. Smith's frozen apple pie or a Sarah Lee pound cake or a couple of Pepperidge Farm puff pastries and popping 'em into the oven on the clay stone.

Just a little hint, though. To make all your pies and pastries shiny and golden brown on the upper crust, brush them with a little egg white about halfway through the baking process. Otherwise, just follow package directions.

Other Baking Notes: When you're baking small cuts of poultry, meat, and fish, it's easiest to bake them *uncovered*. When you have to bake thicker cuts of poultry, meat, and fish, especially those you bake in a gravy or liquid, you should bake them *covered* with heavy-duty aluminum foil to keep the moisture in the food and to keep the liquids from splattering.

You can also bake briskets and other tough cuts of meat tightly wrapped in heavy-duty aluminum foil alone. This is more of a steaming process than technical *baking*. The same applies to the use of so-called "baking bags." They tend to "slow-cook" or steam the foods inside of them, because the dry heat of the oven never gets to the food and you end up with only a slight browning effect.

Of course, all pastries, pies, and cakes should be baked uncovered because you want to utilize the dry heat.

And finally, the oven is a great tool for keeping foods warm while you cook the remainder of your meal. Ideally you want to set the temperature somewhere in the neighborhood of 150 degrees and keep the foods slightly tented (covered with aluminum foil but not sealed on the ends).

Oh—I also suggest that you use your oven to warm your dinner plates before serving the food you cook—hot plates keep the food you serve hotter longer ... especially steaks.

DRY ROASTING

Roasting, essentially, is cooking food in the oven while it's *uncovered*. What you're doing is using the dry heat to cook beef roasts, pork roasts, hams, veal pockets, racks of ribs, whole chickens, whole turkeys, oil-brushed vegetables and diced potatoes, and nuts in or out of their shells.

Most roasting is done somewhere between 325 and 375 degrees. That's the temperature range you should be in for rump roast, rib roast, eye of the round, small chickens, venison, veal pockets, and vegetables.

But fatty foods—like pork roasts, baby-back ribs, pork fillets, and whole turkeys—come out best when they are "slow roasted." That means that first you need to brown and seal them quickly (about 10 to 15 minutes) at 500 degrees; then reduce the heat to 225 or 250 degrees and finish the roast over a longer period of time at that temperature. The slow-roasting process also produces slow basting, which constantly bathes the meat in its own juices as it cooks. Consequently, you end up with a virtually grease-free cut of pork, a ham that's juicy, and a turkey that literally falls off the bone.

Incidentally, when you're using the roasting technique be sure to place the roast on something inside the pan that keeps it up off the bottom (chefs call this a *trivet*). You don't want your food resting in the fats and oils. A small saucer or wire rack makes a good trivet; but the trivet I like best is a large onion cut in thick rings, a couple of ribs of celery, and a few peeled and quartered carrots placed on the bottom of the pan. As the roast cooks, the drippings fall into the vegetables and cook them! In the end, you get a great *au jus* (pot liquor) that you can easily transfer to a skillet and convert into a sauce.

By the way, don't ever wash the dirty pan you use to bake or roast in until you first "deglaze" it. Know all that stuff that sticks to the bottom of the pan after the meat is done? That's your sauce fixins! Why would you want to wash it away with a Brillo?

Instead, pour a can of Campbell's chicken broth into the pan while it is still hot, take a wooden spoon or spatula, and gently loosen all the stuck-on "stuff" with a back and forth action until it dissolves. Then transfer the broth to a skillet, bring it to a boil, pour in a little wine, or maybe a little lemon juice, and thicken it up with about a teaspoon of cornstarch mixed with ¼ cup of water (it'll thicken as soon as it comes to a boil!). This is called "deglazing," and always, always deglaze!

Finally, as I teach with all the other forms of cooking, baking and roasting should be gauged for doneness not by minutes to the pound, but by the internal cooking temperature of the food. So whenever you're roasting, use a thermometer. A complete cooking chart is included in the previous chapter.

One more thing—when you're roasting baby-back ribs …

1—Remove the silverskin on the back of the rack—it peels off easily with the help of a small paring knife. When you remove the silverskin, the ribs are more tender. And,

2—As with cooking on a grill, don't boil ribs before you roast them! You lose a lot of flavor that way. Instead, season them to your taste and slow-roast them. They come out greaseless, beautifully browned, and tender enough to fall off the bone.

I recommend you cook them on a meat rack. Take a baking pan, put about a cup of water in the bottom, place your rack on top of the pan, and set the well-seasoned ribs directly on the rack. As the ribs roast, the fat drips down into the pan, it prevents flare ups, and the steam from the water pan further tenderizes the ribs. It's the only way to do pork ribs!

POT ROASTING

Most folks think pot roasting can only be done on top of the stove. And the truth is, that's how most folks cook a "pot roast." But …

I'm here to tell you that you should *start* your pot roast on the stove (you need to brown the meat all over) but then slide the roast and the pot into the oven and *finish* it there.

Follow me closely on this one!

Take your black cast-iron (or heavy aluminum) Dutch oven and sauté the seasoning vegetables in a small amount of oil on the stovetop until they caramelize and soften. Then brown whatever meats you're cooking (chuck roast, chicken, venison, pork, lamb, etc.) along with the seasoning vegetables.

Then set the oven at 325 degrees, adjust the oven rack to make room for the pot with the lid on, and slide the pot into the oven. All you do from this point on is let it cook! You don't stir it! You don't stand there and watch it! You just let it cook!

You're gonna find out that most meats will make a little gravy on their own using the pot-roasting technique. But I suggest you peek in the pot about halfway through the cooking process. If you want more gravy than you're getting from just the natural juices, pour in a can of Campbell's chicken or beef broth, or cream of mushroom soup, or creamy onion soup, or a half-cup of wine, or a can of V-8 juice. Stir it into the au jus (the natural pot liquor), put the lid back on the pot, and let the dish finish.

You'll find that accurately timing the food is not that important when you "pot-roast" in the oven because unless you totally forget about the pot … the food will rarely burn (the cast iron and lid protects it!).

This is also the way to cook a "one-pot meal." Because not only can you pot-roast a chuck roast, you can pot-roast a cut-up chicken, a stack of beef ribs, a rack of pork ribs, a piece of venison, or anything else that you don't want to watch on the stove. And don't forget to drop in your peeled carrots, some whole mushrooms, and a few potatoes. When the roast is done, so is the rest of the meal. Call it a stew if you want to! But it serves up and eats great!

By the way, this is the best way to make chili and hot tamales, too. Start them on the stovetop, but finish them in the oven. The flavors intensify so richly you won't believe it!

BROILING

Another thing you can do in the oven is broil. It is one of the healthiest forms of cooking we know since it uses little fat to cook and renders out most excess fats contained in foods.

Just remember that "broiling" is a very fast way of cooking, because the food is exceptionally close to the heat source, which means you have to stay with it when you broil. Unlike pot-roasting in the oven, walk off for only a few minutes and leave the food unattended ... and you're out to Burger King if you wanna eat supper! Believe me, it'll burn that quickly!

Now that you understand that, know that you can broil:

Round steak, rib eyes, porterhouses, New York strips, hamburgers, sausages, liver, pork chops, chicken breasts, veal cutlets, fish fillets, oysters, shrimp wrapped in bacon, soft-shell crabs, lobsters, and tons of other things.

The way you broil is to take a lightly greased shallow baking sheet or heavy broiling pan, place your seasoned food onto it, and slide it under the broiler (top rack in your oven). Then after a few minutes—say 2 to 5, depending upon whether you're cooking seafood or beef—you turn the food over with a spatula and broil the reverse side. When what you're cooking is nicely browned on both sides, it's done!

Technically, broiling temperature is 500 degrees. Note that you will get a little bit of natural liquid out of most foods you broil; but the heat will be so high it usually will evaporate (except for fish—you get a nice sauce from broiled fish ... and I like to add a splash or two of wine to the sauce to flavor it up).

You can try it if you want, but I don't recommend you broil vegetables! They never come out right, to my liking.

MAKING CASSEROLES

And finally, the last thing you can do in the oven is make *casseroles*. A casserole is quick and easy to do, it's a great one-dish meal, and it can be cooked in advance and reheated for other meals.

Rice, pasta, and potatoes are the building blocks for most casseroles. What you do is cook your rice, pasta, or potatoes and let them cool. Then using a gravy made from a roux, a sauce made from chicken broth and cornstarch, or a couple of cans of your favorite Campbell's creamed soups, mix the main ingredients of your casserole—tuna, crawfish tails, cocktail shrimp, julienned chicken, ground meat, or sausage—into the sauce ... *then into the rice, or the pasta, or the potatoes.*

Vegetables can be made into casseroles too. Use the gravy, or creamed soups, or reduced heavy cream and mix it thoroughly with a sautéed mirepoix and your *steamed* veggies—broccoli, green beans, cauliflower, chopped spinach, and so forth—and mix everything together.

All that's left is to top the casserole with a layer of buttered bread crumbs or a handful of shredded Monterey Jack or cheddar cheese and slide it into a 350-degree oven. By the way, most casseroles are cooked ¾ of the way *covered* ... then finished *uncovered* so that they brown nicely on the top.

So there you go—all the basics of cooking in the oven! Lemme suggest that you read over these pages a few more times; then give these techniques a try. You'll be surprised just how proficient you'll be the very first time out! I promise you can do it!

The Spice of New Orleans ... the Easy Way!

You know all those great New Orleans dishes I rave about throughout the pages of this book? Well, suppose you find that you don't have time to put them all together from scratch. Can you still do them and still capture that real *N'Awlins* taste?

Absolutely! You simply take the basic recipe and short-cut it! Here's how.

See, since the trick is in the seasoning and since a lot of seasonings we use in New Orleans cuisine are not available in other parts of the country, in addition to writing this new cookbook, I've also developed a complete line of spices and seasonings that's authentically *Crescent City*. I'm telling you, whatever you cook with them ends up tasting just like it would had you been born and raised smack-dab in the middle of the French Quarter.

And check out the selection you got!

There's *Sicilian* (it's like Italian, but better!) ... *Bronzing* (which is like blackened, but a whole lot healthier) ... *Wild Game* (I make the only wild game seasoning on the market) ... plus *Seafood, Vegetable, Poultry, Pork, Beef, Sprinkling Spice* (which you use instead of salt and pepper), and *No Salt* (for folks on a sodium-restricted diet)—plus the best doggone *Fish Fry* you ever used and a gourmet blend of liquid *Crab Boil*.

I've created every one of them with the highest quality ingredients I could find. Honestly, I really don't think there's anything better on the market! And because you get 6 to 8 ounces of the seasonings instead of just 2 ounces, you save a ton of money! You gotta try 'em!

So how do you do that? Simply call a 24-hour toll-free hotline and order what you want by telephone. The number is 1-800-742-4231 and I promise you that nothing you'll ever cook with will come closer to *"Cajun, Creole, and Crescent City."*

Talking Pots and Pans Again!

The last time I took notice, a lot of folks are still having trouble deciding which pots and pans to use for cooking different dishes ... and which ones to buy as replacements when the old ones wear out. Well, without getting into a lot of hi-tech gibberish, let me give you a few rules of thumb.

The bottom line is *heavyweights*—heavy cast iron, heavy aluminum, heavy stainless steel. The problem you're going to run into is only cast iron and aluminum will be affordable for home use. Heavy-duty stainless steel is cost prohibitive; you'll need to own an oil well in Lafourche Parish to buy a set.

And face it—thin metal pots and pans do not (I repeat) *do not* cook uniformly. You can't get a consistency in your recipes with thin metal. Heat is not diffused, hot spots form, and more often than not a lot of your foods will burn. So for that reason, you should cook only things like soup and stock in thin stainless steel. Oh—it might look pretty, but it rates poorly as a cooking utensil unless it's fitted with a heavy, expensive copper bottom.

On the other hand, cast iron is outstanding. But you have to go through the hassle of curing it before first use and keeping it cured. Otherwise, it's going to rust and just about everything you cook is going to taste rusty. Of course once it's cured properly (and I've explained how to do that on page 244 of *Frank Davis Cooks Naturally N'Awlins*) you got it made for life ... provided you don't ever again wash it with soap!

Which brings me to aluminum. Most professional chefs and just about everybody else who considers himself a really good cook uses aluminum— polished or anodized. I know, we've all heard the stories about Alzheimer's disease, but aluminum is still the most popular cooking medium.

I guess the bottom line is ... it's your choice. But whichever you buy, buy professional quality.

HOW CAN YOU TELL WHAT'S PROFESSIONAL-QUALITY COOKWARE?

Whether you're looking for skillets, frypans, roasters, Dutch ovens, or stockpots, look for the plain metal varieties (with no filigree, pastel flowers, or baby teddy bears on the sidewalls).

Professional cookware also has plain metal handles (not plastic ones). And the standard indicator in the industry is that those handles *must* have 3 rivets in them where they attach to the pot—less than 3 ... not professional!

Now expect to pay a premium price for good cookware. But know that what you pay is well worth the price. They'll last a lifetime, they'll cook with precision, they can go right from the stovetop into the oven, and they'll clean quick as a wink every time.

So when it's time to replace ... replace professional!

Index

Hot sausage, 99
Hot tamales, 244
Hunting camp baked turnips, 204
Hush puppies, Cliff's Southern
    fried, 246

I

Instant potatoes, 225
Internal cooking temperatures,
    chart of, 277
Italian salad mix, 42
Italian salad with Caesar
    dressing, 41
Italian sausage and pasta in red
    gravy, 100

J

Julienned carrots in a brown butter
    sauce, 202

L

Lagniappe meat and vegetable
    gumbo, 56
Lentils and Italian sausage, 195
Lobsters, spicy Cajun boiled, 188
London broil, spicy, 68
Louisiana lagniappe gumbo, 54
Low-calorie vanilla ice cream, 268
Low-cholesterol vanilla ice
    cream, 270

M

Mardi Gras roasted steaks and
    potatoes, 70
Marinated chicken, 119
Marinated grilled tuna, 135
Mary Clare's Sicilian tomato gravy
    (sugo), 256

Measurement equivalents, 275
Meat and vegetable gumbo,
    lagniappe, 56
Meatballs, Italian, 75
Meatballs and spaghetti (in Italian
    tomato sugo), Italian, 76
Miraculous mousse, 272
Mirlitons, shrimp-stuffed
    N'Awlins, 159
Mock crabmeat, 144
Mousse, miraculous, 272

N

Nectar syrup, 258
Nora's "don't tell me you can't
    make these!" hot tamales, 244

O

Onions, pickled, 242
Oriental fried cabbage, 206
Oven-baked baby-back ribs, 11
Oven cooking, 291-97
Oven-fried chicken, 126
Oven temperatures, 276
Oyster po' boys, 185
Oyster pudding, 187

P

Panéed pork chops, 105
Pasta d'Roma, 215
Pasta Peppina, 213
Pasta, tips for boiling, 248
Pecan fudgey pudding, 266
Pepper steak, 72
Perfectly grilled steaks, 66
Pickled onions, 242
Picky-quickie shrimp, 162
Pommes petites, 220
Pork chops, orange-glazed, 102